Journalism Studies

As the world of politics and public affairs has gradually changed beyond recognition over the past two decades, journalism too has been transformed. Yet the study of news and journalism often seems stuck with ideas and debates which have lost much of their critical purchase. Journalism is at a crossroads: it needs to reaffirm core values and rediscover key activities, almost certainly in new forms, or it risks losing its distinctive character as well as its commercial basis.

Journalism Studies is a polemical textbook that rethinks the field of journalism studies for the contemporary era. It is the politics, philosophy and economics of journalism, presented as a logical reconstruction of its historical development. This book offers a critical reassessment of conventional themes in the academic analysis of journalism and sets out a positive proposal for what we should be studying.

Organised around three central themes – ownership, objectivity and the public – *Journalism Studies* addresses the contexts in which journalism is produced, practised and disseminated. It outlines key issues and debates, reviewing established lines of critique in relation to the state of contemporary journalism, then offers alternative ways of approaching these issues, seeking to reconceptualise them in order to suggest an agenda for change and development in both journalism studies and journalism itself.

Journalism Studies advocates a mutually reinforcing approach to both the practice and the study of journalism, exploring the current sense that journalism is in crisis and offering a cool appraisal of the love–hate relationship between journalism and the scholarship which it frequently disowns. This is a concise and accessible introduction to contemporary journalism studies and will be highly useful to undergraduate and postgraduate students on a range of journalism, media and communications courses.

Andrew Calcutt is Principal Lecturer in Journalism at the University of East London, where he leads Master courses in journalism and magazines. He is vice-chair of the London East Research Institute and editor of *Proof: Reading Journalism and Society* (www.proof-reading.org). Previous publications include *White Noise: An A–Z of Contradictions in Cyberculture* (1999) and *Arrested Development: Pop Culture and the Erosion of Adulthood* (1998).

Philip Hammond is Reader in Media and Communications at London South Bank University. He is the author of *Media, War and Postmodernity* (2007) and *Framing Post-Cold War Conflicts* (2007) and is co-editor, with Edward Herman, of *Degraded Capability: The Media and the Kosovo Crisis* (2000).

Journalism Studies

A critical introduction

Andrew Calcutt and Philip Hammond

Routledge
Taylor & Francis Group

LONDON AND NEW YORK

First published 2011
by Routledge
2 Park Square, Milton Park, Abingdon OX14 4RN

Simultaneously published in the USA and Canada
by Routledge
270 Madison Avenue, New York, NY 10016

Routledge is an imprint of the Taylor & Francis Group, an informa business

Typeset in Galliard by Taylor & Francis Books
Printed and bound in Great Britain by CPI Rowe Ltd, Chippenham, Wiltshire

British Library Cataloguing in Publication Data
A catalogue record for this book is available from the British Library

Library of Congress Cataloging in Publication Data
Calcutt, Andrew.
   Journalism studies : a critical introduction / Andrew Calcutt and Philip
Hammond.
      p. cm.
   Includes bibliographical references and index.
   1. Journalism–History–21st century. 2. Journalism–Ownership. 3.
Journalism–Objectivity. 4. Citizen journalism. I. Hammond, Phil, 1964- II. Title.
   PN4815.2.C35 2011
   070.4071–dc22
                                2010031680

ISBN13: 978-0-415-55430-5 (hbk)
ISBN13: 978-0-415-55431-2 (pbk)
ISBN13: 978-0-203-83174-8 (ebk)

Contents

Acknowledgements

For stimulating discussion and convivial company, we should like to thank our colleagues and students at the University of East London (UEL) and London South Bank University. We owe a particular debt of gratitude to Richard Sharpe at UEL, not only for introducing us to the work of Tom Wicker but also for excavating the 'natural history' of concepts such as mediation.

We are very grateful to those friends and colleagues who read and commented on the manuscript, especially Mark Beachill and Dr Graham Barnfield. Needless to say, any errors that remain are our fault rather than theirs.

Finally, we would like to thank our respective partners, Alka and Nena, for their forbearance as we pursued a project that may sometimes have seemed to have no end in sight.

Introduction
Journalism in question

The title of this introductory essay sounds like the title of a university seminar. Rightly so, since its authors are employed in the academy, and the academy is bound to question its objects of study or it can hardly claim to be studying them. Questioning professional journalism is thus the everyday activity of everyone involved in Journalism Studies. Today, however, journalism faces another line of altogether different questioners, this time from outside the academy. Advertisers, publishers, readers, viewers and listeners – and even journalists themselves – are all questioning journalism, wondering what it is for and asking whether its professional, paid-for incarnation provides anything that digital media users are unable to supply for free.

This line of inquiry may have been initiated at the same time as 'Web 2.0', i.e. around the turn of the twenty-first century, but at that time it was pencil thin. Since then the question mark hanging over journalism has been cross-hatched by a combination of cyclical advertising recession and fundamental economic downturn, with the added complication that each of these has now segued into the other, making it almost impossible to distinguish one cause from another's effects. You know the score: we only know that the tally of journalism's casualties (titles closed; publishing houses brought down; hacks no longer hunting in packs, but singly, for jobs) will be higher by the time you read this than it was when we wrote it.

Questioning journalism has become much more than an academic exercise. In today's context, the hardest questions are framed by the turn of events outside the academy. Surely this should have some effect on those inside the academy and the way we go about studying journalism. If it was one thing to question the moral authority of professional journalism while its commercial viability looked assured, it must be another, lesser thing to kick at journalism when all its doors are open and unguarded.

Now journalism is down, the academy will only confirm its irrelevance – and there is no shortage of those looking for confirmation – if it carries on kicking in the same way that it did when journalism was on the up. On the other hand, while external events are combining to deconstruct journalism, Journalism Studies could distinguish itself by contributing to journalism's reconstruction.

Instead of continuing its dog-bites-man routine (Not All Journalism Is Good – Shock! Horror!), perhaps the best outcome for the academy would be for academicians to make the most effective case for dogged, professional reporting.

We certainly think so. In today's context, the most pertinent part of critique, we believe, is that which pertains to reconstruction: logical reconstruction of the historical development of journalism, undertaken in the attempt to show the logic of its future histories. Though we are not qualified to determine which version of journalism's future will prevail, our book is an unreserved attempt to develop a version of Journalism Studies which supports what is best about journalism and plays some part in today's struggle to ensure that journalism has a future.

To this end, we reject the kind of negative labelling which the academy has readily practised on journalism. There may have been a time and a place for something along such lines, but we think it is intellectually and morally wrong for Journalism Studies to stay within its established tramlines now that journalism has been bounced out of its own routines – almost to the point of being disestablished. Especially in today's conditions, uncritical continuation of 'critical thinking' will add little more to the understanding of journalism's past, still less to the prognosis for its future; moreover, it can only have a corrosive effect on the academy's relationship with media and society.

This does not mean that we find all journalism defensible. Some of it has been truly culpable (such as the erstwhile role of the British press in legitimising state racism or its regular propaganda service in wartime), and it is the responsibility of Journalism Studies to make their own culpability comprehensible to journalists, i.e. to explain it in such a way that journalists can recognise themselves in the explanation. But this, too, is a responsibility that Journalism Studies has not often lived up to. All too often, Journalism Studies has talked past journalism rather than addressing it.

Neither is it for Journalism Studies to address itself to the day-to-day requirements of commercial journalism or its public service counterpart. Even in the abstract it would be self-defeating for the academy to suspend judgement and turn itself into an industrial training provider; but in today's circumstances this turn would be doubly disastrous. If we in the academy were to rehearse our students to perform for journalism as it was, we would be failing to prepare them for what now is. Equally, there is little point in drilling students in the established patterns of today's industry, since they are not yet confirmed: at present, whatever may become the new pattern has barely begun to emerge from the disestablishment of old-style journalism.

Desperately seeking solutions

Journalists, publishers and their associates have been trying to find consistency in the midst of today's uncertainty, largely without success. Typically, brash attempts to settle the future of journalism by one means or another soon give way to the unsettling realisation that any such vehicle could be more harmful than helpful to journalism. In one week of March 2010, for example, we heard or went to hear various solutions being talked about and came away with the sinking feeling that one journo's lifeboat might easily be another's torpedo. Uncertainty was the only unavoidable outcome, repeatable across the board.

There was noisy trumpeting of Apple's iPad as the tablet with journalism's future written on it. But we could not help wondering why the iPad will not launch even more of the user-generated content (UGC) which allegedly spells the demise of professional journalism. Others insisted that the answer lies in a new business model, either the pay-to-pass firewall as pioneered by Rupert Murdoch's *Wall Street Journal* or the collaborative collation of micro-payments mooted by Google and various magazine publishers. Perhaps one of these will prove commercially effective, or maybe both; but even so, it is naive to expect them to solve the problems of journalism. If we can now convince ourselves that new business models are the solution to the problems of journalism, we must also be able to forget all those earlier criticisms of journalism (going for the lowest common denominator, etc.) in which the old business model and its dominant influence were said to be the cause of journalism's problems. The turn-of-the-century experience, when journalism's crisis was existential before it became financial, should be a sufficient reminder: there is more to this than meets the accountant's eye.

Not everyone is fixated on private sector business models, however. At 'Democracy Without Journalists? The Crisis in Local News', a seminar held in March 2010 in the annexe of the House of Commons, the coinage common to a number of speakers was the idea of journalism as a 'public good' which merits public funding.[1] Thus the General Secretary of the National Union of Journalists (NUJ) introduced his union's 'economic stimulus plan for local media' (Dear 2009), which called on government not only to invest in local journalism but also to assess which media organisations are 'genuinely local' – genuine enough to qualify for financial support. Indeed, the journalists' union should have a policy response to 'the sapping away of resources from local newsrooms and a failure by major companies to invest in quality journalism' (NUJ leaflet). But is it advisable for the elected representative of journalists to be inviting the state to play a bigger role in journalism? Is state intervention representative of journalism's current interests? In the peculiar conditions pertaining today, perhaps it is; but, before rushing to answer, or, still worse, assuming the answer without even recognising the question, we should consider the historical record of state attempts to control journalism and bear in mind that resistance to state control on the part of journalists has been among the formative experiences of journalism; moreover, it is one of the characteristics of journalism that make it worth saving.

This should be borne in mind along with the recent attempt to co-opt journalism into the fieldwork of the therapeutic state, resulting in a flurry of government-funded publications that promote 'well-being', 'participation', and 'community'. While it is hardly unusual for journalistic copy to be composed in ideological terms, we suggest that not since the Restoration period has so large a portion of published material come directly from government. If you live in a British city, you are certain to have seen one of these publications, and you are almost certain to have noticed that, though 'genuinely local', they are not issued from that place in our minds which looks upon all manner of events – local, regional, national and international – as if from the outside. Their content results from a selection process, but the eyes which made the selection are not those of an outsider. Such publications are state-funded but are by no means characteristic of the state of mind required for independent journalism. It is questionable whether copy-writers whose livelihood depends on a funding stream that flows towards this kind of publication would be in a position to retain or even attain the independence of mind required for journalism. Their position would seem to be precarious (even if, in this age of austerity, funding were found to secure such titles), and their predicament resembles that of journalists already working on 'contract magazines' in the private sector, whose role is to promote comparable or identical values – 'sustainability', 'engagement', 'community' – oriented towards corporate brands instead of the state.

Please note, we are not saying that government funding prohibits genuinely journalistic activity outright; there is no more basis for this sweeping statement than for the assertion that contract magazines contain absolutely no journalism. What we are saying is that the relationship between independent journalism and government funding is especially fraught; and, in March 2010, in the run-up to the British general election, we were surprised to find the NUJ appearing to pay little attention to this in its 'stimulus plan'. We think it foolish to enter into a revised version of this relation without careful and continuous scrutiny of the terms of engagement. Similarly, not to apply such scrutiny would endanger journalism instead of securing its future, i.e. the opposite of the desired effect.

None of the available solutions are above suspicion. The other examples given above show that private-sector solutions are equally in need of thorough scrutiny (just as the world we live in all but demands the level of scrutiny applied to it by journalism itself). But who is in the best position to serve journalism as its own scrutineer? Of course, the public will have the final say, but the problem with the 'final say' is that it comes at the end. When all else has been said and done, the public's verdict on journalism still comes too late to have a proactive effect on the preceding process. Similarly, journalists have inside knowledge of their own activity, but the problem with 'inside knowledge' is that it does not look out upon that which it knows; often, its very proximity to internal pressures also limits its powers of observation and evaluation.

Neither professional writers nor everyday readers of journalism, therefore, are in the best position to think long and hard about journalism and what it should be doing. On the other hand, it seems to us that the academy is a strong candidate for this role, but only if Journalism Studies learns to scrutinise not against journalism so much as for and on behalf of it. To illustrate what we mean, we now present an example of each kind of scrutiny, negative and positive, as recently practised by Journalism Studies upon journalism.

'Big Media' vs. DIY journalism

Journalism Studies is a young academic discipline, having emerged in the UK as a discrete area of study – distinct from Media and Cultural Studies on the one hand and from journalism training on the other – not long before the turn of the twenty-first century.[2] It has, of course, a considerable intellectual inheritance – most recently and, certainly in a British context, most importantly, from sociology and Media and Cultural Studies (Wahl-Jorgensen and Hanitzsch 2009: 6). But part of our purpose is to interrogate how far that inheritance remains useful and how far it may be holding Journalism Studies back by making it more difficult to see what is distinctive today. The problem, we argue at various points in the book, is that the post-1968 political context that shaped the radical sociology and cultural theory of the 1970s is long gone, yet the theoretical shapes from that period are being applied to the current context as if it could be moulded to fit ready-made formulations from the past.

A case in point is the critique of the influence of commercialism in journalism. There is a long and initially honourable tradition of criticism of the ill-effects that market constraints can have on journalism. Radical critics have long pointed out that ever-larger media businesses reliant on revenue from advertising sales do not deliver the plurality of perspectives that liberal theory has traditionally claimed for the 'marketplace of ideas'. Yet this enduring concern with commercialism now often seems to produce not an increasingly sophisticated understanding but a caricature of 'big media'. Anthony DiMaggio's study of US 'mass media and mass propaganda', for example, describes a process of 'extreme corporate consolidation and conglomeration of media' which means that 'views reflected in the news are [...] homogenized' (2008: 217). To make the point, DiMaggio portrays Michael Moore's difficulties in publishing his book *Stupid White Men* and in releasing his film *Fahrenheit 9/11* as examples of the marginalisation and exclusion of dissident voices. Yet, as DiMaggio himself notes, *Fahrenheit 9/11* was 'the most profitable documentary ever made' (2008: 153), generating $220 million in revenue, while *Stupid White Men* stayed on the *New York Times* best-seller list for over a year. The fact that Moore has enjoyed enormous commercial success with works that explicitly criticise mainstream US political culture surely demands critical analysis rather than complaints about 'progressive' critics being silenced by monolithic commercial media giants. The assumptions of the past do not necessarily fit the present.

Similarly, in order to sustain the argument about the extreme 'power of corporate media', DiMaggio dismisses concerns about declining news audiences and intensified competition for advertising as exaggerations (2008: 309). The strength and dominance of 'big media' are simply assumed. From this perspective, size is not just an important factor, it is the determining factor: big media are bad because they are big; 'Progressive-Left media outlets' are all the more progressive because they are 'far smaller [...] [with] much more limited audiences [...] [and] less influence with the mass public' (DiMaggio 2008: 24). Were such media outlets ever to gain in size and influence, presumably they would be left less progressive. This logic leads DiMaggio to suggest that CNN was a better, because smaller, outfit under its founder Ted Turner than after its takeover by Time-Warner (2008: 308). Yet this is the same Ted Turner who described media owners as 'a lot like the modern chicken farmer':

> They grind up the feet to make fertiliser, they grind up the intestines to make dog food. The feathers go into the pillows. Even the chicken manure is made into fertiliser. They use every bit of the chicken. Well, that's what we try to do with the television product.
>
> (quoted in Pilger 1999: 476)

Turner drew this comparison in 1994 – two years before Turner Broadcasting Corporation was bought out by Time-Warner; yet in DiMaggio's account Turner is cast as the plucky little critic of 'the perils of monopoly domination' (2008: 308). Rather than illuminating the contemporary relationship between journalism and market imperatives, the routine denunciation of 'big media' seems to miss the point.

Concern over the commercialisation of media, first expressed for the radical Left by the Frankfurt School in the aftermath of the Second World War, grew stronger in the 1990s in the context of debates about the growth of 'infotainment'. Serious journalism, many critics argued, was being squeezed out by the trivial and frivolous in a bid to increase profits – a trend that is often seen as further evidence of the strength of corporate media. Daya Thussu's study of 'global infotainment', for instance, describes the 'growing power of global info-tainment conglomerates and their local clones' (2007: 13). These 'news factories', he argues, signal the worldwide dominance of neo-liberalism, eroding journalism's capacity to serve the public good and promoting a shallow consumerist culture. While there is little doubt that news agendas have indeed become 'dumbed down', with a preponderance of trivia, celebrity gossip, scandal and so on, this development could just as easily be indicating not the strength but the weakness of media businesses. That is to say, although the trend since the 1990s has in one sense been towards maximising profitability by making the news more 'entertaining', the context has been one of declining audience numbers – largely as the result of widespread disengagement from public political life. Thus, as larger numbers of the people formerly known as the electorate have become further alienated from the political coverage that was once the very bread and butter of journalism – even commercial journalism – so media businesses have been under pressure to win them back with new kinds of jam, up to and including the honeypot of celebrity. In this reading, the divorce of journalism from serious coverage is not reduced to the simple love of money on the part of big media corporations.

For most critics, however, the chain of cause and effect is that profit-hungry big media drive out the serious in favour of the trivial, thereby undermining political engagement. Indeed, Thussu maintains that in this sense 'infotainment' can be understood as 'an ideology for a neo-imperialism of neo-liberalism' (2007: 13). As he argues:

> Infotainment, especially in its global context, entails much more than dumbing down: it works as a powerful discourse of diversion, in both senses, taking the attention away from, and displacing from the airwaves, such grim realities of neo-liberal imperialism as [...] the US invasion and occupation of Iraq; the intellectual and cultural subjugation by the tyranny of technology; of free-market capitalism and globalization of a profligate and unsustainable consumerist lifestyle.
>
> (2007: 9)

This scenario draws on a long tradition of critique in which all-powerful media provide an alibi for the weakness or failure of radical politics. Yet surely a more credible explanation is that people are not so much 'diverted' from serious political issues as simply uninspired by a political culture which, after the end of Left and Right, is almost entirely devoid of vision. As it happens, the issues highlighted by Thussu – anti-consumerism, suspicion of science and technology and an individualistic, 'not-in-my-name' opposition to war – constitute something like the common sense of the age: there is little evidence that people are 'diverted' from holding these familiar views. But the larger point here is that in an era when the character of political life is given by technical managerialism rather than compelling ideals, it does not take a global cabal of media moguls to turn people off politics.

Inside the vicious circle of declining audience interest in the stuff of journalism, of course, media owners and managers have seized opportunities for cutting costs while grabbing as much as possible of a dwindling audience share (the context in which Turner was so determined to wring every last drop of value from the 'product'). The strategy to achieve this – making the news glossier, lighter, more user-friendly – may, in turn, have further discouraged popular engagement with the public sphere; but, rather than the media causing disengagement, in reality it has been the hollowing out of politics by politicians, and the electorate taking itself away from this increasingly empty shell, which prompted various attempts to connect with the news audience in a different way. Hence, for example, in the numerous revamps of British television news during the 1990s, the explicit concern was to find some point of connection with the audience. In 1997, Channel Five's controller of news, Tim Gardam, promised a 'non-elitist and bottom-up' approach and said that he aimed to prevent the news from being 'painful' by featuring 'less politics and more consumer, sports and entertainment news' (quoted in Franklin 1997: 11–12). The same year, the BBC's Head of News, Tony Hall, embarked on a 'search for new audiences' which would reportedly entail 'less on political ding dongs at Westminster and more on technology and consumer issues'. By the end of the decade, Independent Television's flagship

News at Ten programme had been dropped in order not to clash with films and entertainment in the evening schedule, and a new magazine-style programme, *Tonight*, was launched with the slogan: 'the stories that matter to *you*' (quoted in Franklin 1997: 11–12). As it turned out, such innovations were not very successful (in ITN's case, viewers complained about the absence of the *News at Ten* and switched over to the BBC, which had promptly moved its own programme to the 10 p.m. slot). But the clear intention was to retain audiences by lightening up and focusing less on traditional political stories. 'Tabloidisation' in the broadsheet press can be understood in similar terms – attempting to retain readers via restyled formats and lifestyle content – with similarly disappointing results. At nearly every turn, the public has rebuffed the news executives and their charm offensive. Received ideas about the evils of 'big media' turn reality on its head, however, portraying these lame responses to the worsening health of the news industry as if they were a sign of economic and ideological strength on the part of neo-liberal, mega-media corporations.

The rise, over the past decade or so, of various forms of web-based journalism and UGC has to some extent been understood, either negatively or positively, within the same framework. Efforts by established media organisations to solicit 'citizen journalism' and to encourage 'users' to be content-generators is sometimes understood as simply a cost-saving measure, getting the public to supply for free what might otherwise have to be paid for (Deuze 2009: 255). In fact, news organisations have incurred considerable costs in concerted attempts to encourage and process users' photos, stories and other contributions: the BBC's UGC hub, established in 2005, for example, employs more than twenty people to handle the 10,000 contributions it receives every day, checking stories, verifying pictures and selecting what to use.[3] The BBC has also sponsored research into how to elicit more UGC from its viewers and listeners (Wardle and Williams 2008; Wardle 2010a, 2010b). Of course, it might be argued that more, free UGC ultimately means less paid journalism, but encouraging audience 'interaction' appears to be a greater priority than any cost savings.

More upbeat assessments of citizen journalism usually understand it as presenting a challenge to corporate media. According to Dan Gillmor (2006), for example, whereas 'Big Media [...] treated the news as a lecture', the Internet allows 'news reporting and production [...] [to] be more of a conversation, or a seminar', thereby giving 'new voice to people who've felt voiceless' (Gillmor 2006: xxiv). Such optimism, common in early accounts of web journalism, has been tempered by more sceptical appraisals of the idea that digital media have an inherent democratic potential (Hindman 2009; Markham 2010). The point, however, is not to write off the positive potential of new technologies but to arrive at a realistic judgement about how it might be realised: the claim, for example, that the Internet provides 'a radically reforming (if not revolutionary) tool for globalized, social-movement-based activism' (Atton and Hamilton 2008: 4) lacks credibility because of its fantastic projection of incipient global radicalism. Besides this exaggerated opportunity, there is also the equally exaggerated threat which is said to be posed by media corporations in their 'cynical attempt to recuperate radical forms of representation for the purposes of marketing, to take emerging forms of alternative journalism and rework them in order to add a contemporary sheen to dominant practices' (Atton and Hamilton 2008: 141). A more sober assessment of the relationship between citizen journalism and the mainstream is suggested by documentary film-maker Adam Curtis:

> Now our presenters plead with us to send in our photos and videos. They proudly present it as a new kind of open democracy. But in reality it's something very different. Because the journalists don't understand what is going on in today's complex, chaotic world, they have had to revert to their old habit of finding someone in authority who will tell them. But this time, it's not the politicians – it's us, the audience, that they've turned to. The only problem is that *we* don't have a clue what's going on. Particularly because the journalists have given up on their job of explaining the world to us.
>
> (Quoted in Meikle 2009: 194–5)

Though tongue in cheek, Curtis's comments capture the way in which major media organisations are seeking to incorporate their readers, viewers and listeners in a diminishing spiral of reciprocal uncertainty. But they are reaching out to audiences, more because of a loss of professional nerve on their part; much less in the attempt to deactivate a radical, alternative viewpoint. Even among minor media organisations there is little to suggest that the latter really exists. In contrast to the 1960s and early 1970s, when setting up a small shop usually entailed piling into the monolithic foundations of post-war, consensual thinking, being small is no longer cognate with Big Ideas.

Exemplary work

Amidst a stampede of stories about the death of journalism, in the title of his March 2010 inaugural lecture as Head of Journalism at City University, Professor George Brock took the bull by the horns. 'Is News Over?', he first asked, before answering, no, not at all, if only journalists prove their worth by 'narrowing down the elements which make the core of what they do' – elements identified as 'verification', 'sense making', 'witness' and 'investigation'. Professor Brock also hazarded a definition of journalism as 'the systematic effort to establish the truth of what matters to society'. He added: 'it follows that expertise and experience, for example, should count for something' (Brock 2010).

To us, Brock's contribution seems commendable on a number of counts:

1   It identifies professional journalism with a consistent quest for truth in the interests of all humanity – a form of identification which has fallen into disrepute for all the wrong reasons.

2   It associates journalism's claim on truth with its claim to public attention and, by implication, the preparedness of the public to pay for what it attends to.

3   In approaching the problems of journalism, Brock acts as its critical friend.

Brock's friendliness is hardly surprising, since he himself was only recently a journalist (Managing Editor of *The Times*, Editor of *The Times* Saturday edition), but in his new-found, professorial role, he is not afraid to voice sharp criticism such as when, in his lecture, he compared the recent course of journalism with that of the *Titanic*.

Positioning himself as something like an external examiner of journalism, who is sympathetic to journalism and its ambitions while remaining critical of their imperfect realisation, Brock seems to us to personify the kind of positive role which Journalism Studies should be playing in today's circumstances. Moreover, Brock's selection of 'elements which make the core' of journalism accords with our emphasis on journalism as the organised fulfilment of a cognitive capacity that is socially constructed. In other words, we think that besides politics and economics there is also a philosophy of journalism – a whole aspect of journalism which has tended to be either sadly neglected or erroneously negated but which merits much closer attention, especially in today's context. We are confident that journalism and the academy's relationship to journalism would both benefit if more attention were paid to this aspect of journalism as it is sketched out in our book. Indeed, these are the ends to which our own contribution is meant.

About this book

This book has grown out of our dissatisfaction, as academics interested in news and journalism, with many of the inherited assumptions of the field. Not only has journalism itself changed but the broader world of politics and public affairs has been transformed beyond recognition in the past two decades. Yet the study of news and journalism often seems stuck with ideas and debates which have lost much of their critical purchase. *Journalism Studies* both offers a reassessment of conventional themes in the academic analysis of journalism and sets out a positive proposal for what we should be studying. The book is organised in three sections, addressing the contexts in which journalism is produced, practised and disseminated.

Part I: Ownership

In Chapter 1 we discuss some key examples from the history of journalism to show how developments in journalistic technique correspond to the changing social and historical context in which they arose. In tracing this evolution we attempt a logical reconstruction of the changing relationship between the press, politics and patterns of ownership. This understanding of journalism's past, we suggest, should make Journalism Studies wary of reductionist approaches which identify editorial content too closely with bourgeois ownership (as in the denunciations of 'big media' discussed above). As an alternative, in Chapter 2 we set out a different view of the news industry which takes account of its dual character, involving both private appropriation and social production. We propose a new theory of media as a form of mediating activity – that is to say, a form of activity that mediates between the indirect relationships of capitalist production and the direct, interpersonal relationships between individual human subjects. In the history of capitalism, mediating activity has sometimes been monetised, just as culture is often produced as a commodity. But in the 300 years since Joseph Addison and Richard Steele wrote the *Spectator* as well as owning it, the history of journalism has also entailed the relative divergence of ownership from obser- vation. Thus, though they may be in the same building, the reporters' room (with its concerns) and the boardroom (with its priorities), are not normally identical, and academic signage that points to them being in one and the same place tends to be unhelpful, if not misleading.

Part II: Objectivity

We turn next to the question at the heart of journalism: is it true, and how do we know? Chapter 3 outlines the various academic objections to journalistic objec- tivity, either as a desirable ideal that has rarely been reached in practice or, more often, as an impossible and misleading claim. Reviewing accounts of the historical rise and fall of objectivity, the chapter goes on to argue that the critique of objectivity itself needs to be seen in historical context, largely as a response to circumstances that no longer exist. Rather than continuing to repeat the critique – superfluous, in any case, since journalism has internalised it – Journalism Studies would do better to reclaim the possibility of objectivity. Chapter 4 attempts just that, arguing for a new understanding of objectivity as the corollary of human subjectivity rather than something opposed to it.

The critique of objectivity, we maintain, was really a critique of objectivity in its alienated form, whereby 'hack' journalists were likely to become estranged from themselves as subjects producing an object – the story of what happened, while readers were encouraged to become passive: immobilised by the weight of objects known as facts, as they too were alienated from themselves as autono- mous subjects. More recently, the same developments, inside and outside jour- nalism, which have destabilised these erstwhile arrangements, also demonstrate that the meaning of 'objectivity' was not fixed for all time; objectivity is not uniform throughout history. Accordingly, we propose that journalism, supported and perhaps even led by Journalism Studies, can play a significant role in the reconstruction of objectivity in a different, non-alienated form. Whereas alienated objectivity rested on the denial of human subjectivity, non-alienated objectivity depends on the extension of it. This is objectivity produced collectively by self- conscious subjects, not the pretence that knowledge is a ready-made object which lies on the ground waiting to be picked up and packaged. Non-alienated objectivity is now facilitated by digital technology and the subjective interactions which it enables. It is predicated on human subjects producing the world, and it anticipates the possibility of us producing a different one.

Part III: The public

Journalism Studies has long complained of an exclusionary public discourse that fails to take account of difference, yet the opposite problem now presents itself: that journalism addresses not a public sphere but 'separate public sphericules', in Todd Gitlin's (1998: 173) phrase. Chapter 5 addresses this issue, reappraising the claim that the news media construct false unities such as the 'general public', by examining some of the difficulties that broadcasting has historically encountered in conceptualising the public it serves. We then further scrutinise the emphasis on textual representation and discursive construction that Journalism Studies has inherited, attempting to place this approach in historical context as not just a theoretical debate but also a response to a particular set of political circumstances. In order to address the very different circumstances of the present, we argue, both journalism and Journalism Studies need to rescue a universalistic conception of the public.

In the Conclusion, we return to the relationship between journalism and Journalism Studies in light of our enquiry, offering a mutually reinforcing approach to both the practice and the study of journalism. Our focus is the point where journalism as inquiry into the world meets academic inquiry into journalism. While others may wish to serve as the conscience of journalism, we would act as its consciousness.

Part 1

Ownership

Chapter 1

Ownership and the news industry

One of the most famous examples of mid-twentieth-century professional journalism is Tom Wicker's account of the assassination of President John F. Kennedy, which first appeared in a special edition of the *New York Times* published on the same day that Kennedy was killed (22 November 1963).[1] Kennedy's assassination came at the high point of the post-war boom and the peak of American influence over the rest of the world (before the USA was seen to fail in Vietnam). Wicker was prominent among a generation of journalists writing news for an industrial society – journalists whose news writing amounted to an industrial process in its own right.

Wicker's account of the death of JFK is a fabrication. This, we hasten to add, does not mean that he made any of it up, but that he *composed* it; Wicker constructed his account, building a structure out of what he had observed that day in Dallas. Wicker's structure is streamlined. He presents a stream of information lined up in order of significance, starting with the assassination of probably the most important man in the world and moving down through the hierarchy of information (and people) to encompass Jackie Kennedy's bloodstained stocking and the bullet wounds sustained by John B. Connally Jnr. Not only because of his lesser wounds but also because he is a lesser mortal, the Governor of Texas does not appear in the body copy until the tenth paragraph (though there has been a fleeting glimpse of him on the fourth deck of an eight-decker headline).

If we were conducting a class on news reporting, we would say that the lines formed by Wicker's structuring of this world-famous event comprise a pyramid (or triangle). But there is nothing ancient about this formulation, or Wicker's use of it; instead, it is consistent with the modernist mode of abstracting from appearances and the order in which they first present themselves, the better to understand that which is being presented. Wicker re-presents JFK's assassination in much the same way that a Cubist painting presents reality anew. Wicker's representation bears the same sort of relation to raw experience as Picasso's depiction *Three Musicians* (1921). In Wicker's case, he has travelled backwards and forwards in time so as to shape the occurrence he is describing. Similarly, Picasso captured the presence of three musicians by depicting them from different angles which would not normally present themselves to the same viewer at the same time. In each instance, immediate sense impressions have been taken out of their real-time setting and organised into clearly identifiable, geometric shapes (pyramid, cube). But these formulations are not only for form's sake. In drawing words, sentences and paragraphs together into the formal development of his story, Wicker has also replaced the line of events as they occurred in time – a flat timeline – with a sequence of information presented in descending order from primary importance to supplementary significance.

This presentation is the final movement in a three-part manoeuvre on Wicker's part. First, as a trained observer, he will have made a mental record of events as they occurred in real time. Second, although he actually wrote it on a portable typewriter at the scene, in his mind's eye Wicker must have stepped far enough back from the scene to extract key elements from the raw footage going on in his mind and to identify in these elements what would become the crucial components of his story. By now it is as if he has already drawn another line, dissecting the timeline of events and reaching as far back as the mental position from which to review them. Finally, he takes these crucial components and edits them into a hierarchy of descending significance (since you need to know this, you may also wish to know that which follows on from it; since you must have wanted to know that – or you wouldn't have read this far, you may also, etc.). Having constructed the story according to this logic, Wicker has also drawn another line starting from his own, internal viewing platform, stretching not only back to the original setting in all its vivid detail but also forwards, in the direction of his readers. This last line is the one that puts them in touch with the scene, via the reporter's reconstruction of it. In the way he wrote the story, in effect, Wicker took the flat timeline of events and drew two more lines, sharply angled against this first one, so that together they form a triangle (or pyramid structure).[2]

Line by line, Wicker's story bears out the shaping process described above. The priority at the top of the story is: 'President John Fitzgerald Kennedy was shot and killed by an assassin today.' This is an abstraction from the real-time sequence. The motorcade has been wrenched out of its Dallas setting and replaced by a simple statement of the utmost importance: Kennedy is dead. The level of abstraction upon which the opening line rests is underwritten by formal identification of the dead man. Referring to him by his full name and the title of his elected office removes him temporarily from the realm of ordinary, interpersonal relations and transports him to a higher level in the public domain. As Wicker proceeds with his composition, however, he leads the reader back down towards personal detail and the passing of real time. He subsequently tells us that it was 2 p.m. when Jackie Kennedy left Parklands Hospital, walking beside the bronze coffin containing her husband's body. We also learn what has happened to her famous coiffure: 'she had taken off the matching pill box hat she wore earlier in the day, and her dark hair was windblown and tangled.'

In rearranging events so that his construction of them moves from the abstract to the concrete – something like an aeroplane coming down through the clouds towards the runway – Wicker offers far greater insight than could have been provided by the chronological reiteration of events. It transpires that information arranged according to a descending order of significance rises to a new level of meaning, thereby adding to its own descriptive power. Wicker's considerable craft is formally realised in expressions which are all the more telling for being so economical ('Mr Johnson is 55 years old; Mr Kennedy was 46'). Equally remarkable, and perhaps even more substantial, is the way that he presses vivid details ('Mrs Kennedy [...] still wore the raspberry coloured suit in which she had greeted welcoming crowds in Fort Worth and Dallas') into service on behalf of a strict hierarchy of information in accordance with the pyramid structure. Wicker was commuting back and forth between sensory impression and causality, and the pyramid was his vehicle for making the journey.

In Wicker's rendition of it, the pyramid construction is able to encompass abstraction from events and something of the real-time moments in which they actually turned. Far from being a barrier to meaningful information, or a shield against the intensity of being there, as Wicker constructs it the formality of the pyramid is designed to give readers more content – greater knowledge – than they might have acquired if they had been there on the day. Thus the information in Wicker's story on the front page of the *New York Times* is infinitely richer than real-time, amateur film of the assassination, such as the footage currently available on YouTube, and it is more composed even than the consummate TV professional, Walter Cronkite, seen struggling to anchor CBS coverage as news of Kennedy's death rolled out before his eyes and in his earpiece.[3]

Wicker's account is a superb example of what has been described as the view from nowhere (Nagel 1986), apparently devoid of personal positioning on the reporter's part (disingenuously so, some would say). His view is clear and far-sighted, but what comes out of his viewing is, above all, constructed. In the best sense of the word, this is the *manufacture* of news. Of course, we recognise that in reference to news, the word 'manufacture' is normally used negatively. Among media academics, it is customary to put a negative construction on the story construction which Wicker exemplifies. For these critics, either the pyramid is jacked up too easily – an automatic, journalistic routine which precludes fresh observation and obstructs original insight; or else it is too much of an effort, and too big a claim – a sad case of the deluded reporter straining for godlike independence and inevitably failing to reach it. This is the case against objectivity, which we will discuss in detail in Chapter 3. Moreover, the pyramid is taken to be the structured form of writing which most clearly represents the industrial structure of news manufacture and the system of private ownership that both generates and contains it. The correlation of these three dimensions – (professional) story, (industrial) structure and (private) ownership – has led to the academic modelling of modern, industrialised news production as if private interest were its only driving force and publication merely the projection of journalists' and publishers' private concerns onto increasingly cynical readers, viewers and listeners.

In this chapter, we show that such a model is reductionist, i.e. it reduces a multi-level process, which entails the recurring aspiration to tell the truth, to the lowest common denominator – the bottom line. While we acknowledge that commercial turnover has usually been the precondition for professional news production, telling the story of news largely in these terms is like covering a flower show by reporting almost exclusively on the vases in which the flowers are arranged. Of course, the flowers could hardly be shown without vases to support them, but they also stand for something in their own right.

To make a case for the substantial (though never absolute) independence of news production from the blinkered self-interest associated with private owner-ship, we have selected some tableaux from the history of journalism, chosen because they represent significant moments in its development. Our approach to each of these encompasses something of the journalistic techniques involved, alongside the social and historical contexts from which such techniques evolved, together with recognition of the correspondence between these two paradigms (developments in technique, developments in society), utilising each to shed light on the other.

By tracking the development of journalism and the development of society, and by cross-referencing one with the other, we seek to show that journalism has been partly but by no means wholly accountable to private owners. Conversely, we aim to explain how private ownership has been essential to the development of journalism not only as its commercial basis, in which capacity it is often seen as unwelcome and unavoidable in equal measure, but also in the actual practice of journalism and the performance of its social role. In short, journalism and commercialism have flowed through history as complementary but non-identical streams.

If it seems laborious to go the same ground thrice over, it is surely better to do this than to keep revisiting the same territory any number of times, without moving the debate any further forward. To us there appears to have been something like trench warfare between professional accounts of the emer-gence and development of modern, commercial news production, told in terms of individual endeavour, timely innovation and journalistic autonomy, and academic studies, with their emphasis on social and industrial constraints, sys-tematically enforced in the context of private ownership. Our aim is break this stalemate with a logical reconstruction which, though admittedly short on historical detail, nonetheless identifies and explicates the essential contradiction in journalism, namely, that it has striven for truth on behalf of the majority, while operating for the most part in conditions of minority ownership and private gain.

Furthermore, having reconstructed some of the most important elements in the *previous* development of news reporting and journalistic manufacture, we will be better placed to review the recent debate about objectivity and to specify the strengths and weaknesses of professional reporting in *today's* context (the task to which we come in Chapters 3 and 4).

Being there

> June the 16. our men having made a breach in the Castle, assaulted it, but
> found the Enemie desperately resolute, reviling and calling them English dogs,
> Parliament Rebells, Puritan rogues, and holding up some of their best apparell
> and linnen at their sword points, and topps of Pikes, and setting fire unto them
> burnt them in our sight, saying, look here you pillaging Rascals there is pillage
> for you, and when our Gunners shot, they cryed shoot home you rogues, Cap-
> taine Stutuile having thrown in at the breach some hand grenades, part of
> the house took fire, which some of them seeing, resolutely burnt their armes,
> goods, and lastly themselves therein, others cryed for quarter, but none being
> granted but to the women and children, they resolutely defended themselves,
> and kept our men almost two houres at the breach at push of pike [...].

This quotation is from the first part of 'A Perfect Diurnall of All the Proceedings
of the English and Scotch Armies in Ireland', published on 18 July 1642, attributed to one Master Godwin, and selected by Joad Raymond (1993: 46) as one of
three examples of 'early newsbook descriptions of battle'. In writing this report
for circulation, Master Godwin was compiling a list of all that had happened in
battle, or, more precisely, all he recalled as having happened, so that his comrades
in arms might come to know of it. The lines quoted above are about half the
number selected by Raymond in his extended extract from Godwin, but at the
end of Raymond's selection, even at twice the length of the section quoted
above, neither the author nor his first sentence have yet arrived at a full stop.

Godwin's 'Diurnall' was 'perfect' in that he wrote down just what his memory
retained of the events of the day. In his writing there is no sign of formal structure or hierarchy of presentation; it is simply a chain of linked words which reflect
the actions and reactions of those embroiled in battle. Godwin has not *constructed* his report in the same way that Wicker did, three centuries later; indeed,
it is not even clear whether the occurrences Godwin describes are formed as
separate events in his mind's eye. In writing down his account, Godwin may well
have been reviewing these occurrences in the same way that perhaps he first
experienced them, as an uninterrupted stream. By the tenses that he has used, we
know that Godwin was not writing his account as the battle raged around him:
'our men *having made* a breach in the Castle, *assaulted* it' (italics added). The
past tense puts Godwin writing about the battle after it had occurred. But it does
not put him at the same distance from the battle as we have since come to
associate with news reporting. Nor can his positioning be understood as an early
example of the 'journalism of attachment' (see Chapter 3 for further discussion of
this), since the latter was a late-twentieth-century reaction against levels of
detachment which in Godwin's time (1640s) were not yet widely adopted, either
in writing or in the orientation of human beings to their surroundings.

It would be wrong to say there had been no previous manifestations of any such
detachment. Something like it is discernible, for example, in the self-examination

of the Shakespearian soliloquy, when leading characters come down stage and out of the action in order to address the audience, and in doing this they look askance at themselves as the audience itself would do. Similarly, the delineation of separate scenes on Shakespeare's part, distinct from the flow of medieval mystery cycles, underlines the construction of the play and indicates that Shakespeare was occupying a new kind of social position from which to construct it. But the dual spectatorship entailed in Shakespearian drama – the audience viewing characters on stage and onstage characters viewing themselves – also suggests that the Elizabethan theatre was an unusual place of uncharacteristic self-consciousness, set apart from the normal run of largely unexamined lives.

From today's vantage point, if we look back at Godwin's newsbooks as an early episode in the history of reporting, it comes naturally for us to say that they show the necessity of reporters being there, on the scene they are reporting. Similarly, it would be easy to suggest that, whatever its faults, the 'journalism of attachment' has restated the importance of this. But both statements are equally facile. Human beings have always been there, since 'there' is where we are, necessarily. What differentiates Godwin's news from ours is that the reporter's position of being one step removed, the default position from which to file copy, is hardly there for him to occupy, still less for him to deny. There can be no question of Godwin questioning the validity of detachment and opting for attachment instead, since the position hardly exists (at least, not widely) from which he could choose to adopt or reject either one of these.

The battle in which Godwin took part (he took both parts, having written on behalf of both sides in the English Civil War) was part of a war for the right to rule England. It was a war fought between representatives of opposing modes of government: theocratic autocracy versus parliamentary democracy (though the 'demos' in this democracy was narrowly defined and largely confined to the nascent merchant class and their collaborators among the landed gentry). In modern eyes, a conflict between two sides such as these implies that there is a choice to be made between them, and, moreover, that there is a third position from which to make choices. Regardless of whether we make our decisions out of self-interest or in the public interest, or a compound of the two, for much of the modern period we have tended to assume that the process of our coming to a decision is undertaken from a vantage point that is raised above and apart from the immediate options; indeed, if not from such a position, though we may have a stronger interest in following one, particular course of action, there is no ground from which to make a deliberate choice, no space in which to make our choice the outcome of a process of deliberation, and, without this, it is more that the 'choice' chooses us, rather than the other way round.

The historical development of civil society is tantamount to the formation of the third position at the mid-point between two comparable possibilities. Seen in this light, 'civil war' in the mid seventeenth century was not the breakdown of civility or the abandonment of this position so much as the violent anticipation of it. But it really was to be anticipated, rather than something which existed there and then in the 1640s. The brief episode of the Putney Debates, immediately followed by brutal suppression of plebeian elements within Oliver Cromwell's New Model Army, shows that the debating position – the space in which material interests might be laid out as logical propositions – was not yet sustained by historical conditions.

To say that this kind of mental positioning was barely conceivable before the modern period is not to say that choice was hitherto unknown to human beings; but choice on the part of human beings was understood to be trumped by fate, i.e. the element in our existence which we cannot stand out from and which turns out to be the factor that determines whether or not our existence will continue, and on what terms. In other words, fate was the pre-modern concept for the confinement of human agency within prescribed conditions and their corresponding outcomes. Far from being confined to the ancient world, the concept of fate was reasserted as recently as the early modern theology of Calvinism in which it was recast as divine predestination. In Godwin's day, not even the Puritans had progressed all the way to the modern expectation of mind as the out-of-body experience which positions us beyond both our immediate, physical existence and also the non-human element previously thought to condition that existence – our fate.

Recently, the existence of such an independent position has been called into question, but the questioning is so widespread that it has the effect of confirming the theoretical possibility of this position even while denying its practical reality. As often as it is said to be historically impossible, the more it is acknowledged as a logical possibility; and since what's at stake here is the possibility of exercising logic in human affairs, this is all that is required to confirm it. Even in their protest, critics of the independent position do much to confirm its existence in modern times.

It would be wrong to assume, however, that the modern position was readily available to Godwin, even as a theoretical possibility. Instead, we must recognise that the English Civil War was in some ways a war to establish this position, to liberate especially the members of the merchant class from a situation in which they were mentally and spiritually enclosed within a theocratic way of thinking and doing, even though the definitive aspect of what they were already doing – their expanding commercial activities – had brought them to the very boundaries of the pre-modern condition and thence into military conflict with its institutional forms. For the purposes of our presentation, the point is that there was as yet no easily occupied, widely available vantage point from which Godwin could have looked down on the events in which he had only recently participated, and, if there was no such external position from which to look into them, neither was there an easily accessible form of writing in which to compose an account of what he was seeing, as if seeing it from the outside.

For Godwin to have been able to compose an account of these events in this fashion, his mind's eye would have to have been positioned outside the battle and outside his own composition also. He would need to be looking in at both of them and taking up a position equidistant from each. But in England in the middle of the seventeenth century this positioning was barely developed in ordinary life, still less formalised in everyday writing. Accordingly, in Godwin's work and that of his contemporaries, there was as yet no 'diurnal' form of writing up what is being described as if the writer is standing largely outside the content of his own description, just as writers themselves could hardly stand outside their immediate context. This, in turn, suggests that we should be cautious about tracing the genealogy of journalism as far back as ballads and other forms of description which were largely contained within the communities they served; because of their communal character, though they were descriptive, these forms of expression could go only some way towards what we now understand as the position of external independence that characterises journalism. En route, however, there was no such recognition of what was only later revealed as the culmination of an historical progression.

The ferment of civil war prompted the publication of thousands of newsbooks and pamphlets. While these contained diverse accounts of various occurrences, more often than not they were presented in facsimiles of pre-existing forms of writing; as quasi-military despatches (see above), letters, legal documents, political argumentation and theological tracts. Such writing may have been appropriate to its time but it does not *appropriate* in the modern manner; it does not move from outside in, like an invisible hand taking hold of its subject matter. All newsbooks expressed an outlook, since they looked out from the point of view of either the King or Parliament. But the converse aspect of *outlook*, which entails looking in on events as if from outside, was a habit still to be spread wide, and without this external positioning, there must be some doubt as to whether the occurrences so described were composed as discrete events, either on paper or even in the minds of their authors.

Thus, at the time of the English Civil War, there was a growing number of writers whom we might call journalists, but what they wrote in 'newsbooks' was not *sui generis*, it had yet to find its own form as journalism. Similarly, the position from which to formulate journalism as a specific type of writing was only now – in the act of war itself – in the process of being established. Not that the end of the English Civil War was also the completion of this process. As late as the late 1670s, the first page of the *London Gazette* (Monday, 17 November 1679), published by 'Authority' (the government of Charles II), suggests that there was still some way to go before journalism was fully established in the distance between reports and the reported. Instead of being a report of the proclamation 'for the more effectual discovery of Jesuits', the page simply is the proclamation (reproduced in O'Malley 1986). It is hardly true to say that it is a full reproduction of the proclamation, since even this implies the possibility of a shortened version and the mental position from which to compose a brief account of its full significance. As yet, however, neither of these has become the default position which we tend to take for granted, even when we are criticising it.

Looking at society

Perhaps not all, but the title says most of it: the *Spectator*. On Thursday, 1 March 1711, Joseph Addison and Richard Steele published the first issue of their own periodical (following the recent demise of their *Tatler*). It was to be a publication that looked upon society as if, at least momentarily, the two main authors, publishers and owners were not themselves participants in it but the eponymous spectators of it. In the scenario of the *Spectator*, as they themselves set it up, Addison and Steele were always outsiders looking in on whatever they were writing about, even when writing about themselves; which is also to say that their publication positioned them outside their subject matter. This was how they wanted it – their specified preference. Unless Addison and Steele had been making a point of looking in on their topics from without, they would hardly have picked a title that positioned their publication as the *Spectator* and identified its author-publishers as spectators. As Addison put it in the first issue, 'Thus I live in the World, rather as a Spectator of Mankind, than as one of the Species' (Steele and Addison 1988: 199). Below the title of the first edition ('NUMB. I The SPECTATOR'), the nearest thing to a headline was a quotation from the Roman poet Horace pointing out what a writer should aim for in his writing:

> Non fumum ex fulgore, sed ex fumo dare lucem
> Cogitat, ut speciosa dehinc miracula promat.
>
> He thinks not to produce smoke from radiance, but to give light from smoke
> So as to draw out handsome and peculiar things.

The next line announced that publication was 'To be Continued every Day'; it is followed by the date of this first issue (1 March) and then the opening lines of the first column of the first article:

> I have observed that a Reader seldom peruses a Book with Pleasure, 'till he knows whether the Writer of it be a black or a fair Man, of a mild or cholerick Disposition, Married or a Batchelor, with other Particulars of the like nature, that conduce very much to the right understanding of an Author. To gratify this Curiosity which is so natural to a reader, I design this Paper, and my next, as Prefatory Discourses to my following Writings, and shall give some Account in them of the several Persons that are engaged in this Work. As the chief Trouble of Compiling, Digesting and Correcting will fall to my Share, I must do myself the Justice to open the Work with my own History.

The first formulation is particularly pertinent: 'I have observed that a Reader seldom peruses a Book with Pleasure.' In other words, not only am I stating that I have been looking at something but the something I have been looking at is itself the process of looking at something – a book, which in turn is the result of its writer looking at something else – the subject of the book; bearing in mind that the something I have been looking at (readers and the way they like to look at books that look at things) is separate from I who have been looking.

Similarly, the Reader is someone who 'peruses' a Book. That is, readers are understood to go through ('per') books, making use of their contents, in such a way that what is contained in the book is taken to be distinct and somewhat distant from the person(s) perusing it. Furthermore, though we know it was Joseph Addison who wrote this opening article, the drop capital 'I' with which it opens is not a reference to Addison directly; instead, the article is presented as the work of Mr Spectator, one of a cast of clubbable characters whose writing populates the pages of Addison and Steele's periodical. 'Mr Spectator' is the product of Addison looking out at the London society which he inhabited and opting to create a quasi-fictional persona through which to be seen looking out at the London society he lived in. Thus, in its opening paragraph, the *Spectator* raises the curtain on a hall of mirrors, in which real people and quasi-fictional personae are shown reflecting on a chain reaction of their own reflections. At each point in the chain, each individual personifies the new subject position from which to look out upon the world before acting in it; and in their particular personification of that position, the same individuals are also cast in the role of objects for the person next in line to 'peruse' and read like a book.

The whole venture hinged on the possibility of describing the things that people do and the kind of people that they are, and of doing this from a quasi-fictional position simultaneously derived from their common characteristics and distanced from traits peculiar to particular individuals. This duality is discernible in the prospect of Addison reinventing himself as Mr Spectator; and it was no mean feat. In the shape of Mr Spectator, a public persona is presented who is not quite identical to that private individual who invented him, Joseph Addison; indeed the presence of the former depends on the absence of the latter, at least to the extent of Addison suspending his individual activities and private interests in order to become the exemplary spectator and to speak with his voice. In this arrangement, Addison is the ventriloquist; Mr Spectator the dummy who purveys intelligence.

In the 300 years since Addison configured his own dual existence in this way, we have become accustomed to the distinction between narrowly self-interested activity and the fulfilment of a professional or public role, even though in the past half century especially, there has been growing cynicism about the real existence of this distinction. We reserve a fuller discussion of private and public for Chapter 5. At this moment, suffice it to say that at their moment, in England in the early years of the eighteenth century, Addison and Steele were among those introducing a qualitatively new version of the possibility of this distinction. (Daniel Defoe was another such innovator; his *Review* [1705] also captured the possibility of looking anew.) Their capacity for commuting between subject positions was so novel, so different and so distinctive that they felt the need to make the transition a literal one. To establish a spectator's position outside their private selves they were obliged to create literary characters other than themselves; hence the invention not only of Mr Spectator but also his clubbable contemporaries, Sir Roger de Coverley, Isaac Bickerstaff et al. With hindsight, these ruses seem unnecessary, but they only became superfluous when both journalism and the surrounding culture grew more adept at negotiating public and private interests and commuting between the subject positions entailed in their varied expression.

The *Spectator* and Mr Spectator were hinges that articulated the private self looking out on the world with a public self looking in on oneself as the outside world itself would do, and out of this articulation arose a stronger sense of one and the same selfhood. To put it another way, these subject positions (particular interest, general interest) further distinguished themselves as and when conditions and mechanisms jointly arose which allowed their articulation. By their articulation, each element matured, and their compound became more substantial. Private individual and public persona: each was distinguished, and both were reinforced by continual cross-referencing.

But this was also a delicate process, open to rude interruptions. In an essay entitled 'Mischiefs of Party-Spirit' (*The Spectator*, No. 50, 27 April 1711), Addison sought to protect it against growing factionalism between Whigs and Tories. 'If this Party-Spirit has so ill an Effect on our Morals', he warned, 'it has likewise a very great one upon our Judgments' (Steele and Addison 1988: 445). Addison referred back to the English Civil War and its divisive, destructive effects. He wrote from the vantage point of the new century (Addison was as many years away from the English Civil War as we are from the Second World War); also, from a viewpoint in which he expected his contemporaries to present themselves for others to view and to arrange themselves and their actions in anticipation of what others would make of them. In the hall of mirrors, spectatorship was the process (participatory and self-conscious in equal measure) in which one's actions and motives would be scrutinised by many, and because scrutiny was now to be expected, sensible persons would scrutinise themselves in advance and act only in ways acceptable to one's many external scrutineers. Thus, for Addison and Steele, a new level of self-consciousness was the means to articulate self-interest and the public good. Reciprocal relations between private interest and public good were to be arrived at in polite conversation and formulated in its written counterpart – periodical journalism.

In the eyes of the twenty-first century, this process looks very fine – as if the world were made of lace – and absurdly mannered, for the same reason. But compared to the levels of mystification entailed in earlier forms of social reconciliation, it was much more down to earth. In pre-modern times, at relatively low levels of socialisation, magical thinking and its institutional presence (religion) were the only means of addressing such discrepancies. By contrast, Mr Spectator and his clubbables were representations of human society, without resort to any *deus ex machina*. By referring explicitly and almost exclusively to *human* self-consciousness, the *Spectator* was itself an actor in the real world of the early eighteenth century. At the same time, in its undue reliance on human *self-consciousness*, it proved to be more ideal than real; furthermore, its idealism was realistic only for a relatively short period of time.

Addison might have gone on to say that Mr Spectator and his cronies could not have been created while the Civil War was raging, nor even while its legacy remained paramount in the period after 1660, dubbed 'the Restoration' because the son-king, Charles II, was brought back from exile and installed in the hereditary role of monarch, even though his father, Charles I, had been executed by order of Parliament in 1649. When Charles II died and was succeeded by his brother, James II, a Catholic who harked back to his father's belief in the divine right of kings, it seemed as if regicide might make a comeback also. But in 1688, in an event referred to as the Glorious Revolution, sections of the English aristocracy formed an alliance with the merchant class to depose James, and, instead of killing him (the fate of his father), they sent him into exile, replacing him with the Dutch prince, William of Orange, who was married to James's daughter, Mary, and, crucially, favoured the further development of England's mercantile economy. Although there was military conflict in Ireland at the Battle of the Boyne (1690) and in the subsequent, Scottish rebellions of 1714 and 1745, with first James and then his son as their figurehead, all this occurred without civil war breaking out throughout England. (In 1745 the rebels came as far south as Derby, but their incursion was soon beaten back.)

The temporal climate was conducive to trade and associated procedures such as negotiation and litigation. In place of civil war, there was a disposition towards civil society. Moreover, negotiation occurred on human terms, without reference to divine right and by diminished reference to Almighty God (thereby diminishing the 'almighty'). There were to be transcendent values, but perhaps for the first time, these were explicitly man-made. Instead of calling on God to judge them, parties to negotiation were called upon to refer their personal interests to the court of human interest and to defer to its judgement. Common humanity – the interests we have in common – was the new sovereign lord, occupying a new space which was built from self-interested trade yet stood one step aside from its continuous exchanges.

At the turn of the eighteenth century, London was riding high on the wealth accrued from trade, and, as it scaled new heights of commerce, so it became the site for the construction of a new viewing point from which to look down on all kinds of human activity, beginning with, but not restricted to, trade.

In locations such as early-eighteenth-century London, where there are very many commodities for sale, and where there is more than one seller of the same kind of commodity, the buyer is in a position to choose between commodities of the same type. In the moment before exchange (the exchange of commodities for money, which has become the universal equivalent of all commodities available in the market), when there is the possibility of exchange with various parties, the buyer finds himself in a position which is one step removed from any of the exchanges into which he may enter. From this position, he can look over the range of commodities on offer and choose the best one. If he is a merchant, with a view to selling on the commodity he is about to buy, he will make his choice according to generally applicable standards, as he himself interprets them. Though he is doing this because he wants to obtain the particular commodity for which he himself will afterwards obtain the best price, i.e. in his own interests, nonetheless in making a judgement he will have subordinated all such commodities, and his own personal preferences, to a social standard. Moreover, it transpires that, once established in one area of human activity (trade), the position from which to apply social standards to commodities for sale is itself applicable to commercial and non-commercial activities alike. Thus, people's behaviour comes to be judged from the same viewing platform as commodities and according to similarly social standards.

Indeed, in a mercantile culture such as that which existed in London at the turn of the eighteenth century, it was not only possible but necessary to take up this position. For the sake of one's own interests, the capacity to see goods (one's own and other people's) and people (oneself and others) from the point of view of the general interest was a requirement. In a culture based on trade – moreover, trading activity that was as prolific as it was continuous – this was the new position from which men came to see the world and themselves in it. In this sense, they had to be spectators upon their own lives. The position they were obliged to occupy was that of the spectator, and this obligation was directly referenced in the title of the *Spectator*. To announce a publication with this title was thus to announce the establishment of this social position. Only with the publication of the *Spectator* was it fully established as a fixed part of everyday, London life. Similarly, only in the conditions of relative stability after the Glorious Revolution was it possible for the merchant class to act in its own interest by establishing another subject position from which its individual members viewed their own behaviour with something approaching disinterest or, more accurately, with interests other than straightforward advance from their own, personal, starting position, regardless of the consequences. In place of strife, the relative stability engendered by the Glorious Revolution thus enabled the reciprocal realisation of private and public interests – as a possibility, at least.

Never identical but now complementary, these subject positions were articulated in the new form of London's periodical journalism. Such was the significance of this development that from this point on even the most particular self-interest would be expected to present itself in terms of the general interest. Once they had been brought together in this way, no man could presume to put these interests entirely asunder. To do so would necessarily mean undermining one's own social position. Of course, this does not mean that henceforth everyone shared the same interests or voiced them in the same way. As Addison himself was forced to admit, divisive parties were already exerting a destructive effect on his beloved society; and the social forces driving the development of these parties would soon prove too much for the society of spectators. Nonetheless, the formulation of general interests through the continuous scrutiny of one by many, the comparison of particular and general interests, testing the former in terms of the latter and the degree of self-consciousness required to perform such tests – all of these were developed in the *Spectator* and the culture in which it was embedded, and they have all played an enduring role in the modern world.

In his depiction of truth standing 'On a huge hill, Cragged and steep', the poet John Donne had already pointed to a third position located above direct exchanges between human beings (quoted in Smith 1978). Anticipating Addison, in the *Review* of 17 April 1705, Defoe had 'declare[d] himself sincerely desirous of the general peace, abstracted from the prejudice of parties' (quoted in Speck 1986: 51). Afforded by the conditions of the day, Defoe's private abstraction from politico-religious parties suggests not only the development of cognitive abstraction but also the contribution of abstract thought (and the position from which to think it) to the idea of the public interest, and this in turn re-entered the conditions of the day as a material factor in their continuing development.

Both the distinctive character of private interest and disinterest (in the public interest) and the possibility of one complementing the other were further represented in the ownership of early-eighteenth-century periodicals. Addison and Steele were not only author-editors of the *Spectator* but also its owner-publishers. As such, they had a vested interest in the publication; at the same time, they had vested in a project which depended on disinterest, both as a contribution to contemporary culture and as its selling point. What Addison and Steele owned, therefore, was their own capacity for disinterested observation combined with the means to produce and disseminate an account of what they saw – a combination which was itself counted as a commercial venture.

That such a variety of functions could be fulfilled within one and the same individually owned, personally produced, socially derived enterprise may serve to show that these various orientations are not wholly antithetical. Or, it might be argued, the short lifespan of both the *Tatler* and the *Spectator* (in their original incarnations) not only indicates an unstable admixture but also suggests that private ownership and self-interest are always in contradiction with disinterested observation and the common good. In the following section, however, we seek to substantiate the proposition that, in its origins, the journalist's disinterested orientation to the world is akin to that of the commodity owner approaching the market and, also, that both these closely related viewpoints first came together in a culture of Enlightened mercantilism.

The Age of Enlightenment: commerce, philosophy and journalism

In first the *Tatler* and then the *Spectator*, Addison and Steele created what had to be a new form of writing because there was now a new role for this writing to perform. On the European continent, by contrast, a closely related role was more likely to be played by philosophy, and in philosophical circles something akin to the articulation described above was more readily accommodated in the philosophical discourse of subject and object. In England, especially London, the terminology was different and the primary medium was journalism rather than philosophy. Nonetheless, the correspondence between contemporary journalism and philosophy is clear from Addison's declared intention that his own journalism should play a part in bringing 'philosophy out of closets and libraries, schools and colleges, to dwell in Clubs and Assemblies, at Tea-Tables and in Coffee Houses' (*Spectator*, No. 10; quoted in Price 1982: 174). While John Price has established that 'almost overnight, Addison made Locke in particular, and philosophy in general, not only respectable but fashionable' (Price 1982: 174), we are concerned with relations not only between early-eighteenth-century journalism and philosophy but also with the relation of each of these to the mercantile economy that underpinned them both. As we shall show, in conditions of relative stability the latter not only financed both journalism and philosophy but also informed their reciprocal development.

In analysing sentences for their grammar, we customarily distinguish between 'subject' and 'object', respectively, that word in the sentence describing a person (or thing) who is acting and that other word which describes a person (or thing) who is being acted upon. For example, in the sentence 'I hit him', 'I' is the word describing the active component (subject); 'him' is the element that is acted upon (object). Alongside their significance for grammar, these terms are also used in philosophy. Nowadays, there are people who reject their philosophical usage as 'theological' without realising that the counter-position of subject to object was once remarkable in that it counterposed theology to a new, non-religious view of the world and a uniquely human-centred way of living in it; in other words, in the days of Addison's *Spectator*, the philosophical usage of these terms was quite the opposite of 'theological'.

The historical period in which 'subject' and 'object' came into their own as a philosophical (non-theological) couplet is known as the Age of Enlightenment. In England, the coming of this age is associated with the Glorious Revolution of 1688 in which a rational-instrumental alliance of leading aristocrats and prominent merchants substituted William of Orange for the increasingly anachronistic James II and thus established Britain's constitutional monarchy. The climactic ending of the Age of Enlightenment may be said to have occurred across the English Channel, in the turmoil of the French Revolution (1789) and its tumultuous legacy. The Age of Enlightenment was also the period in which the economies of Western Europe moved decisively (though by no means simultaneously or concertedly) from rural, agricultural production to an urban culture based on commercial trade, and, subsequently, towards national, industrial production. Indeed, the proliferating references to 'subject' and 'object' should be seen as the philosophical expression of this transition. In the following paragraphs, we explain why this is so; we also explain why both this transition and its philosophical counterpart are pertinent to the development of journalism.

From pre-modern to pre-industrial

In pre-modern cultures oriented to agriculture, no amount of human effort, whether individually performed or collectively undertaken, was ever enough to decide outright the size of the annual harvest or the quality of life throughout the following year. In quantity and quality, human life was unavoidably subject to the forces of nature, though the latter might be considerably modified by human effort. Even to the Ancient Greeks, who were among the first to consider their own humanity, being human was not so much self-actualising as actualised (in large part) by natural forces. Another way of making the same point is to say that their response to nature was much less mediated than ours.

The combination of limited human capability and the decisive, seemingly infinite capacity of nature was the constant reality of pre-modern times and the stuff of recurring, religious fantasy. Accordingly, as natural forces were represented in the various, partly humanised forms known as 'God' so further human effort, i.e. ritual observance, was frequently invoked in an effort to mollify them or simply in the attempt to connect with them. In the Catholic mass, the mysterious moment of consecration is one such example. In the context of pre-modern, natural economies, when the priest held up the bread and wine in order that they might become the body and blood of Christ, he was holding up a mirror to the mystery of natural forces in the annual growth of crops. Something really was going on in the fields that remained unexplained in human terms – natural growth. As this was crucial to human survival so it was also inexplicable in human terms. Instead it was addressed as 'transubstantiation', the divine word for the magical moment when each of two (earthly) substances – bread and wine – becomes another (holy) one – the body and blood of Christ, respectively.

Just as it remained unclear when and to what extent human beings were the subjects (active components) of their own lives and at which point nature would inevitably take over, in pre-modern conditions the philosophical distinction between 'subject' and 'object' was not likely to be clear or sustained. Similarly, relations between 'cause' and 'effect' could be only partially clarified since 'effect' often resulted without any scientifically known 'cause' having produced it. But there came a point in human history when the quantitative expansion of trade, and the development of a whole way of life around urban centres of trade, including the further development of human self-consciousness as described in the *Spectator* and elsewhere, jointly served to put both commerce and culture at a considerably greater distance from the effects of natural forces. Instead of being so directly responsive to nature, they emerged as 'effects' with largely human 'causes'.

By the end of the seventeenth century, London, the largest city in the world at that time, already occupied such a position. The London markets were a magnet that attracted goods from all over the world; the magnetic pull of London's commerce had also attracted 575,000 inhabitants to the city and its environs, rising to 900,000 by the beginning of the nineteenth century

(Brown 1991: 419–20). Throughout the eighteenth century, London's population growth was fuelled by the expansion of trade and the secondary activities that supported it. Unlike provincial towns or even cities, the London economy was not dependent on local crops or the manufacture of a small range of products in a specific locality. Instead, London's wealth came from its role as the centre for monetary exchange (buying and selling) of all the world's goods, as famously celebrated by Addison in the *Spectator*, No. 69 (19 May 1711):

> There is no Place in the Town which I so much love to frequent as the Royal Exchange. It gives me a secret Satisfaction, and, in some measure, gratifies my Vanity, as I am an *Englishman*, to see so rich an Assembly of Countrymen and Foreigners consulting together upon the private Business of Mankind, and making this Metropolis a kind of *Emporium* for the whole Earth.
>
> (Reproduced in Mackie 1998: 203)

Positioned as the whole world's 'emporium', London's commercial life was no longer conditioned by nature as it pertained locally. Whether the sun shone in London or it rained for weeks on end, the markets would continue to open. If the harvest failed in one region, the same crop might well have thrived in another; wherever it came from, the crop would come to market in London. There might be drought or famine elsewhere, but never a shortage of things to buy and sell in the markets of London. The commercial life of the markets would go on; and the way of life based on buying and selling would continue to proliferate. At this point in London's development, its inhabitants were no longer subject to natural forces in the same way that their forebears had been (or as their provincial cousins were still). True to their own reality, they saw themselves acting, more often than not, as subjects (active components) with sovereignty over their own existence. They no longer lived their lives in fear of nature's rude interruptions, nor did they define themselves primarily as functions of natural forces or, conversely, as functionaries of divine order.

Furthermore, as indicated in Addison, the metropolitan markets were a microcosm of the whole world, with each region of the world represented by the objects it had produced. Again, in keeping with this reality, in the mind's eye of the metropolitans, the whole world came to be represented as a collection of tradeable objects. The metropolitans were living in a different world – different from the past, different from their rural contemporaries; hence, they saw the world differently, largely as a series of objects of which they had the power to dispose. Furthermore, in a commercial culture based on buying low and selling high, their own activity was paramount; thus, they saw themselves as the foremost actors in a world primarily determined by their own actions. Here at last is the uniquely modern sense of self, in which we act as subject, and the world is the object to be acted upon; moreover, we are as we are, and the world is as it is, largely because we subjects have acted upon it.

This is how the philosophical usage of subject and object was originally conditioned; and these are also the conditions in which modern journalism emerged, in the shape of London periodicals such as the *Spectator* (1711) and its predecessor the *Tatler* (1709). As writers, editors and publishers of these titles, Joseph Addison and Richard Steele were subjecting other people's actions to scrutiny. In other words, they were extending this new way of life to a secondary level, where they reported on (acted upon, in words) other people's actions, and these actions became the objects of further scrutiny, just as the scrutiny of primary objects (commodities) was already the established practice of the London markets and a central feature of the way of life oriented towards commodity trading. Furthermore, having read the *Tatler*, *Spectator* and other publications in order to acquire intelligence concerning recent actions by other subjects, reader-subjects would be able to act more intelligently: they would know from various news-sheets how to play the markets and, from the *Tatler* and *Spectator*, how to play the topics of the day in polite conversation.

Thus, the way of life based on the expansion of trade past the point where natural forces might at any moment contract commerce and terminate human life soon came to include reporting on actions undertaken by human subjects and making these reports available in further, new objects called periodicals; similarly, the expectation that human activity would normally trump 'acts of God' was a key factor in philosophy's new emphasis on human activity and its effects, often conceptualised in categories such as 'subject' and 'object'. In journalism and philosophy, the actions of human subjects upon the world and its objects were described and analysed. By such means, these actions also became objects – objects of study, objects of reporting, objects of philosophical contemplation – and, in such guises, these objects went on to inform the next round of further actions by human subjects. But for all their variety, each round of social activity had its origins in the mobilisation of ownership, i.e. the transfer of ownership in the continuous exchange of commodities between old and new owners.

In his magisterial account of the Enlightenment, Peter Gay observed that journalism and philosophy were correlated almost to the point of being cognate: 'Man, *Spectator* in hand, was enlightened man. The Enlightenment of the *philosophes* would be no shock to him' (Gay 1979: 55). Gay also observed Addison correlating commercialism and humanism in a 'slightly cloying ideal' (Gay 1979: 49). Yet, though they were cognate, the journalism of the period was not identical to its philosophy. Thus, it would not be true to those times to drift unawares from that register of expressions that includes 'intelligence' and 'periodicals' to the other (philosophical) mode of understanding couched in terms such as 'subject' and 'object'. As publishers, editors and writers of the *Tatler* and the *Spectator*, Addison and Steele were as keenly interested as the philosophers in the acting and the being acted upon. But whereas journalists monitored a fairly large number of the most active individuals in society and followed the life stories of multiple, tradable goods which these same persons had dealings with, the philosophers of this trading epoch did not speak so readily in plural terms, whether of people or things. Though 'merchant' and 'commodity' were the subjects and objects underlying the utterances of both groups, the philosophers were more inclined to talk in singular terms, to say 'subject' and 'object' and even to dignify these words with capital letters: Subject and Object. Thus, in their depiction of the world, what it was and how it worked, the philosophers of the Enlightenment tended to move away from the day-to-day business of individual subjects with legal titles to particular objects, i.e. owners and their commodities, to speak of humanity as a whole, the Subject, in relation to the Object, the world in general. There were a number of reasons for this.

While there was much greater expectation that urban, trading culture would withstand natural hazards as a whole, there was no such reassurance for individual traders operating within it. The more they sailed the high seas, the more merchant ships were lost (not to mention sailors), while the risk of one party being badly used by another was inherent in the core business of buying low and selling high – a risk recognised in the motto *caveat emptor* (let the buyer beware). Faced with the discrepancy between varied, individual fortunes (some down as well as others up) and the relatively fortunate, consistently improving position which the trading culture had gained for itself overall, philosophers tended to invest in the prospects for humanity as a whole; hence, they formulated a prospectus not so much for individual, legal subjects (property owners) as for the Subject that was taken to be the whole of humanity and for the Object, understood as the whole world which humanity was making for itself.

There was another variation which also informed the philosophers' preference for a form of words – Subject, Object – which referenced the new reality of human existence in a general category rather than particular examples. Though many of Europe's newly expanded cities shared a common culture, it turned out that the cities where trade was at its most expansive, such as London, were not always the same as the cities where philosophers were most active, such as Heidelberg. If their own cities' pickings from trade were not so rich, it is hardly surprising that the philosophers' terms of reference showed a preference for the general capability of humanity to act upon the world, rather than emphasising particular instances of commercial activity in which they and their fellow citizens were not necessarily the most prominent participants.

However, even if the tendency to ascend from particular instances to a pair of singular, general categories, Subject and Object, was, in part, the philosophers' response to their own distance from the realm of specific, prolific commercial activities, nonetheless in a different aspect this tendency was also in keeping with the expansion of trade and the new quality of life which it engendered.

Commercialism, journalism and idealism

For commerce to have become a whole way of life encompassing entire cities and regions, participants in this way of life must have spent a considerable, perhaps definitive amount of time looking, again and again, at goods on sale in the markets and making comparisons between them in order to establish the value of each. In these conditions, the commercial *value* of tradable goods was arrived at from an assessment of their difference from other such goods and, simultaneously, an appraisal of what they and the other goods had in common, as observed by intelligent, calculating subjects and ratified as a number or price. Thus, price emerged as the monetary form of a general category, value, and value came to be a relation enacted at point of sale by legal subjects (owners) continuously comparing one commodity with another.

A commercial culture that depended on making comparisons between objects and putting a figure on the relative merits of tradable goods, i.e. pricing their relation, will have entailed recognising their commonality at least as much as spotting the differences between them. The look of the potential buyer upon goods which he might or might not choose to buy also involved the comparative analysis of these goods with other goods which he may have previously opted to purchase – or not. Thus the oft-repeated comparison of commercial goods was crucial in establishing their value. In addition, the oft-repeated comparison of objects prompted the further comparison of subjects – the comparative analysis of people rather than commodities, who, similarly, came to be seen in terms of what they had in common as human beings, i.e. their common humanity. In this way, the particular conditions pertaining to the expansion of commercial trade were conducive to a world view in which the world was seen as a series of objects to be traded according to their particular representation of general standards, i.e. value. As value is a social reality (more than mere convention), so mercantilism supported a philosophical outlook which tended towards general categories. With one foot in the grubbiest of money-grubbing activities, the Age of Enlightenment also turned its other, slender ankle towards the most rarefied abstractions, up to and including Subject and Object.

To sum up: the expansion of trade had the effect of increasing the proportion of human existence that was dependent on human activity, compared to that portion which was conditioned by natural forces. Quantitative change led to new life of a different quality. As they expanded the field of their activities, so the traders and their associates saw themselves acting on the world and the world as that upon which they were acting. If this sounds unremarkable today, this is because in much of Western Europe and the USA we have continued to think (much) like this for more than three centuries. But 300 years ago, when Addison and Steele published the first issue of the *Spectator*, human activity had only recently gained priority over natural forces in determining their particular existence; and this only in particular cities and specific regions. Since that time the generalisation of this quality of human life has been so uneven that some parts of the world have only recently achieved it, and a few are yet to do so, even now.

As the eighteenth-century traders and their associates saw themselves acting on the world, so they described what they saw of themselves in action. The journalism of Addison and Steele offered one such description; the philosophical discourse of Subject and Object provided another. Both these descriptions were drafted into the expanding pattern of commercial and cultural activity. In each of them alike, reporting the things that people had done was largely inseparable from giving directions on the things that people should do, what they would become by doing so, and how, by so doing, they would become more like themselves. Hence Addison and Steele developed an essay format which did not observe the distinction between reporting and editorial – a distinction that was not much made until the nineteenth century. Meanwhile, a line of thinkers culminating in the German philosopher G. W. F. Hegel identified the progressive manifestation of rational spirit with the realisation of humanity as the Subject of history. As Hegel himself expressed it: all that is real is rational, all that is rational is real (Hegel 1820). In this formulation of the unfolding relation between real and ideal, there is less and less separation between what really is and what really ought to be; rather, historical reality unfolds to reveal more of the rational idea. Idealism was to reach its high point in Hegel's philosophy, but Addison and Steele had already formed the essay into the very ideal of society, thus locating their journalism partly within this philosophical tradition.

We acknowledge that the preceding section is schematic and abrupt, but we hope it is sufficient to reveal something of the Age of Enlightenment in a critical mass of comparable subjects and tradable objects, massive enough to engender the humane ideals of Addison and Steele's journalism alongside the philosophical idea of humanity as the Subject of history and history as the realisation of the Subject. But in this same period, there was also a philosophical counter-tendency: the empiricist view in which objects are seen in their own right and the empirical approach in which Object, not Subject, is the starting point for knowledge and human activity occurs in response to the logical priority of objects.

Empiricism and mercantilism

From this point of view, it is the Object that approaches the Subject, just as objects present themselves to human subjects. This they demonstrably do, both in the markets, where sellers are present only as representatives of their wares (otherwise they have no *business* being there), and also in empiricism, which prioritises objects in the same way that idealism promotes subjects. For empiricists, the Object, in presenting itself for examination, impinges on the eye of the beholder; it gives out data which the human Subject is only there to observe and record. Thus, objects, including commodities that exist only as a result of human activity, are momentarily more active than inquiring subjects whose temporary role is to be impressed by these objects, to soak them up like blotting paper, so that the specific character of particular objects is stamped upon their consciousness. At this point, what was the 'object of study', in the terminology derived from idealist philosophy, has become the empirical 'subject', as in 'subject matter' or 'the subject under discussion'.

There is much to be said in favour of this approach. Not only is it possible to see the world, and ourselves in it, from this starting point; it is necessary, at some point, to do so. In their reporting role especially, journalists must first be open to what was there before they themselves came on the scene to report it. Similarly, the initial obligation of scientists is to address themselves to objects as they present themselves. Though at some stage scientists may act upon their objects of analysis in their imagination and by means of experimentation, posing such questions as 'what if?' and 'what else?', normally this line of active questioning on the scientists' part occurs only after they have first taken the object of their analysis as they found it and taken from it as much as they can learn from the way it presents itself to them.

The scientific approach is in keeping not only with philosophical empiricism but also with the activities of eighteenth-century merchants who scoured the world or as much of it as was known to them, scrutinising objects and taking home the best of those that they had found, in the hope of finding a higher price for these objects than the one they took them for. In this respect, the merchants were taking (home) the world as they found it; they were empiricists, too, and in the mercantile cities, though people conversing in coffee houses were crucial to both commerce and the surrounding culture, in an important sense it was the commodities that spoke first, announcing their own qualities while buyers and sellers were obliged to stand by and listen. These tradable objects all but introduced themselves; they were the essential subject matter of the marketplace. Thus, the object-oriented character of empiricism was partly prompted by the primacy of objects (commodities) in the marketplace.

Empiricism and idealism

In their empirical aspect, eighteenth-century Londoners recognised that they must address the world of objects as they came upon it, either in their commercial activity or in the realm of knowledge, or both. Not that recognising this necessity meant that they must also, as of necessity, renege on their belief in human beings as sovereign actors in their own existence. To the contrary, their sense of being the Subject arose largely from their direct address to the outside world, from their new-found ability to separate themselves from the objects surrounding them, to look at the latter unstintingly and act upon them without expecting their actions to be overridden by natural forces or, which largely amounted to the same thing, being contained within their immediate circumstances.

The crucial point about this set of expectations is that it begins and ends with what human beings can do. Accordingly, when objects appear in this order of business, which is also a philosophical schema, they do so as the objects of human capabilities, including the capability for acquisition, the capacity for investigation and even the power of transformation. However, from one and the same reality it is possible to devise a different pattern of existence that begins and ends with objects, that culminates with the weight of objects bearing down on human subjects; and, if this were the point of origin and the default position of existence, the destination to which it inevitably returns, it must also be the vanishing point of Enlightenment optimism.

As it turned out, the hopes of the Enlightenment were not dashed down, once and for all, in a decisive battle of empiricism against idealism. But by the end of the eighteenth century the idealist call to history and perfectibility was answered, though perhaps in less than equal measure, by an empirical refrain that emphasised the burden of all those objects resting on the frail shoulders of humanity. After a century of evolution, these two positions reached their full exposition in two, polar essays by Condorcet (in 1794) and Malthus (in 1798).

In his *Sketch for an Historical Depiction of the Progress of the Human Spirit*, the Marquis de Condorcet made the definitive statement on the perfectibility of human beings. He declared, 'That nature has set no bounds on the improvement of human facilities; that the perfectibility of man is really indefinite; and that its progress henceforth is independent of any power to arrest it, and has no limit except the duration of the globe upon which nature has placed us' (quoted in Avery 1997: 6).

Four years later, Thomas Malthus published *An Essay on the Principle of Population, as It Affects the Future Improvement of Society, with Remarks on the Speculations of Mr Godwin, M Condorcet, and Other Writers*. In his essay, Malthus warned that other people are a threat to prosperity whenever their number rises above a fixed level. Whereas Condorcet's view, echoed in England by the likes of William Godwin, would suggest that more people can achieve greater progress more quickly, thereby accelerating the perfectibility of man, in Malthus's estimation, larger numbers of people tend to cause poverty and thus reduce 'the future improvement of society'.

In the Malthusian view, growing numbers of people are surplus to social requirements. As such, they are hardly their own subjects, certainly not incorporated into the Subject. Instead, they are more like uncalled for objects that present themselves as an unwelcome burden on society, a dead weight on the limited lifting power of humanity. For the second (1803) edition of his essay *On the Principle of Population*, Malthus provided a number of revisions, including a revised subtitle – *Or a View of Its Past and Present Effects on Human Happiness* – and a new preface in which his repeated use of the word 'subject' is notably not that of the idealists and their Subject; instead 'subject' is here subject matter in the empirical sense (what the idealists would have described as an object being studied, or otherwise acted upon).

Equally notable is the attribution to 'Rev T.R. Malthus, late of Jesus College, Cambridge, professor of history and political economy in the East-India College, Hertfordshire'. In other words, the empirically grounded theory in which the world of objects was extended to include large numbers of people (the more the people, the more objectionable they became, in Malthus's estimation), was elaborated by the theorist-in-residence at the management training college of the world's largest importer of commercial objects, England's East India Company. This is not to suggest that Malthus was merely a mouthpiece for mercantilism, but it does indicate a degree of correspondence between empiricist anti-idealism and that part of the mercantile mentality that regarded tradable goods not only as the source of all goodness but as the originating font from which society itself is issued. With these as its coordinates, this object-oriented mentality was bound to be concerned lest the finite source of goods/goodness was outweighed by all those other objects for whom there is no proper place in the market, i.e. the surplus population.

Reporting language

From the way in which we have rehearsed their relations in the preceding section, it seems that the idea of human independence from natural forces obtained its credentials from the expansion of mercantile economies and the concomitant increase in wealth and security while the centrality of tradable objects in this expansion reinforced the empiricist view that objects are prior to whatever it is that human subjects succeed in doing with them. Even before these approaches entered into a battle of ideas during the period of the French Revolution, in England the potential for their conflict was already represented in the complex, contradictory character of Dr Samuel Johnson, the poet, dramatist, journalist, lexicographer, biographer, editor and celebrated wit who seems to have been fairly frequently at war with himself.

In his writing and conversation, Johnson took on the task of resolving the contradiction between idealism and empiricism – in favour of the former but only by detailed engagement with the latter. In the event, though he possessed the perhaps most independent mind and an undoubtedly strong constitution, even Johnson's powers were not adequate to the task.

Unlike Addison and Steele, Johnson never owned much except his own pro-digious capacities, for reading, observing, thinking, talking, writing and drinking (frequently to excess, but with intermittent periods of abstinence). In a famous letter to the Earl of Chesterfield, in which the noble lord was damned with the faintest praise, Johnson called time on patronage as the most important financial mechanism for supporting literature and the arts. He exemplified the writer who is paid a fee for his writing, who plies his trade on the open market and who must write as he is paid, because he has no other means of paying his way. If the publishing careers of Addison and Steele anticipated the future role of the commercial publisher, for much of his professional life Johnson had more in common with the jobbing journalist. Yet Johnson's career also showed that the appearance of those with a direct, pecuniary interest in the labour market for writers is not also the disappearance of disinterested writing. Not being a 'blockhead' (as Johnson described those who would write without expectation of being paid for it) does not make you a hack. To the contrary, Johnson made his living from his life's work (the former coming second to the latter), and his life's work was to wrest writing even further from the realm of the immediate and the strictly personal. Instead, Johnson sought to identify the common interest in the use of language and to identify language and literature as the currency of the common interest.

For the purposes of our discussion, Johnson is even more remarkable for his efforts to achieve this, not by imposition from above in the style of the French Academy but from the bottom up. This direction of travel was Johnson's route for transcending the conflict between idealist and empiricist approaches to the world and the role in it for humanity. It is most clearly mapped in his *English Dictionary* (1755). His two-volume dictionary is the work by which 'Dr Johnson' is best known in Britain. Leading a small team of researchers paid for by private subscription, Johnson laboured on it for seven years. In the *Plan for an English Dictionary* (the prospectus he drew up in order to attract inward investment), he had written that 'attainment' of the English language would be 'facilitated' by his dictionary (Baugh and Cable 1978: 272). This sounds not so far removed from the core idealist notion of development as the realisation of inner essence. Similarly, in the Preface to the finished work, as in the original *Plan*, Johnson declared his intent to 'ascertain' the English idiom (Baugh and Cable 1978: 272), that is, to make it certain, to establish it. But how was it to be established? By having his assistants undertake detailed study of the usage of English words and tracking their change of use – an extensive preparatory process which then allowed Johnson himself to certify words in their correct meaning. Thus, he sought the realisation of language by standardising its real usage at the highest possible level.

Though there are many criticisms to be made of it, Johnson's dictionary gained and retained its influence because in this work at least he was for the most part able to integrate the two meanings of true meaning: Johnson's definitions were 'true' in that they set a high standard of what words ought to mean and how they should be used; but his definitions were also 'true' in that they caught the nuances of actual usage. Thus, the dictionary was partly a report on the configuration of English as expressed in the meaning and usage of individual words – it took an empiricist approach to the subject matter of a living language, and partly the reconfiguration of English, issued as a set of instructions on the corrected meaning and directed usage of its vocabulary. While the dictionary's first role was in line with empiricism, in undertaking this second aspect, Johnson was not far from the idealist approach to language as living expression of the human Subject in the process of self-realisation.

If Johnson was largely successful in integrating these two approaches to language, thereby transcending some of the limitations inherent in each, this does not mean that he was able to solve the philosophical problem of the age single-handed. With hindsight, we may say that he asked too much of language and expected too much of himself as its leading practitioner. For Johnson, the progressive deployment of language – better usage and truer meaning – was tantamount to the development of manners and morals. A society that was teaching itself to speak and write well would also be learning to live the good life, and who better to promote this progressive development than the leading authority on language deployment, i.e. Johnson himself? This was asking more than Johnson himself realised. Language and literature, no matter how well taught, cannot be expected to school a whole society. But it will not suffice to say that Johnson confused questions of language with problems of philosophy, partly because this obscures both the substance of his achievement and the philosophical significance of language but mainly, however, because framing the problem philosophically still does not get to the nub of it.

Whether empiricists or idealists, eighteenth-century philosophers were inter-preters of the social change they themselves had experienced, specifically the his-torical development of mercantile economies and their concomitant culture. This development was ambiguous. That is, there were two, contrasting aspects in which it presented itself: freedom from the direct impact of the forces of nature that prompted human beings to see themselves as the subject of their own life sentences and the close orientation of human beings towards tradable goods – the objects in the marketplace with command even over human subjects. As this duality presented itself in history, so it was re-presented in two branches of philosophy: the ideal and the empirical, subject-led and object-driven. That they should eventually come to blows in a battle of ideas was entirely in keeping with the two-sided course of this specific historical development. Equally, that the Age of Enlightenment should fail to resolve its own battle of ideas was also in keeping with the age itself. For as long as it lasted, there was no further, outstanding historical development that pointed either to a decisively transcendent subject or to an all-consuming object. Conversely, the emergence of precisely these phenomena in the form of the revolutionary bourgeoisie (France) and the onset of industrial capitalism (England) marked the dissolution of the age.

Thus the impasse of subject and object was derived from the essential character of mercantilism and the way of life associated with it. This means that the historic problem of England's eighteenth century was beyond the scope of the under-standably irascible Sam Johnson. In his contrariness (the radical Tory, the most individualistic of systematisers, the moralist who gave short shrift to moralising), Johnson reproduced the duality of the day, but he also made strenuous efforts to transcend such contradictions by digging deep into what seemed to be their linguistic roots.

In this undertaking he was ultimately unsuccessful but in the attempt he demonstrated (and sometimes lost sight of) a particularly pithy kind of writing which was set to become journalism's preferred form of expression. As the pro-tagonist in James Boswell's various accounts of his life and times, Johnson was also the model for what soon became the genre of 'human interest' journalism. In addition, he represented a personality type that was to be closely associated with journalism. Not only in his choice of stomping ground (Fleet Street and the surrounding district) but also in the way he stomped around the area, Johnson set the journalist in type.[4]

From merchant capital to industrial capital

For much of the eighteenth century, the most advanced economies were mainly mercantilist, i.e. economic growth arose from merchants trading an increased number of commodities which they had bought at a low price in order to sell at higher prices. Until the moment at which they bought them, these merchants would have had no previous connection to these commodities; before purchase, they may not even have known of their existence. When they bought these goods, however, they also brought them into an expanding network of market relations. Through this network, commodities travelled freely. Meanwhile, their close escorts, i.e. their owners, subjected commodities and the people who owned them to continual comparative analysis – the kind of scrutiny that was further represented in journalism, when journalists such as Addison and Steele started to *essay* the merchant city of London.

At this point in the history of capitalism (and journalism), goods were only entering into the network of relations between buyers and sellers at the moment when merchants bought them in order to sell them on. By the same token, the production of these goods had already occurred before they were fully incorporated into the system of market relations. They were goods before they became commodities. That they were good for something, i.e. they had a use, suggested that someone would pay for the use of them, i.e. to consume them – hence the merchant's willingness to act as intermediary between producer and consumer. However, the merchant was also an intermediary between the increasingly systematic operations of the market and various, local production arrangements which were contiguous with the market system but not yet fully incorporated into it. In such conditions, for example, though crops were grown and clothes were made specifically for sale to merchants, their production preceded their entry into the integrated system of market relations; conversely, the system of market relations was yet to penetrate production.

This began to change during the eighteenth century when metropolitan merchants started to visit provincial locations of production, not only to buy up finished products and take them for selling on but also to commission their production and organise the production process (Rubin 1979: 153–62). As they did so, the system of market relations which they represented no longer stopped at the front door of the house of production but walked in and took over the premises.

By the same token, the system in which the London exchange had been the meeting point for diverse clusters of otherwise unrelated production was replaced by what came to be a national system (subsequently internationalised) of production for exchange. This, in turn, spurred the development of a provincial press, which drew not so much on local production per se but was more concerned with the new manufacturing and the contested nature of its integration into the wider economy, up to and including incipient conflicts between industry, trade and agriculture. Thus, trends towards the formation of a national economy of production also contributed to the production of provincial newspapers (Wilson 1978).

When erstwhile merchants entered into production as its new master, they brought with them their orientation to the market and their associated capacity for dislodging any object from its customary setting and turning it into a transferable, tradable commodity. Up to this point, the mercantile economy had been mobilising commodities that originated in production practices affixed to particular locations. Now this level of mobilisation was applied to the process of production itself.

In the mercantilist period, commodities were already valued according to an unspoken comparison of the labour contained in each one, but labour was fully commodified only after it had been interred in goods produced for subsequent sale. Now commodification occurred even before production had commenced, in the buying and selling of the labourer's prospective capacity for work in the production of commercial goods. The capacity to work was transformed into the commodity labour power when it became the general pattern for labourers and capitalists to enter into voluntary arrangements whereby the former loans his time to the latter, during which time the labourer is not himself, i.e. his active capacity, and what he makes in the course of his actions during the time specified are made over to the capitalist.

Labour power, like any other commodity, was exchanged in particular quantities (by the hour, the day or the week) against specific amounts of money (wages). Capitalists purchased labour power from the people who owned it, labourers, who thus became merchants of their one and only commodity, labour power. As they traded their labour power for wages, so a market for labour was brought into existence, and as soon as the starting point of production – buying labour power by hiring labourers – occurred in a labour market, it follows that market relations would encompass the whole cycle of production and consumption. Not merely introduced at the end point of production, now its alpha and omega were couched in these terms. Accordingly, on our part, new terms are required to appreciate the significance of this development.

'Merchant capital' is the best way to describe the money that merchants brought with them for the purchase of finished goods. This money was 'capital' in that the stock they bought with it represented an investment directed towards future profit, to be realised when the same stock was sold on at a higher price. But even if it were the same amount as used previously to buy finished goods, as soon as money was widely deployed to employ labour in an expanding system of commodity production, it must answer to a different description, that of 'industrial capital'. Accordingly, the essence of the term 'industrial capital' is to be found in the generalisation of recurring relations between capital and labour, such as occurred when labour power entered the market as a transferable commodity comparable to all other commodities.

Equality of exchange, inequality in production

Buying and selling labour power was now taking place on an open market. Labourers were free to sell to the highest bidder, and capitalist employers, as now they were, could choose whether or not to buy. In this respect, both parties were equal to the exchange. But in another aspect, this exchange was far from open and above board. In the small print of the contract between buyers and sellers of labour power, it transpired that the take-up of labourers' capacity to labour in the process of production would result in the production of much more value than they were paid for. Formally equal but at the same time essentially exploitative, market relations between capital and labour emerged as the most dynamic source of profit for the capitalist, easily outstripping the wealth gained hitherto from mercantile activity.

Stockpiling goods in centres of exchange had served to insure the growing urban population against natural hazards. Trade and the way of life oriented towards it lent joint support to the idea that being human meant being the sub-ject in one's own (profitable) activity. Conversely, the world must be an object for acting upon and, moreover, an object akin to a collection of tradable com-modities. Thus, the mentality common among many of London's inhabitants during the eighteenth century was grounded in London's position as the merchant capital of national and international trade.

By the end of the eighteenth century, the gradual import of exchange relations into the production process meant that production itself, not just its finished articles, was the object of increasing intervention by growing numbers of indus-trial capitalists. It also meant that production had become a transformative pro-cess in not just one, but now in two, complementary senses. There was the familiar sense in which production necessarily entails making something that did not exist before. As ever, this part of the process was visible to the naked eye, although more technical insight was required in order to undertake it. But what was driving the advance in technology? The motive force behind technical advance came from the other sense in which production was transformative – the sense in which it had only recently become so.

Inequality between the market value of labour power and the market values produced by labourers expending their power is not only a recurring phenom-enon, it is the core element in capitalist production, and its defining quality. In the historically specific context of market relations between capital and labour, the rabbit goes into the capitalist's top hat and comes out many times bigger, at which point the much larger creation is pocketed as profit by the capitalist. Hey presto! The surplus produced by people working together magically becomes his and his alone.

In Britain at the beginning of the nineteenth century, the exploitative character of capitalist production in which labour produces much larger quantities of value than the amount of value for which labour power has been exchanged, acceler-ated the production of profit, which, in turn, enabled greater investment of increased profits in the intense development and rapid deployment of new tech-nology. Not only was such investment made possible, it soon became a necessity, since companies that failed to keep up in the race for increased productivity just as soon discovered that their products were no longer competitive. If a particular enterprise lagged behind the general rate of technical innovation in its production sector, it would fall foul of the new law of socially necessary labour time (new because all instances of human, productive activity had never before been measured and organised according to the same standards). In its factories, the amount of labour time required to produce one of its commodities would be higher than the necessary amount elsewhere, in which case the products of the slow factory would contain more labour, and more of this labour would have to be paid for; yet on the open market the more laborious products could only command the same price as those produced less laboriously elsewhere. More time meant less money – and loss of competitiveness. Speed was of the essence: unprecedented profits were available to those companies that kept pace; for slackers, business failure was immediately in prospect. Even among those who managed to keep up, the experience of this great leap forward was a kind of pandemonium (Jennings 1995). It is otherwise known as the industrial revolution.

The revolution in social relations

Historians of the 'industrial revolution' have long debated whether it was really a process of evolution rather than revolution. There is no denying that it took much longer than the quick-fire events associated with modern, political revolution. Nonetheless, the historical developments usually referred to as 'the industrial revolution' were indeed revolutionary in that they eventually amounted to the transformation of relations among the entire population of Britain and subsequently across the vast majority of the world's population. 'Social revolution supported by technical innovation in industry' is perhaps a more accurate description of this epoch-making process.

Previously, the stuff of pre-modern life in Britain had been an aggregate of direct relations between people, lived largely locally, with wider connections confined to intermittent trade, occasional war and permanent religion. As we have seen, the growth of trade created merchant cities that lived in a new mode of continuous comparison and increased connection. Market comparison of commodities served to connect these cities with the different parts of the world that produced various goods. Among the inhabitants of such cities making comparisons became habitual, and from this habit of mind developed a comparative frame of reference which was as readily applied to other people as to the commodities they owned. Thus, the merchants arrived at a comparative mode of existence. But when merchant capitalists became industrial capitalists, they exported the comparative mode beyond the city walls of mercantilism to sites of production and imported it into production itself. As a result, one person's capacity to work came to be comparable and exchangeable with everyone else's. The capacity to work was now a transferable commodity (labour power); conversely, the people who owned it (labourers) were able to transfer themselves from one employer in a specified location to a range of different employers, sometimes in a variety of places during the course of one working life.

The integration of labourers into the capitalist production process also entailed their incorporation into the culture of continuous comparison. The comparative view of the world had been the preserve of the bourgeois milieu, where it was both embedded in the merchant and inscribed in the mercantile journalist. But now it was writ large in the relations of capitalist production. Production relations that rendered the capacity to work into a commodity comparable to all other commodities also rendered the bearers of commodity labour power – labourers – into objects of comparison and, furthermore, trained them in the habit of making continuous comparisons. The comparative frame of reference which already prevailed among owners of other commodities was also fostered among bearers of the commodity labour power; thus, something like the position of the *Spectator* came to be generalised.

In other aspects, however, there was something different about the comparative capacity that was both afforded by and integral to the new relations of capitalist production. Whereas in the mercantilist era, tradable objects were also found objects, bought as they were found before being brought to market and entered into a social system of comparative exchange, the new objects simply had no existence prior to entering into the social system of comparison. Under the new arrangements, the active process of their production was also the process of their socialisation. Conversely, the human subject produced by such arrangements may be called to be more active and creative than the merchants of the previous era.

Although labourers continued to work on particular products, as before, their productive activity was now incorporated into a general system of comparison. As well as its specific outputs, the expenditure of labour in any factory or workshop produced goods that comprised a share of the universe of labour outputs, all of which were comparable not only one to another but also one to many and many to one.

These terms – one to many, many to one – were widely used towards the end of the 1990s to describe the new-found communicative capacity of the Internet. Our usage of these same terms to describe the social relations of capitalist production is more than metaphorical. Such terms really do capture something of the communicative capacity only recently afforded by digital technology, but they are insightful because technology and the communicability it offers have finally caught up with the general comparability inherent in commodity production. This quality arises from the reduction of all kinds of disparate human activity to quantities of their lowest common denominator: abstract labour. It was fully realised as soon as labour power became a commodity and market relations thus co-opted labour relations. In this sense, the Internet et al. is more a metaphor for the universe of social relations as old as capitalist production in Britain.

In this universe, each individual lives in two worlds at the same time. There is the local world of serial connections between people who are relating directly to one another; this sequence continues to exist, apparently the same as before. But now there is also the universal world of production for exchange, in which people all over the world are connected in two further dimensions, one to many and many to one. As this universe is synthesised in the continuous comparison of commodities, up to and including the commodity labour power, so it comprises a system of constantly cross-hatched connections between bearers of commodity labour involved in production.

But who are the primary actors in this universe? What does one have to be in order to take centre stage in the theatre of production for exchange? It turns out that its protagonists are objects. Having carved up the dialogue between them, commodities and the capital required to initiate their production are now hogging the limelight. Despite their active role in the production of commodities and the expansion of capital, in this theatre human subjects are relegated to a supporting role. In an upside-down world, which is both distorted and real at the same time, we really are what Malthus warned we (most of us) would be (though not quite in the terms he foresaw): surplus (objects) to the active population of subjects (commodities).

Thus, the onset of generalised production for exchange, in which human, productive capacity is systematically exchangeable, first suggests that the powers of the human subject will be raised to a higher level. Viewed on its own this development would seem to be the precondition for the realisation of human perfectibility as envisioned in the philosophy of subjective idealism and chronicled in the journalism associated with it. But this precondition is itself conditioned; it comes with strings attached. Alongside the active promotion of social development, capitalist production relations also enact the demotion of the human subject even compared to the objects of its own making. Though this possibility was first suggested in the conundrum of subject and object during the mercantilist period, in the capitalist era the paradox is activated, expanded and exacerbated to an unprecedented degree.

Thus, generalised commodity production has also generalised a system of relations, one to many and many to one, which occurs primarily between commodities and only secondarily between people. This system coexists with an ongoing series of interpersonal relations. The coexistence of system with series means that we are obliged to live in two sets of relations at one and the same time: direct relations that run in series between persons and indirect societal relations in which one commodity producer is related to all other commodity producers, and vice versa, but only indirectly, by means of the commodities they produce. The duality of series and system, and the disjuncture between them, have been at the heart of our social reality since the onset of generalised commodity production, which occurred first in Britain two centuries ago; even today it continues to occupy a central position.

The deep-seated nature of this duality shows that the historic problem of mercantilism was not transcended by the onset of capitalist production; instead, like the higher powers newly available to increasingly productive human subjects, the problems we face were also raised to a higher level. Accordingly, increased powers of observation and intensified problems of representation both made their appearance in the history of journalism during the first half of the nineteenth century. We turn now to the imprint they made there.

Journalism and dynamism

In the journalism of William Cobbett, *actualité* came to the fore, and, compared to that of his predecessors, Cobbett's language was remarkably economical. For example, while imprisoned for debt, Cobbett witnessed the execution of John Bellingham, the failed merchant who had shot and killed Prime Minister Spencer Perceval. This is how he reported the event for his own publication, the *Political Register* (No. 671, 1812):

> [Bellingham] looked attentively at the people, who were assembled to the amount of many thousands, who filled the opposite windows and parapets of the houses and who, notwithstanding an almost continual heavy rain, crowded the sort of triangle which the streets here form, as thick as they could well stand upon the ground.
>
> (Cobbett 1812; cited in Spater 1982: 324)

The traits of modern reportage are readily recognisable: place, mood, anticipation, the presence of 'many thousands' of people at the event, serving to confirm that many thousands more will be interested in reading about it. The triad of relative clauses (who...who...who...), a faint echo of classical rhetoric, means that the scene could hardly have been written during the American century. But on those neo-classical columns there hangs the kind of compressed but evocative detail that would not go amiss in either Hollywood melodrama or hardboiled newspaper reports: continual heavy rain, the thickness of the crowd. Cobbett might almost be sporting a press card in the ribbon of his snap brim hat.

In his *Rural Rides*, which he began writing in the early 1820s, Cobbett combined close observation of life in the English countryside with heated invective against the 'Great Wen' (London) and its debilitating influence on rural affairs. Apart from the observation and opinion which they contain, his essays are testament to the new-found expectation that journalism should entail journalists going out of their way to observe and investigate. Here is Cobbett setting out on the first of his rural stories:

> At Chertsey, where we came into Surrey again, there was a Fair for horses, cattle and pigs. I did not see any sheep. Everything was exceedingly *dull*. Cart colts, two and three years old, were selling *for less than a third* of what they sold for in 1813. The cattle were of an inferior description to be sure; but the price was low almost beyond belief.
>
> (Wednesday, 25 September 1822; in Cobbett 1967: 32; Cobbett's emphases)

This passage contains information about the price of livestock, but its purpose is hardly to let the reader know the going rate. Instead, Cobbett aimed to use this information to illustrate the recent decline in England's agricultural economy; conversely, in riding out of London and into the country, he was testing his own starting point – that the agricultural economy is in decline – against subsequent observation. Of course, he was not the last reporter to find what he was already looking for, but the point is that Cobbett felt obliged to go out and look for it.

Like Mr Spectator, Cobbett expects what he shows to be scrutinised. Unlike Mr Spectator, he has not set himself up in a fixed position aside from that which is on display (as a merchant stands by his goods but not among them). In keeping with the economic dynamism of early nineteenth-century Britain, Cobbett's reporting was also more dynamic: it moves energetically between observation, analysis and polemic; moreover, in moving between them it covers greater distances – between different milieux in various places – than Addison and Steele felt obliged to do. Not that Cobbett supported the economic growth of his day. His purpose in riding across country was to expose the damage done to it by the beneficiaries of financial and industrial expansion. But even as Cobbett criticised them for riding a wave that threatened to drown the rural poor, in the way that he wrote he too was caught up in the currents of social development, and these found indirect expression in the formal innovations for which Cobbett is also renowned. Though conserving the country was the gist of Cobbett's politics, his political journalism was radical in form.

Immediately following the sentences quoted above, Cobbett tells the story of a Mr Fox (aptly named), a member of parliament to whom the British Government granted land near Chertsey after he unexpectedly withdrew support for a parliamentary motion to investigate the activities of the surveyor of crown lands, Mr Fordyce. It is a tale of parliamentary corruption that anticipates the 'cash for questions' scandal in the 1990s and the 2009–10 crisis over British MPs' expenses. For our purposes, however, the tale of Mr Fox is more remarkable on three, further counts. First, in that Cobbett refers the reader to the parliamentary register for the full account of what was said, what was not said and what was withdrawn: 'I have no *books* at hand; but the affair will be found recorded in the Register.' In other words, Cobbett was *referencing* his story in order to substantiate it; that he felt it necessary to do so indicates that the court of public opinion now required a higher standard of proof. Second, for the way that Cobbett concludes his telling of the tale: 'Such are the facts: let the reader reason upon them and draw the conclusion.' This is English written at a new level of compression. It suggests a readership that values speed – speed of communication and speed of comprehension – now called upon to complement speed of production. Though Cobbett opposed the onset of capitalist production, and by his journalism he sought to reverse the accelerated decline of the countryside which resulted from it, his writing also reflects the quickening pace of life – in journalism, as in all forms of production operating within the capitalist law of socially necessary labour time. Third, Cobbett's concluding sentence sets great store by readers and their powers of reason, granting them the decisive role. For journalism, this formulation points towards the distinction between reporting, in which journalists present to readers the results of investigations carried out on their behalf, and editorial, where the editor or his surrogates offer reasonable conclusions to their readership, also on its behalf. In the fourteen words of his concluding sentence, Cobbett also anticipates the key political questions of the mid-nineteenth century. Who are the readers? What conclusion will their reason draw them to? Can reason contain chaos? If so, whose reasoning will hold sway and by what means will it be applied?

Such questions originated in the problematic character of capitalist social relations, as introduced above. That these social problems should be addressed by civil society, and especially through the conduct of politics in civil society, has been widely understood in Britain for more than 150 years. However, at the beginning of the nineteenth century there was no such understanding. To the contrary, the French Revolution and its bloody aftermath provided a forceful reminder that civil war was an essential part of the modern scene, no less than civil society. In the decades after the French Revolution, however, journalism was to play a key role first in establishing the field of politics and in formulating social problems as political questions, and, again, in reformulating civil society in such a way as to contain political questions and restrict the scope for answering them.

Thus, during the course of the nineteenth century, journalism continued to play a role in relation to politics – but not the same role throughout. Whereas in Cobbett's day journalism was largely given over to politics and politics found expression chiefly in journalism, by the end of the century there had been a partial parting of the ways. Having done much to establish politics by being overtly political, journalism subsequently helped to maintain the place of politics and contributed to the containment of politics in a particular place, largely by depoliticising itself.

Journalism and politics

In Britain, the extent of capitalism's social problems, as they were experienced at the time, was most clearly stated by Thomas Carlyle, the journalist who coined the term 'industrialism' (Houghton 1957: 4–5). Recognising that there was no going back to the old way of life, Carlyle complained that the new way of life had not yet taken shape. Marx and Engels did write 'all that is solid melts into air' (Marx and Engels 2010: 25); but Carlyle could just as easily have done so. Subsequently, he criticised the mechanical way of thinking shaped by the machinery of commodity production. In later life, in the attempt to identify a strong leadership which could keep pace with economic change and its social consequences, Carlyle toyed with the idea of high-born (aristocratic) heroism, but in other respects, and in earlier times, his instincts were more democratic.

In his essay, *Signs of the Times* (1829), Carlyle first captured the full extent of contemporary contradictions. If his analysis was consistent and his responses erratic, the discrepancy between these was at least in accord with the glaring contradictions of the moment. Discordant notes were in tune with the new scale of simultaneous threat and opportunity facing Victorian Britain. Various themes presented themselves. At the high tide of British industrialism, marked by the Great Exhibition of 1851, production itself seemed momentarily capable of providing spiritual as well as material wealth (de Mare 1972). After Carlyle had nominated the aristocracy for a leadership role, in 1869 Matthew Arnold proposed the dissemination of 'culture' as the main line of defence against 'anarchy' (Arnold 1993). Eventually it transpired that party politics would be the means of mapping these times and managing their safe passage; moreover, popular participation emerged as an essential element in the make-up of political parties, without which they would remain unable to perform the near-miracle of stabilising the inherently unstable. But this was by no means a foregone conclusion. It was arrived at not by forethought or conspiracy but by the arduous process of history and the tortuous development of its first draft: journalism.

We shall now look briefly at three further examples of nineteenth-century journalism that indicate the protracted process of trial and error in the reproduction of capitalist social relations and the development of politics to this end. Together they also suggest the outline of a narrative for the news industry. Of course, there are numerous other places in which to find a more fully developed narrative. However, the point of our outline is not to tell the story of news production in its own terms but to add to our argument that journalism has never been a simple correlate of industrial production or commercial trade, still less a direct expression of individual owners or even of private ownership. Instead, news and journalism have played a key role in the mediation of social relations; moreover, their essential character is to be found in the performance of this mediating role, which in Britain has been played continuously for in excess of 200 years whether news and journalism have been more or less industrial, commercial or political.

The necessity of political journalism(s)

William Howard Russell was *The Times* reporter who pioneered the use of the telegraph. But some of his despatches were far from telegrammatic. This is the opening paragraph from Russell's report of the battle of Balaclava, which became the best-known event in the Crimean War between Britain and Russia, largely because of Russell's account (it had been sent to London by post before appearing in *The Times* on 14 November 1854):

> If the exhibition of the most brilliant valour, of the excess of courage, and of a daring which could have reflected lustre on the best days of chivalry can afford full consolation for the disaster of today, we can have no reason to regret the melancholy loss which we sustained in a contest with a savage and barbarian enemy.
>
> (Russell 2003: 15)

To say Russell was putting a brave face on it is something of an understatement. This was the 'charge of the light brigade' in which England's finest were cut down by Russian artillery, mainly because of their commanders' ineptitude. In the form of his account, Russell was also putting a classical façade on modern warfare. This is prose modelled on Livy, the Roman historian, written for an upper-middle-class readership which was likely to have read the Classics, i.e. Livy et al., in the original Latin or Greek.

Readers of *The Times* would have been in positions of authority or close to it, and they relied on information such as this to inform the political process through which they took authoritative decisions. In their version of it, however, the political process was also an internal process, largely confined to members of privileged social groups such as their own – and so it should remain. Accordingly, they preferred to receive their accounts of the world outside (written accounts of *their* world), composed in a form of words which was more or less exclusive to them. While the outside world was becoming more modern by the minute, for this readership bad news was slightly better for being couched in words, rhythms and turns of phrase that reminded them of the ancient world and the historical continuity which they themselves claimed to have with it.

But there was already another kind of journalism: popular journalism written with gusto about the new world and what should be done about it. Here is a brief extract from a report on living conditions in the dormitory underneath one of London's industrial schools. Entitled 'A Sleep To Startle Us', it was written by Charles Dickens and published in his own magazine, *Household Words*, on 13 March 1852:

> The whole floor of the building, with the exception of a few narrow pathways, was partitioned off into wooden troughs, or shallow boxes without lids – not unlike the fittings in the shop of a dealer in corn, flour and seeds. The galleries were parcelled out in the same way. Some of these berths were very short – for boys; some longer – for men. The largest were of very contracted limits; all were composed of the bare boards; each was furnished only with one coarse rug, rolled up. In the brick pathways were iron gratings communicating with trapped drains, enabling the entire surface of these sleeping-places to be soused and flooded with water every morning. The floor of the galleries was cased with zinc, and fitted with gutters and escape-pipes, for the same reason. A supply of water, both for drinking and for washing, and some tin vessels for either purpose, were at hand.
>
> (Dickens 1852: 11)

Dickens describes the well-intentioned, progressive but still inadequate efforts of this charitable institution as well as the various effects it has on its inmates. Although his description is not as overtly polemical as Cobbett's chronicles of rural poverty, Dickens ends with a direct appeal for respectable persons to take less of an interest in the finer points of Anglican theology and more interest in the plight of the urban poor. His article is largely reportage, with an editorialising conclusion. The title suggests that Dickens wanted his lower-middle-class readers to be startled into political action as they moved with him (and were moved by him) from detailed reporting to the concluding exhortation.

Although Dickens was horrified by the levels of degradation which he witnessed, he conducted both his reporting and his editorialising (and even his fictionalising, for which he is much better known today) from the position of someone fully attuned to progressive development and the urgent possibility of furthering it. His opening paragraph – the shot, as it were, in which he established the location of his subject matter – begins with the 'broad new thoroughfare' at the top of Farringdon Street, which was 'in a state of transition', before taking his readers down into that subterranean layer of London which had not kept pace with the rate of change as it appeared on the surface of the city. But even among the subterraneans there was some improvement – in ventilation, water supply and drainage. In its vibrancy Dickens's prose is not only alive to the potential for the alleviation of misery, it is also animated by the sense that his own writing could make a direct contribution to the realisation of progressive potential. This was writing to make a difference.

Four years before Dickens's account, on 2 July 1848, the *Observer* carried a report of 'warfare on the streets of Paris'. This is its second paragraph:

> The object of the war is the distribution of property, which would follow as effect follows cause in a social revolution; and the struggle, therefore, is wholly and solely between those who possess that element, and those who do not – a war, in fact, of poverty against property. This is abundantly proved by the facts that not a man of the working classes was to be found in arms against his fellows, in aid of the authorities – that the combat was altogether fought by the Garde Mobile, and the shopkeepers and middle classes who compose the Garde Nationale – and that the feeling of hatred on the part of the 'populace' of that city for the bourgeoisie was manifested during the battle in the most unmistakeable manner. It is consequently a servile war in the strictest sense of the word – the poor against the rich, the rich against the poor.
>
> (*Observer* 1848: 11)

The report from Paris was also a warning of what can happen anywhere if there is insufficient mediation between rich and poor. Unlike Britain, the unnamed author went on to say, where the 'general diffusion of wealth' sufficed to bring more of the poor closer to the rich, in France a 'restricted' middle class had 'become in practice the governing oligarchy'. No doubt the geographical distance between France and England will have fostered greater reserve on the part of the author: he would surely have been more sympathetic to the position of the propertied if the march of the property-less were coming closer to his own home; nonetheless, in this measured analysis, there is a cool calculation to the effect that 'warfare in the streets' is only to be expected in places without the means of transition, where no bridges have been built between social classes.

Out of these three examples of mid-nineteenth-century British journalism, the last piece to have been published was Russell's in *The Times*, and its author was subsequently associated with the latest technology of the time (the telegraph). Yet of the three it is this article which is the most primitive. It was written for a readership which had not yet grasped the full importance of participatory politics in the maintenance of social order and the reproduction of capitalist social relations. By contrast, both the other articles recognised the significance of the popular in the political and acknowledged the role of journalism in fostering their relationship. This approach was also shared by another journalist who was soon to acquire a certain notoriety. His name was Karl Marx.

The two journalisms of Karl Marx

> The free press is the ubiquitous, vigilant eye of a people's soul, the embodiment of a people's faith in itself, the eloquent link that connects the individual with the state and the world, the embodied culture that transforms material struggles into intellectual struggles and idealises their crude material form. [...] It is the ideal world which always wells up out of the real world and flows back into it with ever greater spiritual riches and renews its soul.
>
> (Marx 1842a)

In a supplement to the paper which he edited, *Rheinische Zeitung*, the young Karl Marx attacked censorship and praised the press for its socially progressive role. He also identified the reciprocal relations between press and people, action and description. The 'free press' praised by Marx was the political press of mid-nineteenth-century Western Europe and North America. Not that he praised everything that appeared in all newspapers; to the contrary, he was as frequently opposed to their 'idealised' coverage of events as he was to the 'material' interests underlying their journalism. But in the early 1840s Marx was extremely positive about the role played by the press as a whole. In his interpretation, its ability to 'transform material struggles into intellectual struggles' was the precondition for politics. If the press enjoyed the freedom to translate 'crude material struggles' into the battle of ideas, politics would ensue; the struggle for progressive social development could take a political form. Conversely, where the press was not free to translate material conditions into their ideal representation, there were no politics, either.

As Addison and Steele had championed it in their way, Marx, too, was taken with the idea of journalism as the instrument of civil society. But whereas for Addison and Steele civil society was associated with the suspension of conflict, for Marx it would be realised by the expression of conflict in ideal form; in the shape of a battle of ideas conducted in the press. Note that Marx did not designate political *parties* as 'the eloquent link that connects the individual with the state and the world'; moreover, the 'free press' is not listed as one of a number of necessary links, up to and including political parties. On the basis of his pronouncement, newspapers seem to be the only link required. In another passage from the same supplement, Marx appears to have affirmed their singular role in the formation of political culture. As soon as the press is restrained, he warned, the people turn away from political life to become 'a rabble of private individuals' (Marx 1842a). He did not expect their political existence to be held together by party membership.

When Marx published this supplement, on 15 May 1842, there was intense political activity in Britain, on the continent of Europe and in the USA: the Chartist movement would soon reach its peak; the 'year of revolutions' in Europe, 1848, was only half a decade away. But political parties did not play the leading role in these events – not only because they lacked the necessary machinery but also, more importantly, because the class interests which British and European parties would come to represent were only made clear through these events themselves. (The process of forming modern political parties was further advanced in the USA, where the first national party conventions occurred in 1831 and 1832. In America, however, the direct expression of class interests was retarded indefinitely by the question of 'race'.)

At this point, the mediation of class relations had already become the main business of politics in Western Europe. Moreover, the press served as mediation point, as the centre of mediating activity between classes, with reporters, particularly those reporting what was said on political platforms, serving as brokers. Anthony Smith has pointed out that social order was the reward for conducting politics as a mediating activity in which the reporter had become 'principal broker for the substantial discussion of society':

> The agitation over the Reform Bill in 1831 was attended by riot and disorder; the agitation over the repeal of the Corn Laws a decade and a half later was conducted throughout the nation by means of the platform and the press – two, inter-connected institutions, indeed symbiotic institutions, which depended on clear notes being taken by reporters.
>
> (Smith 1978: 163)

In the continuous, acerbic exchanges that occurred via the press, the material interests of different social classes were translated into various political positions. Conversely, in occupying that third position which stands partly aside from the particular interests of parties directly involved in clashes and exchanges, by its very existence the press was calling upon each of those parties to translate its own interests into an approximation of the general interest. Moreover, at a time when this generality had yet to be blown apart in outright class war between capital and labour, the press, and almost nothing but the press, seemed robust enough to support the articulation of particular and general interests.

For much of the nineteenth century, political groupings tended to cluster around various publications so that publication was the essence of group formation. By contrast, for much of the twentieth century, opposing (and imposing) party citadels, like the ones from which Labour and Conservatives faced each other across a corner of London's Smith Square, gave rise to publications wholly owned by political parties: the manifesto, which independent publications (journalism) were then obliged to report and comment on. In the meantime, class interests and their representatives had dragged themselves into the format of the modern political party, which then became the driving force of politics and the originating source of political activity, but only after decades in which parties lagged a long way behind the political press. Throughout this protracted period, makeshift parties were understudying the press in the role of political protagonist.

Thus, in 1841, Chartist leader Feargus O'Connor described the radical press as 'the link that binds the industrious classes together' (Curran and Seaton 2010: 13), and his address to the radical press duly appeared in one of its foremost examples, the *Northern Star* (16 January 1841). Other papers served to cohere different sections of society. The connections provided by the Cotton press, including the *Manchester Guardian*, contributed to the formation of industrialists into the most dynamic section of the capitalist class. Palmerston's press – those London papers allied to Lord Palmerston – did much to bring about the coalescence of aristocracy and bourgeoisie in Britain, partly by encouraging a division of responsibilities (and power) in which foreign policy came to be seen as the preserve of the aristocracy.

Meanwhile, the class base of each newspaper determined its sources of funding. In effect, each social group paid to be constituted as a social group by funding publications that helped to further its particular interests and to construct its specific identity (with the interests and identity of each class presented as if they had sprung solely from the general interests of humanity). Furthermore, there were various funding models – government patronage, manufacturers' sponsorship through advertising, popular subscription – to fit the social group that each set of publications was intended to characterise. (In the USA, where party politics were already more structured, press funding owed more to party political patronage.) Conducted largely through the press, this was an early instance of identity politics – perhaps the most significant instance to date. Furthermore, in addressing class antagonisms to the general interest, the press also served to identify politics as the preferred means of mediating between opposing social groups and the social contradictions represented in them.

It might have enthused the young Marx, but since the nineteenth century not all commentators have taken to the idea of the press as a semi-autonomous *locus* of power. In his essay, 'The Fourth Estate: The Re-appraisal of a Concept', George Boyce (1978: 20) was prompted to dismiss the concept as 'a political myth' invented by nineteenth-century editors and politicians. Having traced the intricate network of connections between Victorian political leaders and the contemporary press, he maintained that journalism was by no means independent of particular interests or their personal representatives. No doubt he is correct about the links between editors and leading political figures, but to extrapolate from this that the political press was not endowed with any independent capacity is to overlook the extent to which the conduct of politics via the press normally entailed the formal subjugation of particular class interests to the general interest which politics and especially the press were expected to ascertain. Of course, the formality did not necessarily correspond to the reality, but there is no need to be surprised 'that the press was an extension of the political system' (Boyce 1978: 29), since at this time the existence of each depended on their integration. Moreover, the relative success of their mediating role depended on the joint formation of a platform resting on particular class interests but not reducible to them.

Despite differential rates of party political consolidation, on both sides of the Atlantic newspapers were crucial in establishing the range of political positions which the market could do business with, but they themselves were not necessarily businesslike. The mid-nineteenth-century press was central to the process of working out how market relations would be conducted day to day – the stuff of modern politics; but its own processes of production and consumption were not fully integrated into the market. While there *were* precedents for producing newspapers much like any other commodity, represented in Britain by William Clement, who owned a stable of publications including the *Observer*, this model of ownership was not the template for the political press during the first half of the nineteenth century.

At this time, just as the press was at the forefront of politicisation, so newspapers were established primarily to press for the political interests of their owners, editors and readers. They were only as businesslike as they needed to be to stay in *politics*. Accordingly, when the editor of the *Rheinische Zeitung* published a second supplement on the freedom of the press on 19 May 1842, far from seeing himself as part of the newspaper business he famously declared that: 'The primary freedom of the press lies in not being a trade' (Marx 1842b). Marx went on to distinguish the political development of the press from lines of business such as bookselling and printing. These are trades, he said; newspapers are not. Though the latter arrived with a price tag attached, commercial attachments came a long way second to their political engagement. For Marx in 1842 the possibility of the press being absorbed into the market was more remote and less threatening than the likelihood of the Prussian authorities suppressing it.

Similarly, in Britain in the first half of the nineteenth century, journalism could have been industrialised more rapidly: there was the technology. But it seems that the mediating activity undertaken by the press hardly warranted the levels of industrialisation which were already proceeding apace in other branches of production. Close to the onset of the age of steam, *The Times* introduced steam presses in 1814 and trumpeted their introduction in an editorial (29 November 1814) that glows hot with self-congratulation:

> Our journal this day presents to the public the practical result of the greatest improvements connected with printing since the discovery of the art itself.

The reader of this paragraph now holds in his hand one of the many thousand impressions of *The Times* newspaper, which were taken off last night by a mechanical apparatus. A system of machinery almost organic has been devised and arranged, which, while it relieves the human frame of its most laborious efforts in printing, far exceeds all human powers in rapidity and despatch.

But this technical innovation was not rapidly adopted throughout publishing, perhaps because few publishers could afford it – perhaps also because they did not feel obliged to stump up the cash for it. If journalism was hardly a business until later in the nineteenth century, neither was news an industry with its own production dynamic. Rather, at this time, the commercial and industrial aspects of journalism were subject to the performance of its mediating role in the conduct of politics; they existed to support the mediating role of the press, not the other way round. Moreover, when in the latter part of the nineteenth century journalism took on a more commercial guise, even then its commercialisation (and the production techniques entailed in making it so) occurred only when its mediating role was modified in a manner sympathetic to commercial considerations. Perhaps it should not need saying, but, then and now, recognising the significance of mediation is key to understanding media.

Less than thirty years after venting his passion for journalism and its progressive social role in the performance of politics, Marx expressed a much lower opinion of the press – much more in tune with twentieth-century disdain for its powers of distortion. In a letter to Ludwig Kugelmann, written on 27 July 1871, Marx first identified the myth-making capacity of the press: 'The daily press and the telegraph, which in a moment spread inventions over the whole earth, fabricate more myths [...] in one day than could have formerly been done in a century' (Marx 1989: 176). Though written in the nineteenth century, this sentence seems as much in tune with the twentieth. In the 1970s the editors of *The Manufacture of News* made it the frontispiece of their seminal critique of news media (Cohen and Young 1973); and even in the twenty-first century, it continues to appear in Left-leaning Media Studies (Keeble 2004).

In the same letter, Marx complained of being 'overrun' by 'newspapermen and others of every description' (Marx 1989: 176). He explains that they wanted 'to see the "monster" with their own eyes' (Marx 1989: 176). The mythical 'monster' was Marx himself, or, more accurately, the spectre of Marx as created by the press in fabricated accounts of the leading role which he was alleged to have played in the Paris Commune. (In 1871 the workers of Paris led a revolutionary insurrection; within a few weeks it was put down by a combination of French reaction and German military invasion.) According to Marx, 'the daily press and the telegraph' had been spreading 'inventions' in accordance with the forces of law and order.

Less than three decades apart, there is an enormous contrast between the two appraisals of journalism by Marx. In the first, the press itself is a democratic

process of clarification; in the second, it is an instrument of reactionary obfusca-
tion. Moreover, these appraisals of what the press does rest on assumptions about
who owns the press and for what ends.

In Marx's original assessment, the press is more public good than private
property. Though its various outlets give voice to different sectional interests,
whenever these voices are heard in the press they are obliged to translate their
own speech into the idealised language of public interest, and particular parties
are required to account for their actions in terms of the general interest. In this
context, ownership of a publication affords a political platform to one such
interested party, but on this platform rests that party's capacity to present its
interests in universal terms, and unless it can exercise that capacity and perform
this translation exercise, it will not be taken seriously in politics. Indeed, the
political is understood as the pursuit of class interests tempered according to criteria defined in the general interest, and although even these may turn out to be
class interests in disguise, that they are obliged to appear in disguise is what
makes this a political process. Thus, the dialectical relationship between particular
and general interests, first seen during periods of relative stability associated with
English mercantilism, has been animated in accordance with the instability of
capitalist production.

In the second assessment, the press seems to have been pressed into the service
of private property and the social order on which it depends. Journalism's appe-
tite for sensationalism – for seeing 'the "monster" with their own eyes' – suggests
that sensation is now a marketable commodity, a unique selling point in the eyes
of 'newspaper men'. In this guise, the late-nineteenth-century press bears a
striking resemblance to twentieth-century media and their propensity for folk
devils and moral panics.

Market myths

For the past thirty years (as long as the gap between the two journalisms described by Marx), media academics have been inclined to ascribe the degenerative
transformation of the nineteenth-century press to the growing influence of the
market, culminating in the rise of mass media and the emergence of press barons.
This is the view put forward most persuasively by James Curran and Jean Seaton
(1981, 2010). In their influential account (successive editions confirm its
continuing influence), the political character of the press was consumed by
marketisation – a process which they see occurring in the nineteenth century
although what goes on in their account is uncannily similar to the course of
events which many Left-wing critics observed under UK Prime Minister Margaret
Thatcher and US President Ronald Reagan in Britain and the USA during the
early 1980s. Coincidentally, this was the time (1981) when Curran and Seaton
first published their thesis.

Curran and Seaton set out to expose the limitations of Whig history – the
previously dominant account of the development of journalism and society in

which press freedom was more or less equated with market freedom. But closer examination of the social role of the press in relation to historically specific conditions, and especially in relation to other elements and actors in the mid-nineteenth-century context, including the timely formation of centralised political parties, suggests that their critical account makes as many ideological assumptions as its predecessor. In particular, it tends towards the assumption that journalism that exists in market conditions will become a creature of the market and an adver-tisement for the ideology of the market, unless and until the state intervenes to safeguard the independence of the press from the market ideology embedded in newspapers and the copy they carry. Instead of projecting liberal ideas onto the press, as Whig history was wont to do, this seems to project the pressing issues of the late 1970s and early 1980s onto the press history of the 1850s, 1860s and 1870s. It also sets up ownership of the press as a form of market-led dictatorship over the press – a position which press ownership does not warrant, any more than private ownership of car factories necessarily dictates the style or the technical performance of automobiles.

While it cannot be denied that the history of journalism is bound up with the history of the market, the mere existence of the latter does not account either for the earlier exceptionalism of the press – its decidedly political (and non-commercial) character – or, subsequently, for its closer integration into the system of market-oriented production relations. Commodity production was already the mode of the British economy in general when the press was at its most political, at a time when ownership of the press was notably non-economic. Conversely, in the second half of the nineteenth century, when newspapers became economic propositions even more than political ones, politics did not abate; if anything, political struggle grew more intense rather than less.

Disappointed by the sensationalist turn on the part of the press, and spurred on by the defeat of the Paris Commune, in reaction to both, Marx was not alone in insisting that the International Workingmen's Association should focus on party formation as the front-line strategy in a class struggle that was now to be fought at a new pitch. On the other hand, there was perhaps less need for newspapers to idealise material interests or to clarify class antagonism. No jour-nalism could be any more explicit than the corpses on the streets of Paris. For Marx in the 1870s, the pressing requirements were for party organisation and a self-critical political economy that could understand the world of our own making better than the class currently controlling it.

Meanwhile, the newspapermen who attempted to make Marx into a sensa-tional monster for popular consumption had not sought him out in order to clarify class interests. Already they were writing reports in such a way as to take the politics out of the events and the people they were reporting on. Since even this apparently neutral process had political significance, its growth can only have amounted to the partial depoliticisation of the press. Nonetheless, the partial depoliticisation of newspapers towards the end of the nineteenth century did not at this time result in a reduction of the political temperature overall. Instead, it coexisted with the intensification of politics. The disjuncture between partially depoliticised journalism and intensified political struggle came about when the intensification of politics was accompanied by the movement of politics elsewhere. While the press continued to act in the political theatre, politics were restaged so that the centre shifted from press to party organisation. Instead of loose parliamentary groupings dependent on journalism for their identity, highly organised, increasingly centralised parties came to the fore, with political reporting and leader-writing demoted to supporting roles in the political process and juxtaposed to other genres of journalism which were apparently not political at all.

The market alone cannot account for the partial depoliticisation of an increasingly commercial press towards the end of the nineteenth century, not least because its earlier politicisation had itself been a response to the market. In other words, when the press became primarily political it was responding to the generalisation of market relations and the social problems generated in this historical process. Subsequently, the partial depoliticisation and further marketisation of the press occurred at a time when political parties and their mass membership became the primary mechanism for addressing the social problems arising from capitalist contradiction. While newspapers became less overtly political, at the same time party and politics were becoming more directly confrontational – a long-standing process which it took not one but two world wars to contain. Thus, the commercialisation of the press and its partial depoliticisation towards the end of the nineteenth century cannot be held accountable for a decline in political struggle which did not occur until half a century later. Equally, it is not possible to grasp the political character of the earlier period primarily by reference to the changing character of the press, since the press, at that time, was no longer the premier channel for the conduct of politics.

Modern politics, on their first showing in the political press, were not a function of the market. Yet they were nudged into existence by the onset of market relations, and their purpose was to address the social problems arising from market relations not to imitate them slavishly. Similarly, if newspapers later came closer to the market, a crucial factor in the relative integration of newspapers with commerce was the migration of politics from press to party – a transfer of shared expectations and collective commitment driven more by political and even military developments such as the suppression of the Paris Commune and less so by the simple influence of the market that both pre-dated and post-dated this turn of events. Accordingly, market-led accounts of such developments can only be simplistic.

Not that Curran and Seaton were wrong to challenge the false identity of press freedom and market freedom that characterised Whig history. The presentation of press history as a straightforward line of development from suppression in the age of absolutist monarchy to freedom upheld by the two pillars of representative democracy and the market – the liberal account which Curran and Seaton were taking aim at – is only at home with the simple truth of historical social development from feudalism to capitalism but cannot cope with the contradictions inherent in the latter. However, in our logical reconstruction of journalism's history, we emphasise the modern role of journalism in the mediation of social contradiction – a role that entails the composition of contradictions as well as the possibility of addressing them.

Accordingly, it has been our contention that journalistic independence was first posited in a mercantile culture that created and also depended on the median position from which to look back at the two parties directly involved in commercial exchange, which is also the common ground between their potentially contradictory interests. We emphasise this not in the attempt to iron out the contradictions inherent in market relations between capital and commodified labour, or to straighten out the contrary role of journalism in both writing up and writing off the effects of these contradictions, but rather because both parties in exchange-oriented, market-focused culture have been obliged to occupy, at least temporarily, common ground wholly owned by neither (hence it contains the contradiction between them), which is also the basis for journalism. This is also to say that the market, and the activities of commodity owners operating in the market, have been the *locus* of the social as well as the site of its antithesis. Thus, to make a simple equation between scope for the market and the negation of press freedom is no more realistic than their false identity.

Journalism and the clarification of class interests

Both the politicisation of the press, and, subsequently, its partial depoliticisation were prompted by changes in the balance of class forces. In the period before 1848, the industrial bourgeoisie was still experimenting, in print, parliament and government, with the sound of its own voice. In vocal (often raucous) opposition to anachronistic elements among the aristocracy, its interests sometimes coincided with those of the working class. However, as the latter grew more numerous, became better educated and began to identify its own independent interests, so cracks in the coalition between capital and labour developed into the class divide that endured throughout the nineteenth and twentieth centuries. Moreover, the class divide between capital and labour found in politics its form of address and a (limited) mode of redress. (Indeed, without the dual role of politics, class is constituted neither in divisive nor in consensual terms; it simply is.) But to play this dual role effectively, modern politics would have to find its most effective mechanisms, and move towards them; this it did by transferring its own centre of operations from the political press to party organisation.

The transition was slow; even in the 1870s, it remained incomplete. The direct opposition of capital and labour had been revealed for the first time in 1848, with the onset of bourgeois (not aristocratic) reaction against the struggle for democracy. In 1871, democracy took to the streets of Paris again, where it was soon terrorised by the armed wing of capital. In the intervening decades, party political organisation had not featured greatly, but when the Paris Commune ended in bloodshed, all sides undertook a concerted move towards party organisation. At the far reaches of the political spectrum, reactionary forces and revolutionary movements sought to organise themselves more effectively; taken as a whole, Western politics came to be earthed in the new, middle ground of social democracy. Sometimes this territory was occupied by a newly formed party; on other occasions an existing party was reformed to accommodate social democratic elements. In Britain, for example, social democracy first found a home in the Liberal Party but came into its own, eventually, with the constitution of a national Labour Party in 1921.

Thus, class interests continued to unfold throughout the second half of the nineteenth century and into the twentieth. But the earlier clarification of class interests in the press had been superseded by their stark revelation on the streets of Paris and elsewhere, and the latter episodes further revealed the need for new mechanisms capable of maintaining allegiance and containing social conflict.

As an effective means of mobilising support for ideas and policies, parties are the political in its most compressed form. With the intensification of politics around centrally organised parties, the press was no longer the epicentre of politics. Meanwhile, the partial evacuation of politics from the press began to alter the balance between the two main models of press ownership. Whereas until then the businesslike proprietor had been overshadowed by the ink-stained politico-publisher, so that Cobbett with his *Political Register* represented a more influential type than Clement and his *Observer*, now their relative weighting was reversed, and Clement became the archetype first for late Victorian magazine-owners such as George Newnes, founder-editor-publisher of *Titbits*, and subsequently for a new generation of newspaper overlords – the press barons.

For most of the twentieth century, the mediation of social contradiction and the amelioration of concomitant social conflict were conducted primarily through an arrangement of political parties, with the media playing an important but secondary role. However, to say that politics was refocused on party is not to say that the press removed itself from politics altogether. In Britain, for example, political funding for some newspapers continued until the period between the two world wars (and even after that, in the case of the *Daily Herald*). But this is precisely the point: political funding of the press now took place via party organisation, which is to say that the latter had become the senior partner in their relationship.

Conversely, if party had replaced press as the starter motor of politics, then the press need no longer operate primarily as a political engine. Accordingly, a version of the press might now live by means other than the political. Publications could adopt a modus operandi that included political coverage in amongst other kinds of content; if only there was another, suitable social role to be played by this sort of compound journalism.

Indeed, there was such a role, a newly expanded social role which was now to be played by a partly depoliticised press, and the performance of this role, in turn, is what made the press marketable. Equally, no amount of market forces could have depoliticised the press, in and of themselves; neither could market forces revive the fortunes of a partly depoliticised press without the simultaneous development of a significantly modified role for it to play. Furthermore, in the fulfilment of this modified role, an already existing term acquired a new level of significance: 'newspaper' was the term now used to designate print journalism's performance of a modified mediating role.

This concludes our logical reconstruction of the revision of relations between politics, the press and its ownership. In the next chapter, we will continue to weave between the two elements of logical reconstruction and historical presentation, with the proviso that the latter is necessarily a selective presentation in the interests of the former.

For more than a century now, newspaper ownership has drawn its social cachet from the importance of this role in the reproduction of societal relations, hence the succession of proprietors who, as Simon Jenkins (1986: 11) notes, have been 'happy, indeed eager to derive non-pecuniary returns from owning newspapers'. Similarly, the ambition to be a 'newspaperman', often at an uncompetitive salary, reflects the kudos associated with the role of the newspaper as the beating heart of society.

To identify this role and to explain how its performance came closer to the market but without necessarily coming into profit, we need to reconsider the wider relations between members of a society oriented to generalised commodity production (capitalist society) and to revisit the distinction between (direct) interpersonal relations and (indirect) societal relations in this social formation. In order to open up this distinction, and the relations so distinguished, we will advance the proposition that journalism in particular, and media in general, form part of a wide range of mediating activity which is essential to the reproduction of capitalist society.

As part of this proposition, we will make further use of philosophical terms such as subject and object, which previously appeared when we discussed Enlightenment philosophy as the mirror of mercantilism. Moreover, we will use this terminology to show that the further development of what has come to be known as the news industry was driven not so much by industrial machinery nor industrial processes, both of which pre-dated their application to journalism by many years; rather, the development of news, and the increasingly industrial character of its production, came about in fulfilment of a growing demand for mediating mechanisms capable of connecting millions of newly literate individuals across the vast expanse of capitalist social relations.

Chapter 2

Media and mediating activity

The subject of the modern world is comprised of human beings acting upon it in concert. As we apply our subjectivity in constructing the modern world so we also expend our labour in producing it. Yet in current conditions the results of our labour are not ours to dispose of. As human subjects are exploited, so too are the objects of our own making commandeered by another object, capital. Moreover, the capacity to initiate the production of objects also belongs to capital. To say that this object usurps the sovereignty of the human subject is to suggest that the reality of exploitation as captured in economic terms is complemented by corresponding realities requiring cognate terms from philosophy; furthermore, it is to say that both modern philosophy and political economy are terminologies with common origins in capital as a social relation.

The concerted activity of human beings in production is conducted by capital; capital conducts labour. Like an orchestral conductor, capital is the intermediary between various producers. Also in the manner of a conductor capital gives the tempo to labour: it is our maestro. Here the intermediary is also the voice of unwarranted authority. The unexpectedly authoritarian voice accompanying capital's intermediary role is echoed in the way that the market, which in other circumstances might be nothing more than a patch of middle ground where commodities are exchanged, currently holds sway over the production of commodities, just as capital cities, typically the location of the largest markets, lord it over provincial sites of production, even though the authority of the former is ultimately derived from the latter. Similarly, the commanding role of mediation reveals itself again in the humble orientation of commodities towards money, which is the intermediary between them just as they are intermediaries between the people who produced them. Both the fetishism of commodities, as Marx described it, and the fetish of commodities for money are prompted by capital's double life as both mediator and master.

That mediation is central to society should not come as a surprise. As we have shown, modern levels of socialisation emerged alongside the development of a third position, in the middle between two parties – people and objects – which are, respectively, commensurate and exchangeable. Thus the mediating position, to which commodity owners are drawn and from which they look upon the world as a choice between commensurate possibilities and exchangeable outcomes, has been integral to socialisation.

In the contemporary version of this scenario, however, there is also an antisocial element. The antisocial comes to the fore when the mediating position at the centre of society is primarily occupied not by people but by capital. In conditions where the centre is capitalised, the mediating position is not only the place where subjects associate; it also comes to be associated with the domination of objects over human subjects. It is here that the current form of socialisation obstructs further social development.

Capital is the form of mediation which has risen above its station to become the primary social relation of our times. It is thus the intermediary object which displaces the human subject. Indeed, it transcends the distinction between subject and object. It is transcendent; but at the same time dependent. As capital takes on a life of its own, so it relies on the expenditure of human life in the process of capitalist production. Our social reality is formed by this discrepancy, and our lives are lived in the shadow of its countless manifestations. Commodities, the cell form of capitalist production, are hard-wired with that version of it which is presented in the duality of use value and exchange value. Marx set out this duality in the opening chapter of his *Capital* (1887), in order to establish that contradiction is fundamental to capitalist production relations, having previously established (in *The German Ideology*, 1845–6) that the relations of capitalist production are also the societal relations of our time, i.e. they are the primary relations in which society is constituted.

In the three volumes of *Capital*, his summative work, Marx established the essentially unstable character of these historically specific production relations. But his earlier work had already opened up another field requiring further investigation. The dual character of capital, the coexistence in capital of transcendent and dependent qualities at one and the same time, is further expressed in a second field of duality, namely, the simultaneous coexistence of societal relations in which people are subject to capital and interpersonal relations in which they are their own subjects. Thus, in capitalist society, humanity itself comes to replicate the duality of capital as both dependent subject and transcendent object: as subjects we are dependent on the object that is capital; meanwhile, it is only our subjectivity, objectified as labour power, which can transform one object into another, thereby expanding the system of objects that includes capital itself.

In one set of relations, namely, production relations, human subjects are objectified by capital: we become things subject to it. These are the relations by which capital expands itself through the deployment of labour in the production of goods. Moreover, such relations provide the material basis for society as a whole so that what we are is in large part constituted by what we do within these historically specific relations in particular. However, in that capital accumulation depends on the objectification of human subjects – in production we become the commodity labour-power – it is also dependent on the creation and continuous recreation of human beings as interrelated subjects; for if we are not subjects in the first instance, neither can capital expand itself by reducing us to its objects. Thus capital itself is as dependent on this second set of relations, in which human beings are subjects, as it is upon the prior set of (production) relations in which it objectifies us. In order for it to be transcendent, capital turns out to be doubly dependent; it depends on two sets of relations which are at odds with each other; and this further duality constitutes a secondary field which exists alongside the duality already inherent in the prior set of production relations.

Confronted by whole fields of such discrepancy, human subjects customarily respond by trying to put them in order. We have devised coping strategies for our dual existence, i.e. strategies that allow us to cope with its duality; and by our efforts the disjuncture between production relations and intersubjective relations is rendered into a more or less manageable sequence of contradictions. Conversely, by this same process, the distance between these two sets of relations is reconfigured as a continuum that allows each to exist in reciprocal relationship with the other.

Contradictions are not resolved in this process; rather, they are constructed and reconstructed at every point. But instead of an unbridgeable gap between production relations and intersubjective relations, there is now a series of stepping stones, each one representing a field of contradictory experiences. Although they all contain contradictions, each stepping stone is also a form of mediating activity, and the variety of mediating forms includes the state, politics, media and the family. They are unstable but strong enough to enable human beings to speak against (contradict) their objectification, while, to the contrary, capital retains the capacity to objectify human subjects. Thus both capitalist production relations and relations between individual human subjects are sustained, and their coexistence maintained, by a sequence of mediating activities which normally succeed in containing contradiction as well as representing it. Accordingly, both the coexistence of these relations and the discrepancy between them are represented in a relatively orderly series of contradictions.

This sort of mediating activity entails the exercise of human subjectivity upon the discrepancy between the two sets of relations in which we are currently obliged to live. Mediation is not a process that happens automatically (though the seemingly spontaneous reproduction of capitalist production relations could not continue without it), nor is it a process that occurs only in logic. Rather, it is a social process characterised by historical human activity, activity that mediates between the multiple clusters of direct relations among human subjects and the unified system of object-relations in which the self-same human subjects are related to each other only indirectly and in accordance with the continuous movement of capital to labour.

The historical development of capital has conditioned its mediation. Similarly, the continuous movement of capital and labour has repeatedly reconditioned the forms of their mediation and redrawn the relations between one form of mediating activity and another. Thus, what constitutes politics, media and the family is changeable; so too are the relations between them, just as the significance of each relative to the whole is also variable.

The subdivision of mediating activity

In the turmoil of mid-nineteenth-century capitalist expansion, there was as yet no clarification as to which practices might succeed in performing what kind of mediating role. There is no doubt about the two sets of duality to be addressed at that time: the objective side of capital coexisting with its jumped-up role as the active subject of industrial production (and thus the most dynamic component in social reproduction) and the curious coexistence of universal production relations, in which human beings serve merely as the objects of capital, alongside direct relations between fully fledged human subjects (intersubjective relations). For an advanced capitalist society to survive and prosper as a single, unified whole, each such disjuncture would have to become conjunctural – and this by means of the various mediating activities that conjoin them. But to say that the period was tumultuous is also to say that the process of allocating particular roles to specific forms of mediating activity was still at an early stage. Many mediating mechanisms were untried, untested or as yet undeveloped, and, as we have seen, retaining social order was by no means a foregone conclusion.

Ironically, periods of disorder such as the revolutions of 1848 and 1871 had the effect of forcing the allocation of roles to various mediating activities. For example, responding to their differential experience of these events, both sides of what thus became the class divide moved towards the composition of political parties, while each party dedicated itself to the dual task of winning popular support and acquiring control over the state. By the end of the nineteenth century, across Western Europe and the USA, centralised parties were not only the central *locus* for political activity, but also, as mediators between the state and the respective social groups which they represented, their political activity was the primary mechanism for mediating between aspects of capital which were bound to be in contradiction, such as use and exchange value, social production and private appropriation and the subjective and objective roles of capital itself.

But what of that other discrepancy, between societal and interpersonal relations? The leading nations had advanced to the point where they required some form of mediating activity capable of connecting intersubjective relations with capitalist production relations while at the same time maintaining the distinction between them. In this hour of extreme need, help was at hand in the shape of the partly depoliticised press. As the new journalists arranged themselves into something approaching a profession, identified by their purportedly neutral stance, so their arrangement of the world into compartments of 'facts' and 'comment' amounted to a magic system commensurate with the curious coexistence of two sets of human relations at one and the same time.

By the end of the nineteenth century, a two-tier system of mediation was taking shape. Divisive party politics which were nonetheless oriented towards government of the people by means of a unified state, would address the contradictions within capitalist production relations. Meanwhile the disjuncture between that aspect of our lives in which we are subjects and that other aspect in which we are objectified – the contradiction between production relations and interpersonal relations – could now be addressed through the new journalism. Of course, adult literacy was an important precondition for this mode of address, which finally came into its own when most of the working-class population was taught to read in state education systems across Western Europe and the USA.

Empiricism and idealism in the mediating role of the newspaper

While offering some measure of redress against the inequality and alienation inherent in capitalist contradictions, the combined effect of the two-tier mediation system was the maintenance of social order – always contingent upon continuous mediation, always dependent upon relevant forms of mediating activity. One such activity was the production, distribution and consumption of newspapers. As this activity became more widespread, and thus more significant, so its significance was consolidated by the subdivision of news coverage into reporting and editorial; or, as distinguished by C. P. Scott, editor and publisher of the *Manchester Guardian*, 'facts' and 'comment'.

Scott presided over the *Manchester Guardian* for more than fifty years. In 1921, the paper's centenary, he reviewed its record and his own half-century as editor. He also set out what he saw as the role of a newspaper:

> Its primary office is the gathering of news. At the peril of its soul it must see that the supply is not tainted. Neither in what it gives, nor in what it does not give, nor in the mode of presentation must the unclouded face of truth suffer wrong. Comment is free, but facts are sacred.
>
> (*Guardian*, n.d.: 38)

Part invocation, part exhortation, Scott's 'declaration' of the duties of a news-paper mirrored what he thought his readers had a right to expect from it: untainted reporting, independence of character, honesty, courage, fairness, 'a moral as well as a material existence' (*Guardian*, n.d.: 38). An impressive list, which is itself impressed with the growing capacity for gathering and presenting news, just as the world beyond the newspaper office was imprinted not only with the accelerated pace of human social development but also its orientation to capital.

Scott was also concerned with relations between particular and general, both within newspapers and in respect of their role in society as a whole. This is what he had to say about the organic development of newspapers: 'In all living things there must be a certain unity, a principle of vitality and growth. It is so with a newspaper, and the more complete and clear this unity the more vigorous and fruitful the growth' (*Guardian*, n.d.: 38).

He had already set out the relation, as he saw it, between the development of the *Manchester Guardian* and the development of the society surrounding it. This is how Scott's 'declaration' begins:

A hundred years is a long time; it is a long time even in the life of a newspaper, and to look back on it is to take in not only a vast development in the
thing itself, but a great slice in the life of the nation, in the progress and
adjustment of the world.

(*Guardian*, n.d.: 38)

By his own account, Scott was highly sensitive to the relational role of newspapers. His 'sense of duty to the reader and community' was based on the
assumption that newspapers in general, and his newspaper in particular, formed a
connection between the particular reader and the community in general. Thus, in
its relationship with the individual reader, a newspaper 'may educate, stimulate,
assist, or it may do the opposite'; meanwhile, it also 'reflects and it influences the
life of a whole community' (*Guardian*, n.d.: 38). Furthermore, by relating to
both individual and community at one and the same time, the newspaper is the
means by which each is related to the other; and, as such, it is 'in its way, an
instrument of government' (*Guardian*, n.d.: 38).

This last comment is something of an exaggeration. In the strict separation of
'facts' from 'comment' and the prioritisation of the former over the latter
('comment is free but facts are sacred'), Scott's own career had been framed by
the movement of government some distance away from the press, while the space
between them was amply filled by the growth of political parties. But it also
contains a kernel of truth. Even in a relatively depoliticised form more closely
associated with neutral news, the press played a social role so important that
capitalist society would have been ungovernable without it. Its role in support of
social order was performed not so much by smuggling in pro-establishment prejudice (though there was plenty of this in Scott's editorials against the 1916
Easter Rising in Ireland and the alleged fanaticism of suffragettes) but by ren-
dering human activity into an aggregate of separate 'facts' which were themselves
separated from 'comment'.

In the particular performance of this separation, as it occurred in journalism
from the end of the nineteenth century onwards, human activity came to be
represented as both an intractable object and an unfettered subject. This was
partly a restatement of the problem first posed by Enlightenment philosophy,
when it reflected both the extent and the limits of human activity afforded by
Enlightened mercantilism. This problem was subsequently addressed in practice
by the historical development of social relations of production, which superseded
mercantile culture and its fixation on trade with a new orientation towards the
active production of objects on the part of associated human subjects. The new
orientation held out the prospect of resolving the antithesis of subject and object
in favour of human subjects. But the new social relations of production, with
their orientation to productive activity on the part of human subjects, were also
capitalist relations, in which the universal association of productive subjects is
centred on capital, the mediating object which is also the primary connection
between subjects. Thus we have arrived back at a stand-off between subject and

object, now composed in the form of labour and capital; and so the same philo-sophical problem which was partly answered by the historical development of the *social* relations of capitalist production was reposed by the identical process of historical development, i.e. the social relations of *capitalist* production. Further-more, it was posed not only as a philosophical problem which could be acted out in the life and work of a few great men such as Samuel Johnson. In its new composition, social reality as a whole was problematic (and still is) because it could not compose subject and object without them being in opposition. Similarly, these problematic relations condition the continuous requirement for further rounds of mediation both to act out and offset the divisive effects of capital acting as mediator.

By the end of the nineteenth century, therefore, the eighteenth-century problem, which had been partially addressed by the further realisation of human potential in capitalist production, now came to be acted out in various forms of mediating activity, of which newspaper journalism was among the most promi-nent. Furthermore, in the consolidation of 'facts' and their formal separation from 'comment', late-nineteenth and early-twentieth-century newspaper journalism enacted empiricist and idealist approaches along lines previously established in eighteenth-century philosophy: 'facts' as objects found by empiricists, 'comment' as society composed in the leader-writers' room where it exists as an idea to be realised by subjects without reference to the objective nature (social fact) of exploitation. Thus, the newspaper journalism of the day not only followed these approaches but also executed them to a degree that compounded their weak-nesses while fulfilling a mediating role and, ultimately, strengthening social order.

Of course, the reporters and editors who first established this division would have rejected the philosophical genealogy that we have claimed for it. Even if, like Scott, they took a keen interest in the ethics of the newspaper, journalists of this generation saw little need for a philosophy of journalism. However, in their outright rejection of the philosophical, they were labouring under the influence of the established anti-philosophy of the day. This was positivism, which took its stance, and found its distinctive character, in the rejection of Enlightenment 'metaphysics'. Led by the French sociologist Auguste Comte, positivists main-tained that in all essentials human social development had already reached the highest possible level. With priests and princes largely consigned to the dustbin of history, there was no further need either to negate the *ancien régime* or even to develop a critical line of philosophical thought. Instead, we should embark on the process of positively identifying everything about a world that was already ours, cataloguing it in order to get better at managing it. Under these terms, the future would be much like the present, only more so; similarly, under the protection of scientific management, the people (most of them) would realise more of their inherent good nature.

Here was a rationale for stabilising the inherently unstable and a role for sci-entific knowledge in both supporting progress and establishing its limits, thereby configuring social development as orderly progression. Here, too, was a role for the newspaper as the daily echo of such development. In the presentation of 'facts', newspapers were to order the chaotic activity of human subjects into a fixed object: the world on a breakfast plate. In the provision of 'comment', meanwhile, newspapers would re-pose the essential contradiction in social relations as if it could be ironed out (like the master's newspaper) by the application of scientific management and a dose of common sense. Underlying the straight-talking, no-nonsense approach, however, every editorial was to perform a minor miracle: first, each editorial emancipates readers from the objective character of capitalist social relations, inviting them to sign up for social development as unrealistically free subjects; second, it distinguishes between possible and impossible demands, plausible and implausible policies, imposing fixed limitations which lead the reader-subject back to the objective, which now appears more solid than it really is.

Prompted by the contradictions in social reality, in performance of their mediating role, such newspapers swooped repeatedly between object-led empiricism and subject-driven idealism. Moreover, in the twin tracks of their flight path ('facts' and 'comment'), they have tended to objectify human subjects and subjectivise objective conditions. Cognate with the anti-philosophy of positivism, this is both a distortion of reality in its essentially human character and true to the distortions inherent in the current, historically specific form of social reality. With positivism as its anti-philosophical precedent, this is how the modern newspaper has managed the mediation of contradictory realities.

Formulation and formulae

'Bring me a murder a day' is what editors say to reporters, allegedly. Do this, the message goes, and our paper will flourish; so, too, will your career. The famous formula captures the contradictory character of factual news reporting in the modern mode. On the one hand, it's no good if it's not new; for it to qualify as news, something about the murder should have happened today, in which case it is likely to appear in tomorrow's paper. On the other hand, 'bring me a murder a day' is also a plea for repetition: let's have more of the same, please (though, as spoken by many editors, 'please' may be edited out). Alongside the need for novelty, this is 'news as eternal recurrence' (Rock 1973: 73). The contradiction is in keeping with the social context outlined above, in which the human capacity for realising more of ourselves in the expanded world we ourselves have produced is offset by the pressure for stability. While 'all that is solid' continues to 'melt into air', it continues to rematerialise almost as quickly. In its dynamic, capitalism reaches for innovation as it also strives for limitation. This duality means that its reproduction is not set in stone, yet it was partly established on the stone, i.e. in the production and consumption of print journalism.

The sheer energy of capitalist society prompted the zest for capturing that energy on the part of the newspaperman. As these complementary energies have been generated and released, so human beings have realised more of themselves in the wider world; similarly, journalists have increased their capacity for describing our increased capability, resulting in the newspaper as the prime example of secondary realisation. By combining energetic observation with deliberate description, the newspaper has realised again (made conscious) something of that which is already happening to other human beings. Furthermore, in distributing this description to its readers, the newspaper also describes the circle of our shared reality, placing those other people – the people to whom news is happening – at the centre of a circle to which readers are turning; and in turning to its centre – the newspaper – we ourselves have been turned into this circle. This, in turn, offers a representation of our common humanity, and, in this way, the modern newspaper has helped to construct society by the performance of its mediating role.

In his autobiography, *My Paper Chase* (2009), Harold Evans provides a remarkable example of this – not least because it is a particularly intense instance of the everyday business of making a newspaper. He recreates his own frantic activity at the subeditors' table of the *Manchester Evening News* on the day of the Harrow and Wealdstone train crash (8 October 1952) in which 112 people died. As fragments of information came in from the Press Association and other sources, someone had to compose them into the front page lead. News arrived piecemeal; Evans made these fragments all of a piece. Here's how he recalls the process:

> I subbed the best of the new material into yet another version of the story for the noon edition. So it went all day; edit this, spike that, change this, number that, check the number, insert a paragraph here, delete a paragraph overtaken, shout for a proof, mark it and send it back [...] and watch the clock. I was oblivious to all the activity in the subs' room, utterly immersed in a story changing every minute, writing and rewriting the narrative, waiting for the last seconds for the final headline, heart pounding, praying that what I was rushing into metal read well. By final edition the news was much bigger than it had begun. At 4 p.m. I wrote the Late Night Final Edition banner:
> 75 KNOWN, 110 FEARED DEAD IN RAIL DISASTER
> Full platform 'scythed'; Children trapped hours
>
> (Evans 2009: 141)

In piecing together this jigsaw for publication, Evans and his *Manchester Evening News* colleagues were also positioning this piece – the crash and reports of it – into the jigsaw of our daily lives. It occupied a particularly high position in their Manchester paper, because one of the trains involved was the Manchester–Euston Express. Its position in history was secured in a short sentence comparing the collision that morning to Britain's worst-ever train crash (in 1915 a troop train collided with a passenger train near Gretna Green, killing 227). Thus the Harrow and Wealdstone story, and Evans's account of how it became a story, reveal the journalist mediating between thousands of individual readers who jointly comprise society, just as, on the day, he was mediating between the myriad items of information which he brought together to form his finished piece. As already indicated, however, there is more to this mediation process than meets the eye.

Although the newspaper affords a genuine connection between the people reading it and the people featured in it, this connection is complicated by the societal relations in which they are all already connected, these being the relations between commodity producers which occur only indirectly, via the direct relations between commodities exchanged on the market. Moreover, in presenting the world as if the people in it are connected only by news and the way we respond to it, newspapers are necessarily presenting a distorted picture of social reality, even when they are telling the 'truth'. This is a further contradiction, which is itself further expressed in the double standards of standardised reporting. In the way that journalists have measured up to these double standards, the established philosophical duality of empiricism and idealism appears yet again, like a running gag in the double entendre of news journalism.

Not that the reporter would recognise this as any part of his experience. Instead, he experiences something like the competitive law of socially necessary labour time (slower equals loser), which finds its most intense expression in his passion for scooping rivals (and colleagues) and knocking his exclusive into shape in time for the next edition. 'Knocking the story into shape' often means making it fit the formula – an established pattern of predictable variations (or are they variable predictions?) presented in the most readily recognisable vehicle.

News events are frequently made certain by such means. When news has been written up like this, then the event so described can be written off, certified and certificated. Leaving aside the spurious criticism that 'news' is simply an editorial in disguise (this is best left to those who have never been out on a story) and regardless of any slant on the reporter's part or any prejudice subsequently introduced by editors and owners, in its mediating, stabilising role, news production is normally disposed towards this kind of closure. In this respect, there is a little of the obituarist in every journalist, and every news report is something like the obituary of the events represented in it.

Killing the subject

Reporters are generally satisfied, and their editors tend to be happier, if they go out on a story and come back with a singular, identifiable occurrence which can be shown to have happened (past tense). The magic formula is: X has happened (where X is preferably a murder). Traditionally, it is better to say 'X has happened' than 'X is happening' because if you write 'X is happening' this afternoon and print it tonight so readers can have it tomorrow morning, when they get it they will correctly assume that something other than X may well be happening by now, and this only emphasises that the news report is something provisional when almost the whole point is to present it, and the world represented in it, as something fixed and established. Thus, the reporter's ambition to establish what is or has been going on segues into the professional expectation that he will get a fix on it and produce a finished article that reconstructs a fixed entity. Furthermore, when the reporter closes down the story in this way, he tends to relegate the people acting in it to a passive position. To say 'X has happened', where X is murder, is also to say that someone has been murdered (passive mode).

Of course, not all stories default so neatly to the passive. Nonetheless, murder is the ideal story for depoliticised news product – hence the editorial direction cited above; and even the oft-repeated editor's advice to reporters about their writing – be active – confirms our suggestion that the established mode of news production tends to promote the spontaneous use of the passive. If there were not such a tendency, why the need to advise so strongly against it? This is not only a matter of semantics. It means that journalism's descriptions of people in action have tended to render them as passive; conversely, the assumption underlying journalism's semantics is that the people so described are not subjects (active in their own lives as also in the sentences written about them), so much as passive objects who have been acted upon in real life, whose (alleged) passivity is further enacted in the way they are represented by journalists.

Could it be otherwise? After all, news reporting is part of a tradition of empirical investigation which depends on taking impressions and capturing an imprint of people's actions. The imprint of even the most active subjects can only be an object. Objectification of human beings is thus the counterpart of empirical inquiry into their behaviour, and to insist that reporters refrain from it is surely to demand that they stay in the office and become columnists instead.

But it is not the moment of objectification which is objectionable; in and of itself, objectification precludes neither the recognition of human beings as subjects nor the further incorporation of our subjectivity in the news-production process. However much we have recently been conditioned to recoil at the thought of 'objectification', making the world we have made into something outside ourselves – an object momentarily distinct from human subjects – is the precondition for making more of it and realising more of ourselves within it (more of this in Chapter 4). The problem with news production as it was established towards the end of the nineteenth century is that it takes the moment of objectification and prolongs it indefinitely. In the indefinite extension of this moment, human subjects are called upon to remain in this position for ever. Accordingly, in the formation of story types and the stock characters who inhabit them, 'news' has become the account of human beings in the active process of becoming the people we already were, allegedly. Under these terms, there may even be a twist in the tale, but it only serves to confirm that the knife goes in the same way, every day.

True to form

Thus, the exemplary formula among twentieth-century journalistic formulae is the aforementioned, 'Get me a murder a day.' The history of the tabloid, that twentieth-century invention, might even be summed up in it (Williams 1997). In the fourth quarter of the twentieth century, as part of the development of Media Studies, a second formula emerged in order to account for the persistence of the first. According to the second formula, the 'murder a day' formula persists because of the professional culture of journalists who have been trained to work in this way; similarly, readers have been trained to expect news packages produced by this way of working.

The second formula has been almost as persistent as the first; in Media Studies and Journalism Studies it shows no sign of abating. But we find both formulae equally unconvincing. In the next section we offer a new account of each formula which first reveals how formulaic journalism has been truly representative of a distorted present and second how critical accounts of formulaic journalism have tended to replicate its way of working, especially in their spurious emphasis on the legacy of the past.

The journalists' formula cannot be formed only according to the past experiences of those working in accordance with it; it must also be impressed with the demands of the present moment, or else who today would read what are already yesterday's papers? Moreover, the demands of the present are likely to press more heavily than the dead weight of tradition; the past can only talk back when it is galvanised by the present, especially in a quasi-professional occupation characterised by the restless search for new angles, where nobody expects to succeed by repeating 'this is how my fathers did it'. Hence, it is absurd to account for journalistic formulae by observing that they have accrued over time. This is to understand culture by saying that it is cultural. However traditional, the use of any journalistic formula can only continue into the present in so far as it is capable of meeting present demands. If news is 'eternal recurrence', this can only have come about because there is something of the present moment that demands to be presented in familiar terms.

To say that we live in a capitalist society is also to say that the present moment is repeatedly defined by the continuous presentation of capital to labour, and vice versa. Though we (the wider population) may not always recognise it, still less talk about it as such, nonetheless this relationship is our familiar. In addition, we (the authors) have said there is a pressing need for mediating activity arising from this social relation and that the range of such activity includes journalism. More-over, we have explained that mediating activity cannot be confined to the plane of interpersonal relations, since one of its roles is to relate interpersonal relations with the societal relation between capital and labour, thereby connecting the two planes of our dual existence. Accordingly, mediating activity such as journalism is not only the third position to which interacting individuals customarily refer themselves; in modern times it is also positioned – brought into existence – by the interaction of labour and capital, the exchange of one for the other which occurs continually throughout society as a whole. Hence, modern journalism is likely to be imbued with this recurring relation.

But this exchange, as we have seen, is consistently equal and unequal at the same time: equal in that commodity labour power is exchanged for value, in the form of wages equivalent to the cost of its reproduction; unequal in that the value produced in the consumption of labour power during the production process is more (usually much more) than the value contained in the labourer's wages. If this relation is indeed the essential, societal relation – the relation that characterises our society – then we would expect to see it expressed throughout society, including its non-economic aspects; if not, then neither can it be the definitive relation of society, i.e. the relation that gives today's society its definition. But if we accept that labour to capital is the definitive relation of our times, we should also expect this relation to reappear as it is, in its duality; furthermore, we might look for traces of this duality in the middle ground which itself appears out of the exchange relation between capital and labour. Thus we would expect to find the duality of the labour to capital relationship repeatedly expressed in mediating activity, such as journalism, which stands between the major parties and addresses the contradictions arising from their exchange relation. Likewise, if journalistic formulae are indeed derived from this essential relation, surely some of its traits will be discernible in their formulation; also, the persistence of such formulae is likely to be derived from the continual recurrence of this relation, up to and including the present moment.

On the other hand, the derivation of one thing from another is not the same as the two things being identical. Lest we expect to see either capital or labour represented directly in journalism, we should bear in mind that mediation stands aside from either side in the exchange relation between the two of them; by definition, mediation relates to both but differs from each. Furthermore, on the general principle that mediating activity is representative of societal relations but not directly so, in the particular instance of journalism, perhaps its formulae will turn out to be an indirect representation – a mediated presentation – of the dual relation between capital and labour. Conversely, if ever a direct representation of capital or labour is formatted to look like journalism, readers (and writers) may tend to reject this, as indeed they have done, dismissing it with the complaint that it is propaganda, not proper journalism.

As journalism is a space set aside from the labour to capital relation, so it has been specified as the means of looking at what happens between a wide variety of people (normally, other people) on a day-to-day basis. By such means, interpersonal reality is expanded to something approximating to a societal level and thus brought into closer alignment with the other plane of our existence which is already socialised in the labour to capital relation. As a periodical inquiry into the world we make personally but primarily in the shape of this societal relation, journalism is related to but also one step aside from this relation and its manifestation throughout the world we are making. Accordingly, as a stick is kinked in its watery reflection, so in journalism the societal relation requiring mediation is likely to be refracted – put slightly aside – by requirements intrinsic to inquiry. Conversely, requirements intrinsic to inquiry, such as readiness to observe and capacity to report observations, tend to be refracted in line with the overriding requirement for the mediation of social relations.

This suggests that the appearance of journalistic formulae, as recognisable to readers as they are practicable for journalists, really amounts to the consolidated arrangement of such interacting tendencies, now rearranged in such a way as to modify or disguise their contradictory nature. When reporters apply formulae they are bending to continuous pressure for a refracted representation of the world in line with both observable reality and also the experience of societal contradiction in (and only in) its interpersonal form. Hence, it is not (often) true that formulaic journalism is (entirely) false; but neither is it wholly true to the humanity of those described in it (often, it is also partly untrue to the people – journalists – doing the describing). This would also explain how such formulae can have a currency, i.e. derivation from and orientation to the present day, which cannot be accounted for solely by past experience or the learned behaviour of readers and writers. Emphasising their habitus, as sociologists of journalism are wont to do, is only to say again that culture is the result of culture (as if one such saying were not tautologous enough).

News values reconsidered

We shall look briefly at some examples of formulaic journalism from the 1970s, when the concerted application of journalistic formulae contributed to a hostile climate in which heavy, political weaponry was ranged against various social groups including 'black youth'. The most influential, critical account of this process is *Policing the Crisis: Mugging, the State and Law and Order* (Hall et al. 1978), a ground-breaking study that showed how 'black youth' were written into the role of public enemy by means of the moral panic over 'mugging'. We will reconsider only the opening movement in this sequence, i.e. the formation of formulaic journalism; and our task, modest by comparison to the achievements of Hall et al., is merely to identify the combination of societal factors and professional expectations that jointly fostered the journalists' habit of writing to type.

There is no space here in which to dissect the context of the 'mugging' panic or to deconstruct the texts that contributed to it, and, in any case, it would be superfluous, since Hall and his Birmingham research group succeeded in doing it more than thirty years ago. For our limited purposes, cursory reading of only a few of the same sort of examples may suffice to show that writing to type keyed in with contemporary demands on journalism, that it was first of all consistent with the contradictory character of journalism in its role as the mediation of capitalist contradiction; also, formulaic journalism owes more to these dynamics, as outlined above, than it does to the allegedly fixed dispositions that loom large in cultural sociology's account of journalists and their news values, which traces its origins back to Galtung and Ruge (1973), Tunstall (1971) and Tuchman (1972).[1]

For his authoritative account of *Law and Order News*, Steve Chibnall (1977) interviewed a number of crime journalists about their job and their attitudes towards it. One of them reported that they all knew what was expected of reporters:

There is this intangible thing called a news story – I don't know how you recognise it – it's experience, I suppose. It's an odd quality. You can put six reporters in a court and they can sit through six hours of court verbiage and they'll all come out with the same story.

(Chibnall 1977: 13)

Another journalist described his job in the news industry in terms which might have come straight from the pages of the Frankfurt School critics' account of the 'culture industry': 'I regard news as a commodity – it's there to buy, it's there to be processed, it's there to be packaged, it's there to be sold. That's to say, I'm in much the same position as the man who goes to work at Ford's at Dagenham' (Chibnall 1977: 221).

In this account there seems to be recognition of 'commodification' in the 'culture industry' (Adorno 2001), which is not unlike the self-mockery implied in the title of Edward Behr's (1982) account of 'life behind the lines' as a foreign correspondent, *Anyone Here Been Raped and Speaks English?* There is also the suggestion of something much like 'churnalism', but three decades before Nick Davies (2008) coined the latter term.

Chibnall's interviewees identified the routine nature of their job and divulged the extent of their alienation from it. By pointing to alienation, they indicated that the full humanity of the people working in journalism was not represented in their performance as journalists. Despite what some of them may have said to Chibnall, comparing themselves to assembly-line workers, this is not entirely explicable by reference to reporters as the wage slaves of the news industry, since their position has always been more ambiguous than that. We would also suggest that many people depicted by reporters in the mainstream reporting of this era were similarly short-changed. But not normally as a result of outright cheating on the part of (alienated) journalists; rather, the part played by journalism in society, and the parts which go to make up this kind of journalism, were true to life as it was socially constructed at the time – even if the journalism of the time was by no means true to the people it described.

We begin with a paragraph from a 'mugging' story in the *Daily Express* (17 August 1972):

Muggings, a rapidly growing crime particularly among teenage criminals, are causing grave concern to Scotland Yard. London's 'blackspots' are the West End tube stations and side streets of Kennington, Notting Hill and Brixton. Peak hours for attack are 11 p.m. on Friday and Saturday. Average strength of the gangs is four or five and the 'favoured' weapon is the flick knife.

Note that the report has the tone of empirical investigation. The reader is asked to accept that the reporter has either been to the side streets of Kennington, Notting Hill and Brixton or has combed through police records pertaining to these locations and collected enough data to be able to pinpoint 'peak' times of criminal activity; or perhaps he went out on location with officers from 'Scotland Yard' (the name of London's chief police station, used as shorthand for all manner of police activity). But alongside low-key data collection, the report also contains keywords which are intended to unlock additional meanings. For a quick read, the writer has highlighted them with inverted commas: 'blackspots' – perhaps a bad pun on dark deeds and black youth – and 'favoured', the implication being that the (un-British) mugger savours the choice of weapon, in a perverse parody of an English gentleman favouring his old school tie over the regimental one.

A similar pattern is discernible in the *Daily Mail* report (13 October 1972), headlined 'Knife Gang Stole Wives' Shopping Money, Jury Told':

> A gang of four toured London markets and Tube stations picking pockets and robbing people at knifepoint, it was alleged yesterday.
>
> They worked to a system, three jostling the victim while the fourth picked his pocket. And they did it regularly. One of the four was alleged to have told police that he usually 'worked' the Oval Tube station on Thursdays.

Again, there is the matter-of-fact tone, this time with echoes of court proceedings. But the routines of the court are echoed in the outline of a criminal routine, here amplified to suggest the sheer nastiness of someone who approaches violent crime in the same way that the rest of us think about going to work. In an instant, the phrase 'he usually "worked"' raises the story from low key to high resonance. The affective process is reversed in the following paragraph from a feature on The Grove, a street in Handsworth (a district of Birmingham with the same connotations as London's Brixton), which appeared in the regional daily (*Birmingham Post*, 22 March 1973):

> Surely no street in Birmingham is less aptly named. Even on a sunny spring day its ambience is dispiriting; at night it is full of noisome menace [...] the street is the natural – indeed the only playground of the children, a large proportion of them coloured, who live in The Grove.

The passage begins at a high level of rhetoric, and stays there. Perhaps the least colourful language in this extract is the simple statement that 'a large proportion' of the children playing in The Grove are 'coloured'. But this seemingly nondescript clause acts as a lightning rod for all the rhetorical energy running through the surrounding sentences. If life on The Grove is always 'dispiriting' and grey ('even on a sunny spring day'), we know now – rather, we are asked to agree – it's because of the residents' colour and the way of life that is imputed to it.

It is surely too narrow to say that 'racism' was the reporter's only angle all along. In the examples we have re-read, there is too much full-face reporting for them to be dismissed outright as unadulterated ideology. Perhaps it is more accurate to suggest that, travelling in both directions, these stories commute between bone-dry information and succulent rhetoric. Nonetheless, the affective power of such reports was sharply pointed. When they were published in the 1970s, the cumulative effect of hundreds of stories like these was to allow Britain's ruling elite to salvage moral authority by targeting 'muggers' as public enemies, dispensing twenty-year jail sentences to sixteen-year-olds and equating young black males with criminality. The question then arises: what prompted journalists to take part in a racist panic that suited the ruling elite and how much were they aware of the connection between their typewriting and the racial turn in British politics?

The journalists who wrote such reports will have been consciously looking for anecdotes, killer quotes and key words that animate information and elevate it into an acceptable story. As we have seen, they were keenly aware of their role in using such techniques to manufacture news according to unspoken expectations (the formula), and some even felt alienated from this process. But in writing to type – moreover, in helping by their writing to construct a particular type of '[black] mugger' – they surely would have said that they were only doing their job. A legion of critics has pointed out that this is no defence. But to say that their white, middle-class backgrounds readied reporters to do a hatchet job on 'black youth' in the 1970s is to suggest that these journalists were only a ragbag of *petit bourgeois* prejudices waiting to be opened up. This is unduly cynical, and it hardly tallies with the contrary view of journalists as proletarians-with-shorthand.

Perhaps there is more truth in the suggestion that journalists who contributed to the 'mugging' panic were picking up on a tradition of racial thinking and going along with its newly intensified application in British society: racism as a renewed social force. But even this cannot be the whole story. The second part of this suggestion displaces the malign influence of racism to somewhere outside journalism, without giving any reason why hard-headed journalists would have been so open to external influence, while the first part is yet another attempt to project the past onto the present, without explaining how the past can maintain its hold over a time and place where 'all that is solid melts into air', least of all in the social space – journalism – that records it melting.

By contrast, we prefer to trace lines of correspondence between writing to type and the relations that typify capitalist society, thereby reinforcing our proposition that formulaic journalism supplies the pressing demand for mediation at the point where it intersects with the quest for immediate knowledge. If, as we suggest, journalism is produced at the intersection between these two lines of activity, it would follow that news written according to type contains as much (or as little) truth as mediation can currently afford.

Thus the pursuit of truth by journalists is conditioned by journalism's other role in the mediation of contradictory social relations. These activities are different but related. That they have different objectives means that they are often at cross-purposes, but by their interaction they are brought into alignment, in such a way that the discrepancy between them does not come to the fore.

Furthermore, their day-to-day interaction is what we normally take for granted as journalism. Accordingly, the production of journalism results in three product lines: (1) information to serve people in their world-making activity; (2) information in the interests of capitalist reproduction; (3) the means of reconciling (1) and (2). Also, the more that both kinds of information are reconciled in the production of journalism the more they come to resemble each other. Like dogs and their owners, they ape each other's habits and end up looking largely alike.

In this context, the provision of straightforward information is never as simple as that. It is also in line with that aspect of the underlying societal relation in which labour and capital strike a bargain on equal terms. In this transaction, both parties are on the level, in the same way that reporters bring everyone they write about down to the same level as their readers. But whenever it acts as an equaliser, journalism is equal to that plane of our existence which really is on the level; on the other hand, it does not appear to recognise either the societal relation in which inequality is inherent or the ambiguity of these two levels. Similarly, when journalism looks out onto the world at this level, it is prompted by the egalitarian ambition to bring everything down to the same level in order to examine it; but in such conditions this is one and the same thing as the authoritarian pressure to flatten the contradictions out of social reality so that all of it appears in line with the moments of equal exchange between commodity owners and contradiction with inherent exploitation is lost from view, even in the act of looking.

Accordingly, the unstinting character of hard news is underpinned by the frank exchange of wages for commodified labour and the egalitarian character of this relation. Moreover, news would never have formed such a hard patina unless impregnated with the authority that comes from this relationship. However, the equality of labour with capital, as really occurs when commodity labour power is exchanged for wages, is continually contradicted by exploitation in production, where capital mobilises labour to create more than the value required to replenish it. In keeping with this contradiction, seemingly straightforward crime stories are also imbued with the negation of fair play, the disruption of equivalence. Their protagonists are people who have not been operating on the level, hence they are well suited to represent disequilibrium. Thus, the resonance for crime stories on the part of readers and writers is partly derived from the way that they ring true to the contradiction in social reality: their form evokes the formal equality which exists at the point of exchange; their concern with deviance is in keeping with the deviation from equivalence (inequality) which is also inherent in the capitalist production of surplus value. Of course, there are two different kinds of deviation at work here, but the dubious achievement of journalism is that in passing among readers so as to form them into a circle it is also able to pass off one kind of deviation from equivalence (crime) as if it were of the same order as the other (exploitation). Thus, mediation in the visible sense – holding the ring – is complemented by its hidden counterpart, the mediation of equality and inequality, both of which really do occur in the essential relation between labour and capital.

The mercurial capability of journalism was compounded, as we have seen, when 'race' politics were added to crime reporting. In the 'mugging' panic of the 1970s it transpired that journalism could do more for social order without being leaned on too heavily by those in authority. Conversely, it so happened that the formula for crime reporting lends itself to what thus became the racialisation of crime – all this without reporters having worked it out in advance or even, necessarily, at the time they were doing it.

Already at odds with its deviant subject matter, reporting the facts of court cases became especially poignant when the perpetrators being reported (as facts) were members of an oppressed social group, such as the black population of Britain in the 1970s. Being oppressed means that formal equality does not apply to you, either in law or on the labour market. Oppression is thus a further form of inequality (deviation from equivalence), prior to that which normally occurs in capitalist production. When groups of people are oppressed, there is no time at which they enter into a contract with capital on equal terms. But just as it had already disregarded one form of discrepancy (exploitation) and replaced it with a different kind of deviation (crime), the one-sided alignment of standard reporting made it blind to the particular inequalities experienced by black people in Britain.

Judging by the reports of journalists who really were only doing the contemporary version of their job, if life in The Grove was especially dispiriting, the area's downward spiral could only have been the responsibility of its residents, 'a large proportion of them coloured'; the latter had only themselves – defined in terms of their colour and its imputed culture – to blame for the extent to which their lives deviated from normal standards. Similarly, all other things being equal, as indeed they are according to 'colour blind' reporting, the preponderance of young black males entering the criminal justice system was a simple function of them being black; no reference required to the state-sponsored confinement of Britain's blacks to a social position that deviates from the norm. Accordingly, though its ideological effects were a material factor in policing the crisis, the equation of 'black youth' with violent crime did not require ideological conviction on the part of journalists: they did not have to be committed racists. It was almost enough for them to stick with the formula and apply the semantics of formal equality – the facts – to people living in conditions of actual inequality.

Not that the journalists of the day were entirely averse to the addition of rhetorical flourishes; indeed, as we have seen, the formula only flourishes with this addition. But rhetoric itself is not averse to that other aspect of the societal relation between labour and capital: the amplification of value resulting from exploitation. If 'mugging' has persuasive power – the power of persuading people to be fearful – it is derived from the surplus of meaning accrued from it, a psychic dividend over and above the returns from unremarkable, non-rhetorical words and phrases. With the latter, as also at the point of exchange between labour and capital, what you see is what you get. But words such as 'mugging' echo the exploitation in capitalist production relations by exploiting whole fields of extra meaning. In the news reports of the 1970s, it did not take many of these words for the story to end in blaxploitation.

Having first established a distorted picture of oppressed blacks by the simple means of straight reporting, as outlined above, this already distorted picture was then galvanised by intermittent use of powerful rhetoric – all in accordance with the established pattern of crime reporting. Again, it only needed application of the formula for black youth to appear guilty as charged.

In the text itself, the crime news formula was a form of mediation between words in their straightforward meaning, and words with value added. In the context of the times, the circulation of routinely racialised crime stories helped to draw a circle of British respectability against the first in a series of enemies within (Irish 'terrorists' and militant strikers were subsequently identified as such), also drawing a new line of connection between ruling elite and the majority population. Thus, journalism's capacity for establishing who's doing what to whom was subordinated to its mediating capability, i.e. its ability to describe the contradictions in capitalist social relations (call them up and contain them), without revealing the full extent of their essentially contradictory character. Cropping out contradiction meant that the reports of the time were consistent not only with their own tradition, but also with much of what went on. Simultaneously verifiable and distorting, these reports were produced on that single plane of information which does not admit the everyday dualities derived from the essential contradiction in capitalist social relations.

These are the dynamics that determine the production of news according to routine values. Though their routine realisation necessarily occurs within the quasi-professional culture of journalists, it is not sufficient to account for this culture by calling on culture to account for its own existence.

Journalism and the sociology of journalism: approaches in common

From our logical reconstruction of some of the most conventional forms of journalism, it would seem that they operate through the double displacement of our humanity, in which human subjects are first glued into position as fixed objects, then cannoned into orbit by a peculiar kind of negative idealism, now the mirror image of the value added in exploitation, almost as if Godwin had come back as a manic depressive on a mission to reanimate Malthus. We exaggerate, of course – but only slightly. In the modern representation of the world we have made, which journalism represents in its most compressed form, the empirical has a fetish for the ideal, and vice versa. Not because the two sides of this long-standing philosophical tradition are bound to continue their love–hate relationship, but because they are bound together in accord with the fetishistic character of capitalist relations today, whereby the capital value of objects supplants human beings as the subject in social relations.

But if it is correct to suggest that journalism is a way of describing recurring social patterns (without mentioning these directly) as well as the new occurrences which are its only ostensible subject matter, there should be abundant examples of all kinds of phenomena represented in such a way that they too are imbued with the same, underlying patterns. Indeed, there are many such examples, but from these we will highlight only how the same pattern that contributed to formulaic journalism is also discernible in the sociology that sought to criticise it. Formulaic journalism, as we have described it, leaps with alacrity from positivism to negative idealism. This, as we have said, is no exaggeration – journalism really does work in this fashion – but we are also suggesting that the way in which journalism works is an exaggerated version of the workings of Weberian sociology. Conversely, the latter is a more measured operation of the former.

At the turn of the twentieth century, the German sociologist Max Weber confronted the shortcomings of both empiricism and idealism, which had been further revealed during the course of the nineteenth century. He found that empiricism alone could never be sufficient because it could not positively identify 'the absolute infinity of this multiplicity' surrounding every single phenomenon (Weber 1949: 72). This meant that the researcher, 'as soon as he attempts to go beyond the bare establishment of concrete relationships' in order to determine the 'significance of even the simplest individual event', has no choice but to construct abstractions (Weber 1949: 92). On the other hand, the construction of thought and being in terms of simplified abstractions – idealism – was too simple either to satisfy the human mind or to meet the demands of infinitely complex 'concrete relationships'. Perched on the horns of this dilemma, Weber arrived at a pragmatic solution: comprehensive data collection (as far as is practicable), followed by rigorous collation and conscientious selection of data in order to form 'abstract ideal types', plus self-critical awareness that these 'types' were indeed 'ideal abstractions' which could not but reflect the predispositions of the person(s) constructing them (Weber 1949: 92). In this last aspect, Weber was attempting to use consciousness of his predicament in order to effect some kind of escape from it. Instead of entering unreservedly into either empiricism or idealism, he took up a third position between them: a self-conscious position from which to swap from one to the other, also a suitable position from which to conduct exchanges between researcher, research methods and the subject matter to be researched.

From our prior presentation of formulaic journalism, it seems that what journalists routinely do is the fastest possible version of this: their reporting comprises a combination of empirical and ideal elements; empirical data is first collected, at speed, but then selected to form abstract ideal types – on deadline. This is what we have described as writing to type. However, though the journalists who do this may well be conscious of doing it, until recently they have not normally entered their self-consciousness into the story itself; the element of self-consciousness has been largely missing from the published results of their routine, if not from their normal practice (although it may have appeared recently in the penchant for punning headlines and me-journalism, both of which draw attention to the artificial character of the journalistic process). But this missing element is just what media sociology has been supplying, for and on behalf of journalism. The sociological critique of journalism has set itself up as the consciousness of journalism, and its conscience. Thus, the way in which media sociology typically admonishes journalism is cognate with Weber's insistence that research must make a point of admitting to its own suppositions: 'There is no absolutely "objective" scientific analysis of culture [...] independent of special and one-sided viewpoints according to which – expressly or tacitly, consciously or unconsciously – they are selected, analysed and organised for expository purposes' (Weber 1949: 72).

Weber was introducing what would now be described as the need for transparency in the research process; subsequently, many media researchers have criticised the journalistic process for being opaque. But there was another, backward step, implicit in the first, which media sociology has followed Weber in taking.

Not only was Weber concerned about the suppositions of the researcher, he projected this concern backwards onto the human subjects in his research. In his study on industrial workers (1924), for example, he made a virtue out of the researcher's obligation to inquire into the prior assumptions of his subjects: 'Always examine first the influences of social and cultural background, upbringing and tradition, and [...] proceed as far as possible with this principle of explanation' (Weber 1924: 75).

Accordingly, Weber's 'principle of explanation' has been rigorously applied by media sociologists, for whom the principal aspects of journalism are explicable mainly in terms of the 'social and cultural background' of those who practise it. But the problem with this principle is that it often *prevents* explanation from proceeding as far as possible. It is problematic because such emphasis on background (the past) means losing sight of its subordinate relation to the foreground (the present). As we have previously indicated, the pressures of the present select from the past only those aspects of it that correspond to current demands. This is how some traditions acquire currency: not of their own volition but as vehicles for the present. Accordingly, the only parts of the background to be lit up are those that mirror the foreground. In media sociology, however, this order is reversed, as if present-day journalism principally reflects the background of its journalists. This is the world according to Mandy Rice-Davies in which, being the people they are, journalists would say that, wouldn't they?[2]

The irony is that media sociology has been doing to journalists what formulaic journalism does to the people in its stories: formatting them according to their past, writing them to type, building models of them. The commonality in these approaches is their joint aversion to the contradictory character of social reality. Contradiction is ironed out of 'abstract ideal types', whether these models are built by journalists or sociologists; then it is belatedly, hazily recognised but mistakenly identified with the ambiguous position of researcher-reporters, half-in and half-out of two realities (the one they are reporting on and the one they have come from). Thus, the essential contradiction in the definitive societal relation is relocated in consciousness or, unconsciously, in a 'structure of feeling' (Williams 1965: 64–88), and consciousness or 'structure of feeling', on the part of journalists, is taken to be the formative influence over journalism.

But this means losing the location of contradiction in the reality of capitalist social relations and burying the social role of journalism as the mediation of capital's essential contradiction. In turn, the relocation of duality from present-day reality to purportedly pre-existing subjectivity also means losing consciousness of our current capacity to make more than the sum of our previous parts – the self-same capacity, which, in the form of exploitation, capitalism consistently realises. Ironically, capital relies on us becoming more than we were before; our exploitation is also the production of excess, over and above pre-existing models of the world and the people in it. Instead of representing this, however, in the way they assemble our humanity, mainstream journalism and the established sociology of journalism typically tell us that we are bound to stay the way we were, tantamount to our prior existence. Moreover, in emphasising the legacy of *prior*, personal and communal experience, they neglect the extent to which reproducing ourselves as we already were is cognate with the way in which capital *currently* coerces us to stay the same, to take away from production only what is considered necessary for us to replenish ourselves in time to repeat the experience the following day. In order to arrive at this one-sided emphasis, however, it is not necessary for journalists and sociologists to conspire or dissemble (neither is this to say that they never, ever do so), only to lose sight of the contradictory whole and its continual influence over all kinds of human activity, up to and including the representation of human activity in journalism.

Journalism: taking the strain

In Chapter 3, we offer a more detailed discussion of one of the fundamental principles in the academic study of journalism, namely, the scholarly insistence that journalism cannot be objective. For the time being, we return to the immediate objective of reconstructing the historical development of journalism at the intersection between the task of describing the world so that human beings may deepen their engagement with it, and the demand for mediating activity that further describes social reality as if its contradictions were phenomenal rather than essential. Our suggestion is that the news industry has created a range of products that connect individuals with the world around them and the changes occurring in it. In this respect, it has been truly engaging. But as well as addressing change, the news industry is also the servant of continuity. In the interests of social order, its frantic activity provides a mediating service between, on the one hand, unequal relations that constitute the wider world of capitalist production and, on the other, immediate, interpersonal relations in which we live as equals.

The results of such mediating activity are not limited to a moment of objectification, which would allow for the full recovery of the human subject. Instead, as we have shown, the tendency is for human subjects to be rendered into immovable objects, even in news coverage that is necessarily concerned with their action. Thus, the vision of humanity offered in journalism is both extended in line with the expansion of social production in capitalist conditions and, at the same time, contained in the consolidated form of news. While news production has never moved irrevocably in the direction of the latter – it must also gravitate towards the original character of human activity or it will be producing something other than news – neither has it ever been emancipated from the mediating role which it performs on behalf of capitalist social relations.

In the romance of the newspaper, it would appear that the entire news industry, from its lowliest, provincial outlets to the beating heart of Fleet Street or Park Row, constantly aspires to keep pace with myriad, modern developments; moreover, it would appear that pressures arising from this descriptive role determined the formation of news as an industry. But if there really were a strict correspondence between the rate of social development and the industrialisation of news, then British news journalism, for example, would have been at its industrial peak in the middle of the nineteenth century, around the time of the Great Exhibition of 1851. To the contrary, the journalism of the day was not produced to an industrial scale. Mid-Victorian newspapers were not engineered like the railway system, even though technical preconditions such as the steam press were already well met.

News and innovation are not a precise match. Despite what the word 'news' asks us to assume, their correspondence is indirect; and the expansion of news production into an adrenaline-fuelled, industrial-scale process had at least as much to do with speeding up the mediating activity that oscillates between two sets of social relations continually at odds with each other. While the problems of industrial news production are experienced by journalists and editors as logistical ones – interviewees unavailable, copy not ready, money lost whenever presses stand idle – they are also derived from the essentially problematic nature of mediation. After all, mediation in capitalist society involves more than being a go-between; it means going between parties in constant contradiction with each other, and standing out against competing pressures (also being spurred on by them), establishing a third position – the mediating position – in which the terms of their contradiction can be negotiated. Though mediation does not amount to squaring the circle – mediation could not be as conclusive as this without also concluding its own role – it is akin to finding the square in the circle. Moreover, the pressure to square our contradictory experience, over and over again, subjects journalism to a degree of repetitive strain that is often injurious to journalists.

Journalists respond in kind. They have behaved to themselves and each other on the basis that whatever doesn't kill you makes you stronger – Nietzschean shorthand for the negotiation of their own, professional conundrum, namely, that if mediation is an unending, almost impossible task, then the Sisyphean task of not quite fulfilling it is also the excitement of being in journalism. But either the excitement wears thin or the journalist is worn out by it; or, if behaving to type – having depicted everyone else according to such formulae, journalism treats its own the same way – the journalist resorts to alcohol. From the bottom of a glass, it's difficult to discern whether drinking is the hangover from the high that comes from doing journalism, or vice versa. In any case, alcohol has served to submerge the problem which journalism continually poses for journalists. Defined by an occupation that defines itself by looking askance at others, they are bound to look askance at themselves. And, when they do, they are constantly finding out that journalism does not do all it could – and too little of what it should.

The frustrated self-consciousness of journalists explains not only why they themselves have written the best satires of journalism but also why so many journalists identify strongly with the biting self-mockery found in Evelyn Waugh's *Scoop* (1933) and Michael Frayn's *Towards the End of the Morning* (1967). These novels play on the difference between what journalism is supposed to be and what it typically entails. They are reports on journalism that describe the subordination of accurate reporting to the rhythm of journalistic routines, depicted as absurdly fast (Waugh) and preposterously slow (Frayn). Both books ring true to the experience of journalists because they show how keeping the show on the road – not just the newspaper but also the road-holding role of the newspaper in society – acquired the highest priority in the working lives of journalists.

Prompted by the destabilising experience of so many attempts to contain duality in a singular package, the restless self-consciousness of journalists has also found expression in their continuous quest for new forms of journalism and new ways of emphasising the descriptive and/or analytical capability of journalism, thereby diminishing its debilitating capacity for writing contradiction out of existence. In their most innovative phases, it is notable that many of these new forms (and the journalists who performed them) have brought contradiction to the fore. At the close of the nineteenth century, for example, assistant editor Rudyard Kipling broke out of the simplistic routine in which Britons and Indians were neatly divided by the supposed racial superiority of one over the other; instead, Kipling set out to observe and record intimate interactions between the occupying British and the indigenous people of the Indian subcontinent (Allen 2007). But there was almost no room for journalism of this kind in the pages of Lahore's *Civil and Military Gazette*, so he was obliged to reformulate his observation as stories and light verse; and in these forms it became more than acceptable – highly prized, even – in the pages of the self-same publication that could not accept it as journalism.

Journalists of the next generation, led by Americans, borrowed from the formal innovations associated with modernist fiction. They took hold of its deceptively flat language in order to build new structures of meaning, just as they climbed new heights of abstraction in the modernist structure which, in the guise of the pyramid, was soon to become (American) journalistic orthodoxy.

In the personal lives of journalists, and in the constant reformulation of journalism, the unstable contradictions which journalism is meant to mediate have had a destabilising effect on journalism itself. Similarly, the self-conscious rest-lessness implicit in all kinds of modern journalistic activity has also made its presence felt in the reformulation of modern, commercial organisations up to and including news organisations. From the late nineteenth century onwards, wide-spread use of the joint stock company to raise funds and increase investment meant that capitalism as a whole was moving away from the original incarnation of intensely privatised ownership towards something more like public control; yet this partly socialising movement also restated the terms of private appropria-tion, now in the renewed form of share ownership. Thus, the contradiction inherent in relations between labour and capital was partly transcended and partly compounded in the reorganisation of the capitalist company, and this additional conundrum has been further expressed by news organisations in particular. On the one hand, from Northcliffe and Beaverbrook to Murdoch and Berlusconi, by treating their news empires as personal fiefdoms, press barons and media moguls seem to have performed life-size, real-time caricatures of private owner-ship. On the other hand, the ensuing enmity between boardroom and reporters' room suggests not only a further degree of separation between owners and journalists but also the possibility of uncoupling journalism outright from one of its formative influences: private ownership.

Conclusion: journalism and commercialism

In the (pre-industrial) mercantilist period, the way in which journalists looked upon the world corresponded to the mercantile outlook in which all objects are regarded according to their particular embodiment of that property common to all: value. Indeed, the dual meaning of 'property' – what is owned and what it is seen to consist of – confirms the common origins of journalism and mercantilism in the instrumental examination of objects. Accordingly, both journalism and mercantilism were connected to the development of a third position that stands aside from either of the commodities traded in each and every instance of market exchange and from the persons who own them, just as it is also distinct from the personality of the journalist and equally distant from his object of study. This is the median position from which goods are assessed as portions of all that has been produced (judging their claim on value as a portion of the whole), and, likewise, human activity is valued for the good (or bad) that it is judged to bring to society as a whole. In such conditions, therefore, the commercial is not identical to the social – but neither are they entirely discrete.

The third position was developed for commercial purposes, and it continues to be imbued with its commercial origins, but it is also the position in which social reality is realised. For we are all obliged to position ourselves here in order to see ourselves and each other and to observe our reciprocal activity as each of us appears to the other. It may have been established because it was the best place from which to do business. But once established as a commercial vantage point, it has the advantage over all other areas of human activity. In order to write this, for example, we put ourselves in that position; in order to read our writing, you will have joined us there – if only to say that we did not get as far into position as we hoped. The third position is the place where we come together to look back at what has been done, even if, when we get there, we find that we disagree as to what it is. This is the common ground in our consciousness, and, as such, it is no less material to our continued existence than the common humanity (labour) already embedded in commodities. For the purposes of our study, the third position is, additionally, especially important because it is also the wellspring of journalism.

As we have shown, the task of moral evaluation carried out by Addison and Steele in the pages of the *Tatler* and *Spectator* was concomitant with the continuous process of valuation occurring in London's markets. Commodity ownership and journalistic observation were closely correlated; both entailed standing far enough back to get a better look. The outlook common to both reflected a new level of commercially driven socialisation; it also expressed a higher degree of human consciousness. In this period, the writer and the businessman were often one and the same person, and the correlation between ownership and observation was not intrinsically problematic. As writer-editor-publishers, Addison and Steele may have faced a problem of external origin: the imposition of stamp duty by the British state (Williams 1965: 203). They also faced another problem contained within the act of observation itself, as they themselves practised it. From the vantage point only recently constructed by mercantilist activity, the new observer could not fail to notice the maturation of sovereign human subjects, yet equally discernible was the dependence of such 'subjects' on found objects for which they must scour the world, foraging in the somewhat precarious hope of selling on such objects at a high price (and a good profit). Faced with these contradictory findings, the eighteenth-century spectator could hardly decide whether to look to idealism or empiricism. But there was no dilemma about whether to be either a publisher or a reporter: he should, if he could, be both.

If mercantilism owned the possibility of extended observation, as expressed in the development of journalism and the advance of philosophy, it must also own up to the impasse inherent in the observation of its own time. The impasse was as follows: if being human depends on the ownership of commodities but all we do is stand and watch our valuable charges frolicking in the markets like children in the playground we have brought them to, then our humanity remains essentially passive. To be human is to be still; in the way that humanity was defined at the time, the more we move, the less human we are – hence the formality of eighteenth-century life, which was the counterpart of both mercantile and intellectual activity. In this aspect, even our humanity is an immovable object. Yet move we must, in order to make a life for ourselves, especially now we are in a position to make more of our lives. For it is the self-same accumulation of commodities that acts as a break against the forces of nature, which in turn affords us the opportunity to look upon ourselves as actors, as subjects without limitation, in the process of becoming. But what else is there for us to become? For all our anti-aristocratic ambition, how can we be anything other than the courtiers of commodities (the object of objects)?

The crucial problem of the Enlightenment was experienced as a philosophical problem because contemplation was the characteristic orientation of that period in human, historical development: the merchant contemplating commodities as to the quantity of value to be had from them; the philosopher contemplating the qualities of life, and of contemplation itself; and the journalist as the runner between them, running them together in the periodical which might have served as the title of the age, the *Spectator*. The Enlightenment could only have interpreted the world, just as the merchants could only collect its artefacts, ready-made. But by the beginning of the nineteenth century, our humanity was already being redefined in action, and this redefinition would also change the meaning of interpretation.

In Britain, ownership no longer hinged on the mere observation of objects with a view to profitable exchange; instead, owners looked further and entered into the production of exchangeable objects as the most effective source of profit, and in doing so they also produced new people (the industrial working class), who owned but one commodity, i.e. their capacity to work. In this context, merchant (trading) capital became industrial (producing) capital, and the ensuing combination of capital and labour was transformed into the engine of economic growth and social development. In that their relation was active – the one now activated the other – the impasse between subject and object was breached. Instead of the problems arising from mercantile inaction, however, new problems arose in the direct action of capital upon labour. No longer existing in parallel, subject and object were rammed together in the dynamic relation of capitalist production. As their coupling was energetic, it was also perverse. In this arrangement, humanity is capital's passive partner, while capital acquires the active role.

Capital is the subject in congress with labour, the latter in the form of commodity labour power. But, at the same time, labour is also the subject, the active, productive partner, and, as such, it cannot but confront capital, challenging the domination which is both false and true to the contractual arrangements between them. In this context, the median point, the observation platform brought into existence by the continuous exchange of commodities, becomes primarily the platform from which to view the continuous, reciprocal exchange of capital for the commodity labour power and the vantage point from which to address the contradictions inherent in this exchange. Thus, the nature of the vantage point has been changed by the conditions which it overlooks. The place for quiet contemplation, the position from which to be the *Spectator*, comes to be as animated as the relations that condition its new existence. The median point which originated in the limited mobilisation of mercantilism (the restricted character of its socialisation) is now recreated and called into service as the centre of mediating activity, supplying the demands of the dynamic coalition (part-collaboration, part-confrontation) of capital and labour.

In the early decades of the industrial age, journalism, the observation point which mercantilism had established between the two parties involved in every exchange, became the focal point of mediating activity addressed to the contradictions inherent in social relations, now that the latter were defined by the exchange of capital for the commodity labour power and the magic of its value-enhancing properties. Thus, the new level of productive activity (acting on the world) required new levels of reporting on the world, not only to improve our current performance in it but also to mediate the contradictions derived from it (this world that is our problematic performance). The mediation of societal relations and interpersonal relations is not mediation in the abstract. Mediating activity acquired its particular significance from the specific contradictions to be mediated, i.e. in the historical conditions known as capitalism. Thus, journalism in its mediating role is normally angled towards the kind of representation that contributes to the maintenance of conditions conducive to the expansive reproduction of capital. This angle cannot be too narrow or else the information so angled will be unable to serve as the mediation of contradiction; nor is journalism to be understood as a matter of economics alone, any more than capital is only an economic relation.

From this angle, the mass-circulation newspaper that emerged in Britain towards the end of the nineteenth century is seen holding a mirror to the intense contradictions of the day. The newspaper provided a reflective surface not only in the banal sense that its contents echoed day-to-day occurrences but also in the way in which its mediating role offered a working relationship between the dynamic growth of capital and, equally, the limitations grimly imposed by capital on human subjects. Conversely, the journalism of the day became a marketable proposition when commercial distribution proved a viable mechanism for the performance of its mediating role. If the early-twentieth-century newspaper managed to turn a profit, this was because its mediating role had been successfully monetised. It was not as if the market alone invented this kind of newspaper or forced it into existence as a simple reflection of commercial pressures. The essence of modern media lies in their role as the mediation of capitalist contradiction, and this role may be more or less monetised in accordance with a range of economic and non-economic factors.

Furthermore, the dynamic character of capitalist production has conditioned our consciousness so that we expect much more of it than mere contemplation. Accordingly, we have come to expect the journalistic combination of report and thought to play an expanded role in changing our world and accelerating the realisation of our humanity; hence, the composition of the modern newspaper as 'fact' and 'comment', reporting and editorial. But though with this development the impasse in Enlightened observation was opened up, neither capitalist production nor its mediation have managed to resolve the underlying problem. Instead, by its perverse character capital has animated human consciousness in the high-velocity confusion between people acting as their own subjects and the same people being acted upon as the objects of another object, namely, capital. Thus, the fixed problem of Enlightenment philosophy (the problem to which it was inextricably linked, for all its visions of unbound humanity) was activated by the dynamic of capitalist production. Subject and object, which were in parallel (just as they were represented in the parallel lines of empiricist and idealist thought), have been in contradiction ever since.

Similarly, owners of capital and owners of commodified labour power confront each other from their respective positions in the reciprocal exchange upon which capitalist society depends. However, in the realisation of society from the recurring process of exchanging labour power for capital, these two parties continue to converge upon the third position, the common ground in which each party looks back at itself, and especially at the other, all the while referring both itself and the other to common standards which could only have been arrived at in this shared space. These standards are more than rhetorical devices. Though the general interest can only be presented through particular interpretation, it now has a firm basis in the social character of universal production.

Capital is particularly interested in appropriating surplus value for itself; hence its presentation of 'general interests' is partly a mask that belies particular, monetary concerns. Nonetheless, the 'mask' of capital is more than a thin covering; it is more like layers of activity that make up the mediation between contradictory realities. The thickness of these layers is the very substance of mediating activity. Again, much more than mere rhetoric, in modern times the general interest originates in the universal character of labour, which capital translates into the generally equivalent substance of economic value. Mediating activity is the process whereby the social character of labour is further translated from its economic translation into the moral value of that which is considered to be in everyone's interest. The two value-sets are thus related, but by no means identical: the one is not reducible to the other.

Framed by competing and contested references to the general interest, mediating activity operates according to a variety of semi-autonomous terminologies. In the nineteenth and early twentieth centuries, for example, 'truth' and 'progress' were the morally charged terms of journalism and politics in their mediating role. Though the inner connections between these two have been subject to considerable variation, they have often acted together to allow the outlying polarities of capitalist society – social production and privatisation, subject-led interpersonal relations and object-driven societal relations – to coexist in a working relationship.

In the early phases of capitalist development, journalism and politics were more or less synonymous: the press was the premier platform for the presentation of politics; contested 'truth' was a claim to 'progress' which existed primarily in print. Though their paths have diverged somewhat during the later phases of capitalist development, both journalism and politics remain largely oriented to general interests. The typical requirement that journalists must be disinterested has matched the normal expectation that representatives of whichever party (capital or labour) should speak in terms of the common good. Journalists and politicians seen acting 'purely' in their own particular interests usually suffer an immediate loss of credibility.

Similarly, in the initial phases of capitalist production, mediation was not much monetised. In the performance of its mediating role, culture stood largely to the side of commercial production (Williams 1963). We have previously identified culture's capacity to stand aside with the mid-nineteenth-century period when journalism could afford not to be a trade. As much as it is in demand, however, so the supply of mediation is open to capitalisation; hence, subsequent decades are renowned for the marketisation of journalism, the commodification of culture and the monetising of mediation. Such developments really amounted to a new variation of capital which now manages to perform mediating activities, i.e. it acts in the mediation of capitalist contradiction while continuing to operate as capital. At this point, therefore, capital has learned how to act as an economic agent, how to regard and respond to its own economic activity and how to juggle these responsibilities – all at the same time. It is, as are we, simultaneously self-regarding and self-actualising, and if it seems odd to invest capital with human capabilities, bear in mind that it already has the power to move people – to initiate and orchestrate their actions to a degree that is generally denied human subjects.

In the history of journalism, the convergence of mediation and monetisation has also entailed the partial divergence of ownership from observation. This is discernible in the separation of boardroom from reporters' room, an estrangement that approximated to the social divide between sole owners of the means of production and those who solely own their capacity to work. But this does not mean the simple subordination of journalism to newspaper owners and other media moguls. In Britain, for example, the soap opera of Harmsworths and Beaverbrooks shows the extent to which owners were kicked upstairs, leaving journalists at least some leeway to get on with the job of reporting the world. Conversely, in the way they fix the people they are writing about, almost as if these people are commodities owned by the writer, journalists have continued to define themselves by taking up a social position which has its origins in commodity ownership.

This is to reiterate that though journalism is often a business, it has never been only a business. Whether it is more or less business-like, its essential activity is the mediation of contradictions such as that between social production and private ownership, and, as such, it is not reducible to the latter. Even in periods of intense commercialisation, the employment of journalists was also the deployment of that outlook on the world, both self-interested and socially oriented, which originated in the public exchange of privately owned commodities before it was animated in a universal system of commensurate human activity, i.e. the production of commodities. Neither wage slaves nor plutocrats, as befits leading practitioners of mediating activity, journalists are more complicated than that; hence, they have often found themselves occupying the middle ground between the minority of owners and the mass of readers, viewers and listeners. Various attempts to lump journalism in with one side or the other have only performed a disservice to all concerned.

Part II

Objectivity

Chapter 3

The rise and fall of objectivity

The tension that has often existed between the study and the practice of journalism has been felt perhaps most sharply in the discussion of objectivity. Traditionally a core tenet of journalistic professionalism, the idea of objectivity has been subjected to unremitting attack by academic critics of news and journalism. 'It must surely be self evident that objectivity is, and has always been, a meaningless concept', asserts one British journalism professor, for instance, describing even the aspiration to objectivity as 'dangerous' (Gaber 2008). Similarly, Keith Woods, Dean of Faculty at the prestigious US Poynter Institute, declares bluntly that he is 'not a believer in the myth of objectivity' (quoted in Strupp 2008). Today, however, such critics are behind the times. The critique has long since become the orthodoxy: not only is there a consensus against objectivity among scholars of Journalism Studies, but journalists themselves have internalised the critique and often seem unwilling or unable to offer a robust defence of what was once a defining ethic of the profession. In the mid 1990s, the Society of Professional Journalists dropped the term 'objectivity' from its code of ethics, for example (Mindich 1998: 5); around the same time, BBC war correspondent Martin Bell confessed that he was 'no longer sure what "objective" means' (Bell 1998: 18). While scholarly disdain for journalistic objectivity is now so well entrenched that it is almost impossible, in academic discourse, to use the term 'objectivity' without scare quotes, in practice the concept has been so eroded that the critique has become, at best, redundant.

The first part of this chapter reviews the main criticisms of objectivity in journalism, explaining what objectivity is thought to entail and highlighting the different sorts of doubts that have been raised about it. These doubts are of broadly two types. On the one hand, journalism is criticised for failing to achieve objectivity: the latter is seen as a desirable end, but critics try to identify the factors that impede its realisation. On the other hand, objectivity is sometimes held to be impossible or illusory, and journalism's claim to achieve it is denounced as necessarily false. The chapter then seeks to put the concept of objectivity into historical perspective, looking at how it emerged as such a key idea for journalism. It is important to see the rise of objectivity in social and historical context if we are to understand both its limits in the past and its possibilities in the future, though we should also bear in mind that, for many of the critics who have traced the historical emergence of journalistic objectivity, the purpose of doing so was to call it into question. By historicising objectivity, the aim was often to put it at some critical distance – as an idea that could and should be scrutinised and disputed rather than an eternal, taken-for-granted feature of journalism.

Yet just as the concept of journalistic objectivity has a history, so too does the critique. Rather than a set of timeless truths, the critique of objectivity also needs to be seen in context. The third section therefore examines the critique of objectivity in more detail, discussing its emergence against the background of wider social and political developments. The critique that Journalism Studies has inherited (from its antecedents in Media and Cultural Studies and sociology) was forged in circumstances that no longer exist. Debates about political bias in news reporting, for example, often seem to hark back to a past era of clashing ideologies and competing world views that bears little resemblance to our own times. Today the most salient fact about the reporting of politics is that – judging by criteria such as voter turnout in elections or membership of political parties – fewer and fewer people seem to be interested.[1] It is our contention that in today's circumstances, when revelations of 'media bias' are more likely to reinforce popular cynicism than to prompt critical thought, the critique of objectivity no longer makes sense. In conclusion, we consider why journalism has internalised the critique and suggest that, in questioning or abandoning a commitment to objectivity, recent forms of journalism do not offer an improvement on the past.

Objectivity and its discontents

Objectivity in journalism is a complex idea, used to refer to at least three distinct, though interrelated, concepts. First, it primarily entails a commitment to *truthfulness*: reporting factually accurate information. Second, objectivity is often thought to imply *neutrality* in the sense of fairness and balance: seeking to be impartial and unbiased in the process of reporting and, where there are conflicting interpretations of an event, presenting different viewpoints even-handedly. Third, objectivity is also often understood to imply neutrality in the sense of emotional *detachment*: a dispassionate approach that separates fact from comment and allows news audiences to make up their minds about events rather than being offered a journalist's own response. These are interrelated in that – at least in theory – journalists are dispassionate and neutral so as not to let their own emotional responses and political allegiances get in the way of reporting truthfully.

The normative ideals to which journalism traditionally aspires – truthfulness, fairness, detachment – appear to some critics as impossible to achieve just because of human fallibility. Ivor Gaber's contention, quoted at the beginning of this chapter, that the claim to objectivity is 'meaningless', for example, rests on the simple observation that 'journalists […] are human beings':

> That means they have a gender, an ethnicity, a family, a social background, a personal history, a set of prejudices etc. etc. that afflict us all. […] Every

attempt by journalists to argue that they are able to put aside their own beliefs, feelings etc. and become, or aspire to become, genuinely 'objective', strengthens a dangerous canard. For it is when journalists believe they have attained Olympian objectivity that they are in greatest danger of failing to see how their own conscious and unconscious motivations are affecting how they report.

(Gaber 2008)

The objection to objectivity here is that it implies a standard to which mere mortals cannot aspire. This perspective may be informed, in part, by the fact that today it is far less certain who counts as a journalist: in an age when anyone with a blog or a camera phone might be described as a 'journalist', the professional's claim to special status and expertise looks increasingly suspect. Indeed, Gaber contrasts the professionals unfavourably with bloggers who 'make no pretence of "objectivity"' (Gaber 2008).

Journalists' claim to special status is not just hubris, however. It rests on the conviction that becoming a journalist necessitates the acquisition of particular knowledge and skills, either through formal training or via on-the-job socialisation into professional norms. The established routines of journalism, such as fact-checking, seeking out both sides of a story, or seeking confirmation of a claim from more than a single source, have developed as ways to help the reporter rise above his or her individual dispositions and biases. In this sense, journalistic writing is a *discipline* rather than just a personal outpouring of one's own inevitable predilections and prejudices. On their own, though, such routine practices are not enough. They are meaningful only in so far as they support the wider project of objectivity: an open-ended pursuit of truth. If, on the other hand, the norms of professional journalistic practice become hardened into a dogmatic set of rules, then journalism becomes sclerotic, its discipline reduced to meaningless habit.

Critics of objectivity have made just this point: that the routines of professional journalism are mere convention and have little to do with actually achieving objective knowledge about the world. This argument is famously associated with Gaye Tuchman's (1972) critique of journalistic objectivity as a 'strategic ritual'. Objectivity is a 'ritual', she contends, because the routine practices associated with it have little or no bearing on the end ostensibly sought. One such practice, for example, is 'the judicious use of quotation marks', supposedly enabling journalists to '[remove] themselves from participation in the story [...] letting the "facts" speak' (Tuchman 1972: 668). Yet, by choosing whom to interview and which quotes to use, she argues, journalists convey their own opinions or angle on the story while avoiding any explicit editorialising. Such rituals are 'strategic', according to Tuchman, in that they are designed not so much to achieve objectivity but rather to protect the journalist (and, by extension, the news organisation) against charges of bias. For the individual reporter, 'strategic procedures' such as presenting conflicting possibilities in an account of an event, or the use of supporting evidence, are ways to 'claim objectivity' and thereby to avoid 'the risks imposed by deadlines, libel suits, and superiors' reprimands' (Tuchman 1972: 665, 662). Tuchman concludes that 'newspapermen invoke their objectivity almost the way a Mediterranean peasant might wear a clove of garlic around his neck to ward off evil spirits' (1972: 660). It seems likely that Tuchman's method – participant-observation and interviews – may have shaped her findings. Asked, in effect, to justify themselves, the 'newsmen' she studied seem to have defended their decisions in terms of the day-to-day pressures of their work. However, it is also true that the 'rituals' that she describes do not, in themselves, produce objective knowledge.

A good illustration of the issues we have encountered so far is the problem of news selection. Given that the news, in whatever form, can never be a complete account of every event that happens each day, journalism inevitably involves selection – of what to include in the individual story and what to include in the newspaper, bulletin or website, as *newsworthy*. The news media have long been conceptualised as having a 'gate-keeping' or 'agenda-setting' function – deciding which events are judged newsworthy, which issues are put into the public domain (McCombs and Shaw 1972). But how are these selections made? Journalists tend not to theorise such choices – they are for the most part made spontaneously, with little time for reflection. Of course, news organisations may well have definite ideas about their brand identity or their target audience which inform editorial choices in a more or less explicit way, but by and large decisions about what to include and what to leave out are left unexamined, made on the basis of informal 'news sense'. Academic analysts of news, however, have sought to discern what unspoken criteria underpin such choices – not as any sort of operational checklist but as a theoretical abstraction from the largely untheorised decisions of the newsroom. Studies of these underlying 'news values' have sometimes suggested, in line with the idea that objectivity is incompatible with being human, that news reporting is bound to be distorted by the process of selection. Johann Galtung and Marie Ruge (1973), for example, relate their account of news selection criteria to a general understanding of the psychology of perception, whereby all individuals are prone to attentional bias: we tend to notice certain things rather than others, depending on our background and interests. Hence, the process of selection is replicated, they suggest, all along the news chain, from reporters, through editors, to individual viewers and readers: at each stage there is a filtering out that leads to a partial, and therefore distorted, perception of the world. Moreover, where journalism's claims to objectivity imply that selections are made on the basis of professional judgements about the inherent newsworthiness of stories, academic accounts suggest that they are not; at least not in any straightforward way. Rather, judgements are shaped by the demands of news-production conventions, ethnocentric cultural bias and pre-existing expectations about the world (Gans 1980; Schudson 1991).

The picture looks even bleaker when we consider a further objection to objective journalism – in fact, a whole cluster of objections – centring on its heavy reliance on official sources of information. For some analysts it is the

economic structure of the news industry that leads to an unhealthily cosy relationship between journalists and official sources such as government departments,
the police, army and other state bodies; for others, such as Tuchman, it is the
strategic aim of protecting oneself from charges of bias that leads to an over-
emphasis on 'reliable' or 'accredited' sources. Either way, the problem is that if
objectivity is equated with simply following official, elite sources, this undermines
journalism's democratic role. It also means that rather than seeing the news
media as 'agenda-setters', it is elite sources who play the most important role –
as 'primary definers' of the news agenda, in Stuart Hall's phrase – so that journalists are '"cued in" to specific new topics by regular and reliable institutional
sources' and are thereby oriented towards particular 'definitions of social reality'
(Hall et al. 1978: 57–8).

An influential articulation of this problem is W. Lance Bennett's notion of
indexing: 'Mass media news professionals, from the boardroom to the beat, tend
to "index" the range of voices and viewpoints in both news and editorials
according to the range of views expressed in mainstream government debate
about a given topic' (Bennett 1990: 106). Subsequent studies have provided ample
support for his argument – perhaps most pointedly in the case of foreign
policy, war and intervention, where adherence to an 'official line' becomes particularly significant (see, for example, Mermin 1999). Indeed, Bennett develops his
argument with a case study of the *New York Times* coverage of Nicaragua in the
1980s, when Ronald Reagan's Republican administration was seeking congressional support for a policy of aiding the Contra rebels against the country's
socialist government. Initially, the newspaper reflected congressional opposition
to US military aid to the Contras, but after that opposition collapsed under the
weight of a political campaign by the administration, it largely disappeared from
press coverage also. Furthermore, even when debate and disagreement *were*
expressed in Congress, 'opinions voiced in news stories came overwhelmingly
from government officials', and even though opinion polls showed steady opposition to government policy of around 60 per cent, the issues which exercised the
public were treated with 'nearly total neglect' as the liberal *New York Times*
reported polls in a way that 'tended to undermine the legitimacy of public opinion on the issue' (Bennett 1990: 116, 118). The indexing of the range of perspectives available in the news media to those expressed in mainstream politics
fatally undermines any notion of the press acting on behalf of the public as a
'watchdog' against the powerful. It also points up the limitations of 'objective'
journalism if objectivity is equated with relaying the views of elite sources.

A somewhat similar case, but developing in the opposite direction, is media
coverage of the Vietnam War – mentioned in passing by Bennett but explored
fully in Daniel Hallin's authoritative 1986 study, *The 'Uncensored War'*. Hallin
refutes the widespread assumption that, by bringing the reality of the war into
people's living rooms night after night, news coverage helped to undermine
domestic support for American involvement in the conflict and boosted the
anti-war movement. For many in the media, it was a source of pride that

reporters had exposed the truth and had allowed the public to question a dubious military adventure, while for Western governments and military authorities, the lesson of Vietnam was that they should in future control journalists very closely during times of conflict. This 'lesson', however, was mistaken. As Hallin demonstrates, the US news media tended to mirror the official view rather than to challenge it, relying on Washington officials and US military personnel as their main sources of information while presenting a largely negative view of the anti-war movement. What gave rise to the myth of media opposition to the war was that as elite sources themselves became demoralised and divided, media coverage reflected this. In line with Bennett's indexing hypothesis, the scope of media debate about the war was narrowed to the parameters of official discussion: the media gave voice to doubts about the war precisely to the extent that they were 'establishment' institutions.

For Hallin, the US media's uncritical reporting of the Vietnam War stemmed largely from adherence to the professional norm of objectivity: 'most of the reporting, in the best tradition of objective journalism, "just gave the facts". But they were not just *any* facts. They were *official* facts' (Hallin 1989: 25, original emphasis). A telling example is the *New York Times*'s reporting of the August 1964 Gulf of Tonkin incident, when a supposed North Vietnamese attack on US Navy vessels provided the rationale for an escalation of American military involvement. The alleged attack was fabricated – it never happened – but US journalists uncritically relayed official claims about the 'incident' despite having 'a great deal of information available which contradicted the official account' (Hallin 1989: 20). In reporting the alleged attack, the *New York Times* simply stated that the President had ordered retaliatory action but did not mention doubts over whether the 'provocation' had actually occurred. Asked about the story some years later, the reporter responded that it was 'supposed to be almost dead-pan [...] it's supposed to have no content other than what is documentable and quotable fact. No interpretation of any kind. If the president says, "Black is white", you write, "The president said black is white"' (Hallin 1989: 70–1). Hallin concludes that 'The effect of "objectivity" was not to free the news of political influence but to open wide the channel through which official influence flowed' (1989: 25).

The argument that objective journalism is reliant on official sources can be inflected in different ways. On the one hand, it might be understood as implying that by adhering to the professional norm of objectivity journalists effectively abdicate judgement. This is the problem highlighted in the example cited by Hallin above: rather than seekers after truth, reporters become mere conduits for official claims. Similarly, discussing coverage of the 2003 invasion of Iraq, the *Columbia Journalism Review*'s managing editor, Brent Cunningham, identifies 'a particular failure of the press: allowing the principle of objectivity to make us passive recipients of news, rather than aggressive analyzers and explainers of it' (Cunningham 2003: 25–6). Such passivity is indeed problematic, yet it seems illogical to lay the blame at the door of objectivity. As Judith Lichtenberg (1991: 231 n. 9) argues, 'much of what goes under the name of objectivity reflects shallow understanding of it', and it is this 'shallow' or pseudo-objectivity which ought properly to be the target of critique here. After all, to criticise such journalism for its 'destructive agnosticism and skepticism' implies the possibility of a truly objective account (Lichtenberg 1991: 228). Hallin's *New York Times* reporter who appears to equate journalism with stenography is clearly not being objective in the sense of pursuing the truth. Lichtenberg suggests that what underlies this criticism of objectivity as passivity is a confusion between objectivity and neutrality. As noted earlier, objectivity is often thought to entail neutrality – but only in so far as the journalist attempts not to allow his or her own biases or prejudices get in the way of objectivity's primary goal of pursuing the truth. On its own, neutrality does not, of course, guarantee truth if it simply means the unthinking reproduction of official claims. On the contrary, neutrality in this sense is antithetical to the pursuit of truth and has nothing to do with objectivity. As Lichtenberg comments: 'Objectivity does not mean passivity' (1991: 228).

On the other hand, however, the criticism of journalism's reliance on official sources also raises a different objection: not that objectivity entails a *lack of perspective* or a failure to exercise judgement but rather that it *is a definite perspective*: that of the centre, or the mainstream. In his ethnographic study of war correspondents covering El Salvador, for example, Mark Pedelty (1995: 171) argues that 'objective journalism is a political perspective [...] a perspective most closely associated with political centrism'. This point is not necessarily incompatible with the complaint that objectivity is too neutral – journalism might be thought to stay within the political mainstream by default if it simply involves reproducing the claims of official sources. But there is also a larger claim implied here: that what *looks* like 'objectivity' depends on one's political perspective. A good illustration of this is the BBC's response to the early work of the Glasgow University Media Group (GUMG). The BBC was disturbed by the critique of its impartiality advanced in the GUMG's pioneering Bad News studies, and the Corporation's high-level News and Current Affairs Committee discussed how to respond to the Group's work at a 1981 meeting, the minutes of which were leaked. One senior editor, Roger Bolton, argued that 'in one sense the positions of the BBC and that of the GUMG were irreconcilable':

> In an argument between Marxists, who wished to replace the system of Parliamentary democracy, and the BBC which, as successive [directors general] had made clear, was 'for' Parliamentary democracy, and which operated within it and reflected it, there could not be a meeting of minds. To that extent, it could be said the BBC *was* 'biased' and it could not win the argument that in that respect it was not.
>
> (BBC News and Current Affairs Committee minutes,
> 7 April 1981)

The implication of Bolton's remarks is that being 'biased' in favour of the political mainstream is as good as not being biased at all. It may not have been accurate to characterise the GUMG as Marxist (Quinn 2007: 15), but clearly its criticism was seen by the BBC as extreme and beyond the pale of reasonable discussion. Indeed, the BBC has always tended to emphasise not objectivity but rather '*due* impartiality' – that is to say, impartiality within the bounds of mainstream opinion.

This idea is encapsulated in Hallin's model of how the news frames events and issues in terms of three 'spheres' – of consensus, legitimate controversy and deviance. While according to Hallin (1989: 117), 'the journalist's role is to serve as an advocate and celebrant of consensus values', the news is of course also continually occupied with matters of disagreement and debate – but debate within the parameters of the mainstream. In the case that he examines – coverage of Vietnam – opposition to the war was initially treated as 'deviant' and was marginalised as unreasonable and extreme while critical discussion was narrowed to the bounds of 'reasonable' controversy (such as over the tactical execution of the war as opposed to more fundamental questions about its legitimacy). As the elite consensus in favour of the war broke down, however, the boundaries of debate shifted, allowing some of what was formerly 'deviant' opinion to become part of 'legitimate' debate. A similar model of 'consensus', 'toleration' and 'dissensus or conflict' was advanced in relation to British politics by Stuart Hall in a 1970 essay (see Hall 1973: 88). For both authors, the boundaries between these 'spheres' are understood as flexible and changeable, raising the possibility that news reporting does not simply reflect the already-existing contours of political discussion but plays an active role in defining and maintaining them. In the case of the internal BBC discussion cited above, for example, Bolton went on to suggest that giving prominence and airtime to a view outside the mainstream would be seen, rightly, as a 'political act'. One might add, of course, that sticking within the mainstream is also a 'political act'.

This is where many academic critiques of news part company with the everyday discussion of whether the news is objective. Regular complaints by mainstream political parties that a news programme or organisation favours their rivals, for example, are the familiar stuff of day-to-day debate, and news organisations such as the BBC who have a statutory obligation to be impartial are very careful to avoid favouring one party over another. The focus of scholarly attention, in contrast, is on the construction and maintenance of the underlying conceptual ground on which such debates take place. At this deeper level of analysis, critics tend to emphasise the 'constructedness' of news. Unlike the reporter's idea of 'news-gathering', which implies that news is essentially 'out there', waiting to be discovered and picked up, many critics write of 'manufacturing the news' (Cohen and Young 1973; Fishman 1980), or 'constructing reality' (Schlesinger 1997; Tuchman 1978). The idea that journalism is less a *report* of reality than a *construction* of 'reality' has been influenced by a variety of intellectual traditions and shaped by the context in which these were appropriated and used in the development of a critique of objectivity, as discussed further below. For now, however, we should note two main ways in which this idea of the constructedness of news can be developed.

One way is in terms of the concept of ideology, which is particularly prominent in the work of early Media and Cultural Studies writers, such as Stuart Hall, who are influenced to some degree by Marxism (Hall et al. 1978). In this approach, the news media are understood to reproduce the hegemonic or dominant ideologies of capitalist society, in the service of powerful commercial and state interests. The routines of objectivity, and allied concepts such as impartiality and balance, operate – but only within the limits of mainstream politics, constructing a view of the world that is broadly in line with those interests and ideologies. Events are interpreted within this 'consensual' conceptual framework, while political perspectives that challenge the dominant view tend to be marginalised as deviant or extremist. While this means that the news is understood as constructing a distorted, ideological view of the world, in principle this approach does not rule out the possibility of an objective, true account of social reality; indeed, the force of the critique often derives from the implication that an ideological account is in some sense false or partial. In practice, however, the ideology-critique approach often slides into a second, more relativistic, understanding of news as 'socially constructed'. This second approach holds that since all knowledge is inevitably produced from within particular conceptual frameworks there can be no objectivity: there are only competing perspectives, none of them 'true'. 'The belief in objectivity is a faith in "facts," a distrust of "values," and a commitment to their segregation', argues eminent American sociologist Michael Schudson (1978: 6), for example. The implication is that the two cannot really be separated – that what counts as a 'fact' depends upon or is coloured by the values of the person recording it. According to this argument, journalism's claim to objectivity involves a double deception: not only are some perspectives favoured over others but the idea is perpetuated that a true account is possible.

This final point returns us to the view that objectivity is impossible, that to claim it is dishonest and that to strive towards it is dangerous. To say that objectivity is impossible because our knowledge of the world is socially constructed, however, is not quite the same as saying that it is impossible simply because of human fallibility. Rather than the limits of individual subjectivity being the issue, the barrier to objectivity is that knowledge about the world is seen to be shaped *intersubjectively*. This is what puts the 'social' into social constructionism, drawing attention to the way in which different groups, cultures or institutions construct the world differently. It is this which allows the first, Marxist-inspired, approach to slide into the second, sociological approach, since different class outlooks and interests are held also to imply different ways of constructing the world. As we argue later, this slippage is problematic in terms of understanding objectivity and is the reason why the defence of objectivity implied in the ideology-critique approach is rarely followed through. As we have seen, not all objections to objectivity rule out the possibility of a true account, and in criticising journalism's failure to be really objective many analysts imply that it is a desirable ideal. On the whole, however, academic critique has tended towards the view that objectivity is a myth and has espoused a relativist view of knowledge. The reasons for this are discussed further below, but first we turn to historical accounts of objectivity in journalism – accounts which also often aim to relativise the concept.

The rise of objectivity

The history of journalistic objectivity can be viewed in narrow or wide focus. Viewed narrowly, it is a relatively short story that begins properly only in the early twentieth century. While there are seen to be important preparatory steps in the preceding half-century, this approach is mainly focused on the explicit articulation of the concept of objectivity in the years following the First World War. Viewed more widely, however, the history of objectivity begins much earlier, during the eighteenth-century Age of Enlightenment (though again with some important preceding developments). Whereas the first view tends to mark out a discrete moment when objectivity appears, the larger view emphasises continuity. The differences between these two perspectives can result in a somewhat confusing picture. According to Michael Schudson (1978: 4), for example, 'objectivity was not an issue' before the 1830s and only really became important in the 1920s; whereas Stephen Ward (2004: 107) describes editors of 'newsbooks' and 'corantos' as 'announcing their commitment to norms such as factuality – a preference for plain facts, unbiased news, eyewitnesses' accounts, reliable sources, and judicious editing' in the early 1600s. Robert Hackett and Yuezhi Zhao (1998: 31) suggest there have been two versions of objectivity, a progressive nineteenth-century version and an inferior twentieth-century version; while, according to Jean Chalaby (1998), journalism itself is only an invention of the second half of the nineteenth century, when it emerged as a distinctive linguistic field, characterised by the 'discursive norm' of objectivity.

The reason for such differences is not simply to do with length of historical perspective but often indicates differing attitudes towards the concept of objectivity. Accounts which focus mainly on the emergence of objectivity as the explicitly stated ideal of an established journalism profession in the early twentieth century tend to view it with suspicion, as a largely negative development. As we shall see, this is understandable – this period was indeed a key turning point, and the institutionalisation of 'objective journalism' took a peculiar, alienated form because of the circumstances of its development. At the same time, however, viewed too narrowly, the rise of objectivity appears almost as an aberration, cut off from the larger history of journalism and from the larger ideal of objectivity as the pursuit of truth. This is the approach that relativises objectivity: 'journalism has not always been this way', it wants to say, 'there are other ways of doing things'. In saying so, however, this approach sometimes ditches not just the form that 'objective journalism' assumed in the early twentieth century but objectivity as such. The strength of accounts which take a wider view, on the other hand, is that they tend to situate the overt formulation of a journalistic ethic of objectivity as part of the longer history of journalism's role in facilitating democratic debate.

For the same reason, this approach also holds out the possibility of a more positive assessment of objectivity.

Viewed in broad historical perspective, there are three key moments in the history of objectivity: the emergence of the bourgeois public sphere in the eighteenth century; the development of the mass-circulation press as a business in the second half of the nineteenth century; and the institutionalisation of professional norms of objectivity and impartiality in newspaper and radio journalism in the early twentieth century. In the brief historical overview sketched out here, we examine each of these moments in turn, not in order to deconstruct the ideal of objectivity but to show how journalism's ability to fulfil its democratic role has been constrained by the divisions and tensions of class society.

Jürgen Habermas's seminal study *The Structural Transformation of the Public Sphere* describes how, as the bourgeois public sphere took shape over the course of the eighteenth century, 'the press was for the first time established as a genuinely critical organ of a public engaged in critical political debate' (Habermas 1989: 60). This was a specifically *bourgeois* public sphere because it was a forum for the rising capitalist class to challenge established authority, subjecting political affairs to debate and criticism. In this respect, the early periodical press became a kind of print equivalent of the coffee houses, clubs and salons of the era – a public forum in which the reading public could discover and discuss the events and issues of the day. This represented something qualitatively new. Editors of sixteenth-century news-sheets may have made claims about 'truth' and 'impartiality', but these did not necessarily mean the same thing: 'truth' could mean religious truth; factual reporting could mean 'eyewitness' accounts of the discovery of a fantastical sea creature or the birth of the Antichrist (Ward 2004: 116). The eighteenth-century Age of Reason brought a new thirst for objective, scientific knowledge and a new urgency to the public dissemination of news. In the spirit of Enlightenment, the new commitment to rational knowledge extended as much to political and public affairs as it did to the investigation of the natural world. Not only nature but also society could be understood – and remade – through the power of human reason. This is why there was an 'influx of rational-critical arguments into the press', making it 'an instrument with whose aid political decisions could be brought before the new forum of the public' (Habermas 1989: 58).

Habermas describes the public sphere as existing in 'the world of letters', and, indeed, literary figures such as Daniel Defoe, Samuel Johnson and Jonathan Swift were important early journalists. The press of the eighteenth century was certainly different from twentieth-century objective journalism, but it is mistaken to separate them so sharply as Chalaby (1998: 9) does in reserving the term 'journalist' for the press of the later nineteenth century and describing their forerunners in the eighteenth and early nineteenth centuries as 'publicists'. Ward identifies three 'types' among journalists of the eighteenth century: the 'partisan', or political journalist; the 'spectator', who wrote sophisticated essay journalism; and the 'reporter', or news-gatherer (2004: 139–43). The latter's 'contribution to the public sphere', he notes, 'was the provision of accurate, timely information' (Ward 2004: 148). Indeed, Chalaby's (1998: 193) characterisation of the 'publicist' essentially describes the ideal of providing true, objective knowledge: 'Publicists never pretended to their readers that their life conditions were anything but what they really were [...] [and] stressed the fact that these conditions could be changed.' Objectivity is not simply a matter of 'discursive norms'. The eighteenth-century public sphere developed as part of the bourgeoisie's struggle for power, as a space where a new, rational critique of the existing order could be freely debated and developed. Their need to grasp the objective world flowed from the fact that they were engaged in exercising their subjectivity to transform it.

Having tasted power, however, the capitalist class became less of a friend to liberty, and less enamoured of critical discussion. The identification of the interests of the rising bourgeoisie with the general 'public interest' in the eighteenth century was, though partial (restricted to wealthy white men), also justifiable, to the extent that challenging the *ancien régime* really was in the general interest of society as a whole (Habermas 1989: 72). While the press of the eighteenth century 'represented the frustrations and discontent of the middle classes and industrial bourgeoisie', these rising social classes also had a common cause with the mass of working people (Williams 2010: 72, 75). Over the course of the nineteenth century, however, the rise to power of the capitalist ruling class led to a new division of newspapers into 'respectable' and 'radical' titles. As an essentially unequal and exploitative system, industrial capitalism could not properly realise the goals of *liberté*, *égalité* and *fraternité* that had been inscribed on its revolutionary banners. While the radical press held true to the ideals of the Enlightenment era, largely addressing the working class as the agency that could push these goals forward and advocating political and social change, the respectable newspapers adopted a conservative political outlook and supported the status quo. This ideological division was embodied in the different legal status of these two sections of the press: the respectable papers paid the stamp duty and other taxes levied by government, while the radical press was unstamped, printed and circulated 'in defiance of the Law, to try the power of Right against Might', as the masthead of the *Poor Man's Guardian* newspaper proclaimed (Williams 2010: 89). Liberal reformers successfully campaigned for the government's 'taxes on knowledge' to be reduced and then abolished altogether by the 1860s, but this was in the context of the depoliticisation of the press that we discussed in Chapter 1. While the mass-circulation press grew as a commercial venture, it also narrowed the range of what was included in the 'marketplace of ideas'.

The establishment of objectivity as an explicit professional ethic of journalism after the First World War went hand in hand with a concerted and conscious effort to 'manage' a volatile and dangerous public opinion. Stuart Allan (1997: 308) suggests that 'Popular disillusionment not only with state propaganda campaigns, but also with the recent advent of press agents and "publicity experts", had helped to create a general wariness of "official" channels of information.' Perhaps the most important driver of such popular scepticism in the wake of the First

World War was politics: this was a time of militant working-class demands for social change, the era of the Bolshevik revolution, the moment when Communist parties were being established across the Western world. The explicit promotion of journalistic objectivity was in part an attempt to cope with this situation by finding ways to retain credibility with the mass audience. It was also a tool for managing public opinion: the rise of public relations in the inter-war period indicated the elite's pressing concern with handling an unruly and unpredictable mass public by 'engineering' or 'manufacturing' consent as Edward Bernays (1947) and Walter Lippmann (1997) put it.

In Britain, the birth of broadcasting in this period gave rise to the analogous concept of 'impartiality', which served similar ends. Having been established as a commercial organisation (the British Broadcasting *Company*) in 1922, with its potential as a news provider severely restricted on the grounds that it would undermine the press, the BBC's first foray into journalism was during the peculiar circumstances of the 1926 General Strike. The BBC's future direction as a public corporation licensed by Royal Charter had already been decided upon by Parliament earlier that year, but the strike threw all that into doubt. John Reith, the BBC's then managing director, realised that, with newspapers affected by the strike, this was an opportunity to show that 'impartial' broadcasting could be a more credible source of news than the government's propaganda sheet, *The British Gazette*. His implausible formula for BBC 'impartiality' was that 'Since the BBC was a national institution and since the Government in this crisis was acting for the people [...] the BBC was for the Government in the Crisis too' (quoted in Curran and Seaton 2010: 112). Publicly, the BBC was supposedly above the bitter class divisions of the era, serving 'the people' as a whole. Yet, while he fought to prevent the Government commandeering the organisation, Reith wrote in his diary that 'they know that they can trust us not to be really impartial' (Stuart 1975: 96).

The explicit elevation of objectivity did not represent a return to the spirit of open, critical debate of the Enlightenment-era public sphere. But this was not simply because of the industrialisation and commercialisation of the press and the consequent narrowing of the political sphere; nor was it solely to do with the need to engineer consent. As Schudson astutely observes, it was at the very moment of its formal elevation that objectivity was most in doubt. In the inter-war period, 'when the worth of the democratic market society was itself radically questioned and its internal logic laid bare', he observes, the formalisation of objectivity was a response to an elite crisis of confidence (Schudson 1978: 122). Objectivity as a set of formal 'rules and procedures' was emphasised in response to an acute 'pessimism about the institutions of democracy and capitalism' and doubts about 'traditional values and received knowledge' (Schudson 1978: 126). Following the Second World War, such doubts and uncertainties were temporarily suspended through the relatively stable framework of consensus politics at home and the Cold War stand-off in the international arena, but they were not resolved. They resurfaced in the late 1960s and 1970s as the post-war consensus broke down, and one of the ways they were expressed was in the critique of objectivity.

Contextualising the critique

In what Judith Lichtenberg (1991: 217) calls the 'compound assault on objectivity', critics have argued that journalism is not objective, that it cannot be objective, and also that it should not be objective. As she observes, it is logically inconsistent to criticise journalism for failing to be objective while also arguing that objectivity is impossible and/or undesirable. Yet that was the thrust of the critique of journalistic objectivity that sociology and Media and Cultural Studies developed in the 1970s and 1980s. In many respects, the path-breaking studies of those decades continue to set the parameters of contemporary Journalism Studies, yet today's situation is very different. In this section we first look back to see how the academic critique of journalistic objectivity was shaped in particular ways by the context in which it was developed and then go on to evaluate how far it still works in today's circumstances.

One of the few critics of objectivity to reflect explicitly on the historical circumstances which have given rise to the critique they are seeking to make is Michael Schudson, in his influential book *Discovering the News*. Schudson is sensitive to the fact that the critique to which he is contributing is a product of particular circumstances, which he characterises as the rise of an 'adversary culture' or 'critical culture' in the 1960s (1978: 163). Doubts about objectivity in journalism, he notes, arose as part of a broader questioning of the claims of the professions:

> Critics claimed that urban planning created slums, that schools made people stupid, that medicine caused disease, that psychiatry invented mental illness, and that the courts promoted injustice. [...] And objectivity in journalism, [previously] regarded as an antidote to bias, came to be looked upon as the most insidious bias of all. For 'objective' reporting reproduced a vision of social reality which refused to examine the basic structures of power and privilege. [...] It represented collusion with institutions whose legitimacy was in dispute.
>
> (Schudson 1978: 160)

What Schudson describes here as a 'general cultural crisis' (1978: 162) is essentially the rise of the Vietnam-era counter-culture, which entailed a profound questioning of society's established values and institutions. The authority of all received knowledge, conventional wisdom, accepted norms and mores was radically thrown into doubt. The interrogation of news and journalism was an important part of this wider phenomenon, and individual critics tended to see their work in this light, as part of some bigger intellectual and political moment. Schudson (1978: 10) says his own work was conceived as part of a larger history of professions and 'professional ideology'; Tuchman (1978: 216) describes her book *Making News* as 'a study in the sociology of knowledge as well as in the sociology of occupations and professions' and clearly identifies with the women's movement (the subject of a case-study chapter). Similarly, in Britain, pioneering critics such as the GUMG identified closely with the labour movement, for example, and Stuart Hall was a founding figure of the New Left as well as the leading light of academic Cultural Studies.

The critique of journalistic objectivity that came out of the political and cultural ferment of the 1960s and continued to develop over the following decades was always implicitly undercut by the fact that it did not defend the concept of objectivity as such. Tuchman, for example, suggested that 'sociological objectivity' might also be a 'strategic ritual' (1972: 677), disavowing any claim to 'objective truth' and arguing instead that her critique of journalism could also be applied to academic knowledge (1978: 216–17). This conclusion followed logically from the social-constructionist approach adopted by Tuchman and many others: if all knowledge is socially constructed, then there can be no 'true' or 'objective' account, only different perspectives, different 'ways of knowing'. As we noted earlier, however, this relativist approach sits uneasily with a critique of ideology, which implies that the falseness of ideology may be contrasted with a true account. It is the attempt to combine these two basically incompatible approaches that gives rise to the contradictions that Lichtenberg describes:

> Typically, the social constructionist critique vacillates between two incompatible claims: the general and 'global' assertion that objectivity is impossible because different people and cultures employ different categories and there is no way of deciding which framework better fits the world; and the charge that particular news stories or mass media organizations serve an ideological function or represent the world in a particular or distorted or otherwise inadequate way. It is crucial to see that these charges are incompatible. Insofar as objectivity is impossible there can be no sense in the claim [...] that the media are ideological or partial, for these concepts imply the possibility of a contrast. And conversely insofar as we agree that the media serve an ideological function or bias our vision, we implicitly accept the view that other, better, more objective ways are possible.
>
> (Lichtenberg 1991: 220)

What appears to be the most radical edge of the critique – the claim that objectivity is impossible – is actually its weakness, cutting away the ground on which a critical perspective could stand.

Theoretically, the mistake was to confuse a Marxist critique of ideology with other then-fashionable intellectual currents, especially semiotics and a social-constructionist sociology inspired by phenomenology. Hall was not untypical in eclectically welcoming these and other sorts of 'theoretical inputs' as ideas that could be 'integrated' into a 'critical paradigm' (1982: 66). They are, however, not really compatible. Where the distinction between the misleading appearances of society and its real essence is central to the Marxist critique of ideology, phenomenological and semiotic approaches 'bracket out' the question of how far representations correspond to the real world. Whereas, for Marx, the mystified ideological appearances of capitalist society nevertheless derive from its fundamental social relationships, in the phenomenological and semiotic approaches there are only appearances, understood as 'socially constructed' or working through agreed conventions: the 'social' here really just means interpersonal or intersubjective meanings.[2] A good illustration of the problem is the widely used notion of 'professional ideology'. The term sounds as if it must have something to do with the theory of ideology but is actually much closer to the social-constructionist understanding of intersubjective meaning: it refers to the ideas and norms that inform the routine practices of journalists as a discrete professional group. Yet critics write of the 'ideology of news which requires it to be neutral, unbiased, impartial and balanced' and complain that the 'prevailing professional ideology encompassed by the myths of impartiality, balance and objectivity allows the broadcasters to tacitly trade upon the unspoken and dominant ideology of our society – the liberal notion that there is a fundamental consensus' (GUMG 1980: 402).[3] In combining the two ideas (of ideology and 'professional ideology') the analysis slips between criticising the news for being ideological – presenting a false, partial or misleading picture – and criticising it for its 'professional ideology' of objectivity. While the first implies the possibility of an objective, true account, the second repudiates any such possibility. Objectivity itself appears to be 'ideological'.

The question of what would constitute a better, more objective account tended to be avoided in favour of amassing evidence of the ways that the 'neutral, unbiased, impartial and balanced' ethos of broadcast news disguised its ideological character (GUMG 1980: 402). Radical critics made it clear that they were not 'neutral' any more than the news was but did not clarify the issue of objectivity. In the past, the implied relativism of the critique was contained or masked by the fact of active political engagement and contestation. News could be criticised for systematically favouring some perspectives and excluding or marginalising others (trade-union or Left-Labour views in the GUMG's classic studies, for example). In the absence of the clear ideological contest of yesteryear, however, that critique becomes much more difficult to sustain. Indeed, after the collapse of traditional Left/Right politics at the end of the 1980s, as the relativist drift of the critique of objectivity became more apparent, a few critics reacted against it, arguing for a 'rational critique of media content whose validity can be argued for beyond the preferences of a given political subculture' (Philo 1990: 205; see further Philo and Miller 2001). We agree, and would add that, if Journalism Studies is to reclaim the possibility of rational critique, then it ought also to defend the possibility of objectivity in journalism.

The critique of objectivity developed in an era of heightened social contestation as the post-Second World War political consensus broke down. In the USA, issues such as the Vietnam War and the civil-rights struggle polarised opinion, while in Britain the heightened labour militancy of the 1970s signalled the beginning of the end of the cosy 'corporatist' approach to industrial relations. In these circumstances, it made sense to analyse how news reporting played an ideological role by staying within the narrow boundaries of 'legitimate' opinion and defining certain political perspectives as 'deviant'. Today, though, what are the 'alternative' or oppositional viewpoints being marginalised? As some analysts have recognised, the picture of an elite united around firmly established 'consensus' values transmitted through the media no longer seems to apply. Brian McNair, for example, notes that 'Instead of ruling class ideological control [...] we have *mass cultural information chaos*' (1998: 30, original emphasis; see further McNair 2006). Although McNair locates the shift towards 'cultural chaos' as a phenomenon driven by the media, as opposed to the chaotic character of today's political culture, he does at least recognise that it no longer makes sense to continue recycling the same critique. In the twenty-first century, mainstream political debate is narrower than ever, but it is difficult to see this as simply the result of progressive or radical perspectives being marginalised or left out.

If anything, today it is those who think of themselves as progressives and radicals who are often the keenest to narrow the sphere of 'legitimate controversy'. In 2009, for example, Left-wing demonstrators protested against the BBC's decision to allow British National Party (BNP) leader Nick Griffin to appear on its *Question Time* programme. The protestors complained that allowing Griffin on the show would give his extremist opinions a 'veneer of respectability' (Choonara 2009). The problem, in other words, was that the BBC was too open to extreme political views and ought to rule out those of the BNP as beyond the pale of acceptable debate. This is by no means an isolated case. Those who think of themselves as politically progressive today have similarly sought to delineate the bounds of acceptable debate around issues such as 'hate speech', 'Islamophobia' or 'climate change denial'. In the case of the latter, some campaigners have argued that questioning the consensus on climate change should be regarded as a crime (O'Neill 2006), while academic researchers studying news coverage of the issue have argued that balanced reporting of different views is 'problematic' since journalists ought to reflect the consensus view (Boykoff 2007; Boykoff and Boykoff 2004). Having established that the news media play an important role in defining what is 'sayable' in public debate, the aim of those adopting an ostensibly critical perspective now seems to be to police the boundaries of acceptable opinion themselves. If today's journalism is to aspire to the ideal of the public sphere as a forum for vigorous, open and critical debate, it is more commitment to objectivity that is required, not further deconstruction of the concept.

Perhaps the most important difference from the past, however, is that the majority of people in Western societies are not really engaged or interested in the public sphere. Habermas's view – that journalism was no longer able to play the role for which it had seemed destined in the Age of Enlightenment, and that the contemporary commercial media had instead given rise to a 're-feudalisation the public sphere' – has often been seen as overly pessimistic. Today, however, the public sphere does indeed appear to have been 're-feudalised', in the sense that we are more or less passive spectators to a kind of court politics. Yet where Habermas attributed the problem to the media, it seems clear that the real problem is the hollowing out of political life itself: for this reason, his argument is actually more pertinent to the period after its publication in English in 1989 than it was when it first appeared in German in the early 1960s. After the end of Left and Right, the political class has become increasingly isolated and disconnected from the *demos* it is supposed to represent. Established institutions and sources of authority are called into question, not from a critical political point of view but more as an expression of popular cynicism and disengagement. In these circumstances, to go on recycling the critique of objectivity does not move the debate forward: it is at best superfluous and at worst likely only to reinforce cynical attitudes towards the media and public life.

Conclusion: the fall of objectivity

By the mid-1990s, critics and journalists alike were queuing up to pronounce the death of objectivity. David Mindich (1998: 138) argued that journalism's future was as a 'post-"objective" profession', for example; Stuart Allan (1997: 319) predicted that 'The end of "objectivity" and "impartiality" as the guiding principles of an ethic of public service may soon be in sight.' In journalism, perhaps the most striking rejection of objectivity was in the field of war reporting. As we noted at the beginning of this chapter, the BBC's Martin Bell renounced objectivity in favour of a 'journalism of attachment'. Decrying the 'dispassionate practices of the past', Bell argued for a journalism that 'cares as well as knows', complaining that objectivity meant having to 'stand neutrally between good and evil, right and wrong, the victim and the oppressor' (Bell 1998: 16–18). Similarly, in the USA, CNN's star foreign correspondent Christiane Amanpour argued that: 'In certain situations, the classic definition of objectivity can mean neutrality, and neutrality can mean you are an accomplice to all sorts of evil' (quoted in Ricchiardi 1996). Being objective, it seemed, meant complicity with evil. Instead, reporters claimed to be listening to their own consciences, which apparently told them to take sides in the wars they covered (particularly Bosnia – the example pointed to by both Bell and Amanpour). They also sought to make it plain to viewers and readers that they were taking this new approach by couching their reports in personal, often highly emotive terms. Again, war reporting threw up some clear examples of this: Fergal Keane's use of a BBC current-affairs programme to read out a letter to his newborn son in which he reflected on his experiences covering Rwanda is perhaps the most famous instance of the genre (Keane 1996).

Not all journalists subscribed to this new school of war reporting – and some bravely criticised it (see, for example, Gowing 1997) – but its influence stretched well beyond those who explicitly advocated the new approach. In some respects it seems to have attained the status of common sense. In a March 2010 discussion of the ethics of war correspondence, for example, the *Daily Telegraph*'s former foreign editor, Stephen Robinson, declared that 'there is no such thing as objective truth, objective reality'. His comment – on one of the BBC's flagship current-affairs programmes – was welcomed by the presenter as a point of consensus.[4] Moreover, in the 1990s, similar trends became evident in other areas of coverage as objectivity was superseded by the requirements of what Mick Hume (1998) calls 'emotional correctness'. Journalists who did not toe the emotionally correct line risked opprobrium for appearing heartless – as, for example, Kate Adie found in 1996 when her report of the fatal shootings at a school in Dunblane, Scotland, was publicly criticised by a BBC executive as 'forensic'. It seemed that her tone was too cold and factual, failing to hit the right emotional notes (Mayes 2000).

It is notable that the emotive, 'attached' style of reporting that developed in the 1990s has not attracted the level of critical analysis directed at objectivity in the past. Instead, critics have sometimes welcomed it as a positive development. John Eldridge et al. (1997: 118–20), for example, after heavily criticising the 'promotion of the just-war concept' in coverage of the 1991 Gulf War, had nothing but praise for those who sought, through their reporting, to influence 'international policy and action' in favour of 'just war' in the Balkans and elsewhere. Perhaps they were wrong-footed by the fact that reporters who proselytised for international military intervention in the 1990s often presented themselves as critics of Western governments, complaining that political leaders were reluctant to act. Yet in the longer term it became obvious that the moralistic style of 'attached' journalism coincided with the perspective of powerful Western states. By the end of the decade leaders had begun justifying military action in similar 'ethical' terms: in an echo of Bell's formula, for example, British Prime Minister Tony Blair described the Kosovo bombing as 'a battle between good and evil; between civilisation and barbarity; between democracy and dictatorship' (*Sunday Telegraph*, 4 April 1999). Like political leaders going to war because – as Blair said of the 2003 invasion of Iraq – their conscience tells them they must 'do the right thing' (Blair 2003), reporters have attempted to influence policy on the same grounds. In the process, our understanding of contemporary conflicts has been distorted by simplistic narratives of good versus evil, and the sympathies developed by some reporters have led them to welcome attacks on those designated as unworthy victims (see, further, Hammond 2002).

The public has often been ill served by such journalism, but the problem is different from the traditional issue of ideological bias. Rather, journalists confront a similar difficulty to that faced by politicians in our post-ideological era: how to make sense of events when the old framework of political meaning has collapsed. Their response has often been narcissistic, placing their emotional selves at the centre of the story, because the goal has been to resolve this problem of meaning for themselves rather than to inform public debate. As Hume observes, the journalism of attachment 'uses other people's wars and crises as a twisted sort of therapy, through which foreign reporters can discover some sense of purpose' (1997: 18). Journalists are indeed human and have the same sorts of opinions and emotions as everyone else. The problem with those 'attached' journalists who abandon the goal of objectivity, however, is that they tend to 'get their evidence mixed up with their emotions [...] seeing what they want to see rather than reporting all that is there' (Hume 1997: 5). The traditional professional routines of journalism were potentially more than mere 'rituals': practices such as fact-checking or seeking out both sides of a story offered ways to overcome the limitations of one's own subjective impressions and to get at the truth. Today, there is less sense of a necessity to transcend the personal and impressionistic.

Of course, there have been moments in the past when there has been wide-spread questioning of journalistic objectivity, including by journalists themselves. As Schudson notes, for example, the 'adversary culture' that emerged in the 1960s led to a renewed emphasis on 'muckraking', 'enterprise' or investigative reporting in the mainstream and also spawned the literary 'New Journalism' of figures such as Tom Wolfe (Schudson 1978: 187). Some critics contend that today's crisis of objectivity is simply the latest manifestation of periodic 'waves of press criticism' (Broersma 2010: 23). When analysts do examine what might be distinctive about the contemporary questioning of objectivity, the most likely culprit appears to be new technology (Mindich 1998: 139). It is often suggested that traditional forms of journalism have been undermined by the wide avail-ability of sophisticated new kit, as hordes of amateurs with camera phones and laptops present such a variety of perspectives directly to the public that the for-merly authoritative discourse of the professional reporter is reduced to merely one voice among many. Yet it could just as plausibly be argued that – at least potentially – new technologies could help to overcome many of the obstacles to objective journalism. Take the reliance on official sources, for example: Donald Matheson and Stuart Allan (2009: 116–17) contrast the reporting of the 1964 Gulf of Tonkin episode with an analogous event in 2008, when 'the US gov-ernment sought to escalate a military incident between three of its warships and Iranian patrol boats in the Straits of Hormuz'. This time, the official version of events quickly unravelled as the Internet enabled 'a much wider ring of critical voices' to deconstruct and challenge US government claims. What could be interpreted as a positive development for objectivity, however, is today more likely to be seen as yet another nail in the coffin of mainstream journalism. The fact that, to many, the advent of amateur or 'citizen' journalism seems like another reason to question traditional news reporting has more to do with the profession's self-doubt than with the intrinsic properties of digital technology. As Matheson and Allan (2009: 89) observe, the perceived authority of new forms, like the blog, rest on the 'genuine emotion' of the personal testimony, in contrast to the perceived inauthenticity of professional journalism. The mainstream gave positive encouragement to the ascendancy of the 'citizen journalist' – and not just after the fact, by declaring that 'news coverage is a partnership', as the BBC's Richard Sambrook said after the 7/7 London bombings in 2005 (quoted in

Matheson and Allan 2009: 101). The diminished status of objective reporting and the affirmation of the personalised account owes more to the rise of the 'engaged' and emotive style practised by mainstream figures such as Bell and Amanpour than it does to the more recent efforts of bloggers.

The routinism, reliance on official sources and narrowness of debate which critics have associated with the past practice of 'objective journalism' are hardly to be celebrated. And yet, in questioning or abandoning a commitment to objectivity, more recent forms of journalism offer no improvement. In the past, disagreements over different approaches to journalism, just like broader disagreements within society, were generated by the possibility of social transformation. Different currents within journalism responded differently to that possibility – being open to change or reproducing the status quo, as in the nineteenth-century division between the radical and respectable press. Today, though, with the prospect of social transformation off the agenda for the time being, the demand for objectivity is at an historic low. If objectivity is tied to that active process of rational and critical engagement with public affairs which Habermas describes as originating in the eighteenth century, then objectivity's future depends on the extent to which we again come confidently to see ourselves as seekers after truth, able to act on and transform the world.

Chapter 4

The future of objectivity

We begin with two propositions:

The future of objectivity is digital. Constant movement in the workings of digital media accords with the reciprocal activity of human subjects operating upon the world, our object. These human operations comprise what we refer to as 'objectification'. Part of the process of objectification occurs in consciousness, where it culminates in objectivity; and digital technology is well disposed to support this aspect of the objectification process.

Our relation to the world we are making is indivisible from our relations to each other – social relations, enacted in the collective process of making both the world and ourselves within it. Particular forms of socialisation, therefore, correspond to equally specific forms of objectification; and this correlation pertains not only to the social production of objects in general but particularly to objectification as it also occurs in consciousness.

And one hypothesis:

If the workings of digital media correspond to current forms of socialisation and objectification (capitalism), the dynamics of capitalism will be represented in the dynamism of digital media and their disposition towards the social production of objective truth.

In this chapter we shall show how this is so. We will also show how capitalism itself suggests the development of socialisation and objectification beyond their current forms. Furthermore, we will demonstrate that though this potential is already expressed in the workings of digital media, nonetheless they are currently deployed largely against further socialisation and to the detriment of objectification. Our presentation will require reconsideration of influential concepts such as 'network society' (Castells 2009) and 'networked journalism' (Beckett 2010). By such means we hope to move the debate about objectivity out of its analogue phase and into the digital age.

Digital dynamics

The technical composition of digital media content entails a restless process of deconstruction and reconstruction. In one moment of this process, the particulars of each and every message are broken down into general elements – the zeroes and ones from which the term 'digital' is derived. But in another, complementary moment, these general elements are formed into particular combinations that embody the specific content of each, different message. Thus, the bits (general elements) and bytes (particular combinations) of being digital exist in a reciprocal relationship.

Whereas instability is the modus operandi of digital media composition, analogue production has always been oriented towards stability. Analogue media technology was designed to capture an original source by taking the closest possible impression of it. Thus, the analogue recording of Dame Nellie Melba's voice was analogous to the sound which she herself originated. The subsequent history of analogue media production is the improving story of how to obtain fixed impressions of original sources, thereby strengthening the analogy between source and copy. But this relation is absent from digital media. Technically, there are no copies in digital media composition, since each iteration is equally original. Composition and recomposition occur every time media content is rendered by digital means. In their instability, the technical relations of digital media production are consistent with the social relations of capitalist production. While digital media production is based on continuous configuration of bits and bytes, capitalist production depends on continual dialogue between abstract and concrete labour, each negotiating its existence by reference to its complement.

Abstract labour is that which is common to labour when all technical characteristics particular to the production of specific objects have been removed. Concrete labour, on the other hand, is labour in its technical specificity. 'Concrete labour' is a general term for the application of human subjectivity upon particular, technical means, resulting in the production of specific objects for systematic exchange. Like any other concept, 'abstract labour' is an abstraction from reality. But it is also an extraordinary concept in that it refers to a process of abstraction that occurs both in human consciousness and in our historically specific social being.

In today's historically specific conditions, the general exchange of objects does not take place simply because particular subjects, or their owners, have ordained that it should. Furthermore, systematic exchange depends not only on objects being different (though this they must be, or else why swap one for another?); it also occurs on the basis of what they have in common – abstract, human labour. The historical development of the system of exchangeable objects was thus the systematisation of labour in the abstract. Objects came to be universally commensurate at that moment in history when labour became simultaneously abstract and concrete; conversely, the historical expansion of commodity exchange allowed labour to become universally abstract as well as necessarily concrete.

As a result of these reciprocal developments, commodities are now objectively exchangeable, before and beyond the subjective inclinations of those involved in any number of individual exchanges.

Furthermore, the ceaseless exchange between abstract and concrete labour in the production of objects is the objective process that produces the human subject, which is in turn enacted and consumed in the further production of objects. We are what we make: both the world outside ourselves which we have made and also what we have made of ourselves by making it.

Thought and deed

The circumstances in which abstract and concrete labour contradict each other in production also condition our thinking. This means that our consciousness of the world can be as dynamic as the dialectical process in which we came to make it. Although our ability to think in this dynamic way is variable, not constant, even its variations are given by the dynamism of labour and the relation between its abstract and concrete forms.

Just as the human subject makes the world of objects outside itself, so we also remake ourselves in thought; moreover, in these conditions we are able to remake ourselves in thought as if we were outside ourselves (this is the position first established in the *Spectator*). As a collective entity, the human subject occupies both positions at the same time: the position in which we are the subject acting upon the world, our object; and the position from which we regard our own, active self as an object outside ourselves. Objectification is the process undertaken from the first of these related positions; objectivity is the tendency that emanates from the second. Moreover, we can negotiate this duality because our social reality is neither fixed nor uniform. While objects are composed in the continuous relation of abstract and concrete labour, as conscious human subjects we construct ourselves in the continual movement from subjectivity to objectification; hence also to objectivity. Thus we inhabit the reciprocal relations between thought and deed.

This is to reiterate that subject and subjectivity are not only the opposite of object and objectivity. In the historically specific conditions of capitalism, both these philosophical couplets are predicated on universally commensurate labour, and, as such, they also complement one another. For labour is both a verb and a noun; it is the human subject in action, and the essential element embedded in the object produced by human beings – our world. In keeping with this outside world of our own making, the reciprocal relations which have only recently emerged between moving parts in the technical composition of digital media point to (because they themselves are derived from) the reciprocity of subject and object both in capitalist social reality and, potentially, in our consciousness of it.

However, the dynamism lately represented in digital composition has been continually overridden by the passive influence of capitalist social relations. The further paradox is that the human subjects activated in the societal relation between capital and labour are also rendered into passive elements by the performance of their particular roles in this historically specific relation. For example, when capital purchases labour power, it separates this uniquely expansive commodity from its personal vehicle – the labourer – so that the rest of this whole man, apart from his labour power, is left standing on the sidelines of the production process; and this is especially important since production is also the process in which the human subject comes closest to self-realisation. Similarly, when labour power has been expended in production, newly minted products move to the market where they associate freely with each other. Yet the labourer is left rooted to the spot, where his immobility contrasts with the mobility of commodities which he himself produced before they were taken away from him. Meanwhile, the capitalist has no active role to play in production; nor has he ever played such a role. Capital activates labour power, but the bearer of capital is hardly more than a voyeur. Though he may dominate the context of production, in the production process itself he can only watch their coupling.

Thus, the movement inherent in capitalist production also produces two passive personae: the alienated worker and the lumpen capitalist. Both of them look out upon productive activity from a position of inactivity. (This is not to say that either workers or capitalists are individually or collectively immobile; their lives may have been shaped by migration, for example. But neither does this alter the way they are made to stand still in relation to production, viewed as a whole from a higher level of abstraction.) With both of them similarly inactive, it is possible for them to share the same outlook, even though the active elements which each has entered into production (labour power and capital, respectively) are diametrically opposed.

In their fixed character, and the way in which they subsequently attempt to capture activity so that it accords with their fixed character, these personae are to social relations what analogue recording has been to technical relations. But in social relations there can be no simple switchover from analogue to digital; the conservative influence of these fixed figures, arising from the current configuration of our humanity, cannot be turned off at the flick of a switch or turned into the dynamism associated with being digital. Instead, by their passivity, these personae stand out against the dynamic aspects of capitalist production, and by negating this dynamism, they continue to create antagonisms that preceded the digital age but which have not been superseded by it.

The potential for such antagonism is contained in the difference between making the world our object (objectification) and our collective consciousness of doing this as if outside ourselves (objectivity). This corresponds to the distinction between acting as the subject and remaking our actions in thought. As formulated in the preceding sentence, however, this is only a distinction between primary and secondary forms of human subjects making the world our object, which is also to say that acting as the subject (social, productive being) and remaking our actions in thought (consciousness) are related as much as they are distinct, and, thus far, their relationship is not necessarily problematic. But thanks to the passivity of (exhausted) labourers and (inactive) capitalists alike, subjectivity (looking outside myself from a position of passive estrangement) and, on the other hand, being the subject (engaging with the world I am acting upon), not only relate to each other as different moments in an integrated process but also confront each other as alien modes of historically specific existence: passive versus active. This is the basis for the widespread experience commonly known as the mind–body dichotomy and frequently analysed in terms of the division of labour.

As in the system of production relations so too in related systems of thought (social theory), and again in the systematic attempt to know the world we are producing (journalism). Both the active and the passive modes of capitalist society, and the antagonism between them, have all been represented in successive episodes throughout the historical development of journalism and social theory. However, the very fact that these episodes are successive rather than merely repetitive suggests that the passive elements in capitalist society are barely able to maintain its boundaries. To continue the technical metaphor, modern tendencies towards the digital are more marked than the disposition to remain analogue.

The lure of legwork

There's nothing quite like it. Despite the mounting pressures involved, there is something strangely harmonious about being a reporter in the midst of events of which you are required to make sense – when it's your job, and yours alone, to make them into a sensible story. Is this a case of the reporter playing God? Lording it over all he surveys, deciding what will enliven his story, deselecting people to be cut out of the plot and, effectively, killed off? Partly, perhaps. But apart from individual aggrandisement, the lure of the story and the feeling of completion which sometimes arises even when the story itself is still to be written are sensations that come to journalists when their energetic movement – getting out of the office to the place where it's happening, and getting it down, fast – is synchronised with the kinetic aspects of their professional culture and also with the dynamic society which they have been commissioned to represent.

On the other hand, most journalists will have looked in the mirror at some point and seen the face of a cynical hack staring back. This is not only a reflection on them personally. It also reflects the extent to which even the people who perform the productive activity of this society are left ultimately unmoved by their own movements, and this, in turn, is expressed in the hack's muted hostility towards his subject matter – the people in his stories – and, finally, in the way his face is marked by cynicism. Yet still he need not be a lost cause. Unmoved he may be, but the saving grace of the hack is that he usually recognises himself as such (Behr 1982), and, whether or not he admits as much, he normally harbours the desire to get moving again.

Restlessness and routine

The desire to avoid hack work – to move beyond fixed routines of reporting – and the hope of not having to reduce the world to a fixed pattern in our reporting of it, have characterised the best of both sociology and journalism. At the turn of the twentieth century, for example, Max Weber sought to widen the range of academic research and to make it more adequate to its objects of study. He devised a 'method of understanding' that combines 'the conventional habits of the investigator and teacher in thinking a particular way' with 'his capacity to "feel himself" empathically into a mode of thought which deviates from his own, and which is normatively "false" according to his own habits of thought' (quoted in Eldridge 1972: 27).

Weber was calling on the sociologist to describe the world not only from his own vantage point but also from the point of view of those he himself was describing. His aim was to goad sociology into a more active way of thinking, approximate to the restless activity of the world about which it was thinking. For the purposes of our discussion, it is notable that Weber rejected the idea that single individuals could produce objective knowledge. On the other hand, the duality in his method was designed to enable sociology to achieve greater understanding, i.e. as a collected body of work, to make a larger contribution to the objectification of the world in thought, on the part of the human subject.

How, then, was the individual sociologist to contribute to this collective contribution? In Weber's eyes, he should not give up addressing objects of study from the abstract position of the professional inquirer; rather, 'as the situation requires' (quoted in Eldridge 1972: 27), he ought to complement this moment of abstraction by moving closer to the mindset of his objects and concretising their position. Additional, appreciative insight (*verstehen*) was Weber's response to the problem of alienated objectification, as described above, in which human subjects are investigated in such a way that the fixed position of the investigator is imposed upon them in the process of investigation.

Weber remained unconvinced that his own 'method of understanding' was fully appropriate: he doubted that it would ever appropriate the fullness of social reality. For Weber, human understanding of reality could only be provisional. Whereas for his near-contemporary, Lenin, (bourgeois) reality was itself provisional – it provided the opportunity for proletarian revolution, and our understanding would become firmer as the human subject, in the form of the international working class, became stronger.

Though in some respects Weber's life's work was a riposte to Marxist dialectics and their growing, revolutionary influence, nonetheless, the different but complementary moments in his method of understanding came together in pursuit of a similar ambition: to compose a form of consciousness capable of encompassing the liveliness which already occurs in reality. But in Weber's work this ambition was itself complemented by pressure to resolve the lively contradictions of capitalist social reality and to frame them in accordance with the mindset of the passive individual – that loose amalgamation of the bourgeois and the alienated worker, which is variously represented in both journalists and sociologists. Weber acknowledged that the resolution achieved by such an individual would always be imperfect (in thought, as in action), but his pioneering address to the imperfections in such methods also formed part of their subsequent capacity for (provisional) resolution. He may have bent the bars, but neither Weber's discontent with modernity nor his dissatisfaction with established sociology was enough to release him (or us) from what he perceived as an iron cage.

Something of the same ambition runs through the work of Robert Park, erstwhile newspaperman and founder of the Chicago School of Sociology. In Chicago this ambition was partially realised in the development of sociology as a form of super-reporting on social contradiction. Like the big city newspapers of the first half of the American century, Park and the generation of sociologists that followed him were continuously engaged with the contradictions produced by urbanisation. Yet out of their engagement they devised a measured form of intellectual resolution, and their work was duly pressed into active service against the imminent threat of social instability and the possibility of revolution.

Park was concerned with the people who had recently moved into the USA. Immigrants were his object of study; instability and consolidation his underlying themes. Thus, Rolf Lindner (2006: 200) describes Park as both 'reformer and reporter', whose role was to explain the immigrant to the white Anglo-Saxon Protestant, and vice versa. In order to organise lines of inquiry into the lives of immigrants, Park set himself up as 'a city editor in an academic milieu' (Lindner 2006: 94). As their supervisor and editor, he commissioned students to do more than desk research. Instead, in order to report on immigrant communities and their relations with the host city of Chicago, he instructed student-reporters to put themselves in their places, to go into the district, to get the feeling, to become acquainted with people (Lindner 2006: 80–2).

In Chicagoan sociology, Weber's *verstehen* converged with reporter's legwork, not only in the attempt to keep pace with urban developments but also with the effect of establishing the city as a containable site, putting it on record as a place of eventual containment. Drawing on our technical metaphor once more, the digital tendencies in social reality were represented by Chicago sociologists and by their counterparts in contemporary newsrooms, but they were also offset by their joint rendition of the analogue disposition.

In the 1950s and 1960s, the next round in the restless quest to catch up with material reality took the dual form of 'the sociological imagination' (Wright Mills 1970: 11) and the New Journalism pioneered by, among others, Truman Capote, Hunter S. Thompson and Tom Wolfe (Wolfe and Johnson 1975). At almost the same time that C. Wright Mills (1970: 11) was calling upon sociology to imagine its own way out of 'this Age of Fact', Wolfe was failing to meet the deadline for a piece commissioned by *Esquire* because, try as he might, he could not make what he had observed fit the established format for magazine features. Famously, Wolfe wrote a desperately fast, forty-nine-page memo which *Esquire*'s managing editor had the sense to run under an even faster headline: 'There Goes (Varoom! Varoom!) that Kandy-Kolored Tangerine-Flake Streamline Baby' (Wolfe 1968: 9–14). This was journalism as a new way of reimagining the world, in which reporters drove their copy across the page as if the words themselves were custom cars.

Later, in Hunter Thompson's 'gonzo' journalism, words (neck and neck with Ralph Steadman's grotesque imagery) raced reality in a demolition derby. In their coverage of American life and politics for *Rolling Stone*, Thompson and Steadman unearthed the underlying circuits of violence – but violence also embedded itself in Thompson and Steadman. As Steadman later recalled, 'we looked in the mirror and that's where we saw the decadence and depravity' (McKeen 2008: 147).

In his work for *Rolling Stone*, Thompson gave visceral expression to a generation frustrated not only by the world they were inheriting but also with the available means for expressing their frustration. Accordingly, he climbed in and out of his own stories, dissolving the distinction between reporter and reported, and punched his way through the fact–fiction divide like it was a paper bag. Before long, Thompson's predicament *was* the story, as one of his biographers has observed: 'His journalism was usually about journalism: no matter what he started off writing about, he ended up writing about Hunter Thompson trying to cover a story' (McKeen 2008: xv).

Meanwhile, in academic circles, the 'coming crisis of Western sociology' (Gouldner 1970) was becoming perhaps the primary object of sociological study. While there was a notable element of narcissism in this (as there was, also, in some of the New Journalism), it hardly accounts for such a shift in emphasis. Instead, it seems that by the 1970s experimental journalism and imaginative sociology had both reached a point where they could no longer bring themselves to offer much by way of resolution – not in what they found out about (content), nor even in the way they presented their findings (form). Thus, it is hardly surprising that their own ways of working would become their most pressing concern. In journalism, this led to a widening gap between mainstream formulae, which ostentatiously disregarded any such concerns and 'simply' (in fact, self-consciously) got on with the job, and various radical alternatives represented in the 'underground press'. Meanwhile, the academy became more radically estranged – not only from both government and the working class but also from its own traditions – than in any previous period within the modern epoch.

Culture wars and contemplation

In this context, the kinetic aspects of journalism and sociology came into conflict with the analogue disposition to record and contain; indeed, throughout the 1970s and 1980s, this conflict was a formative influence on the overall context of 'counterculture' and 'culture wars'. While the onset of hostilities occurred largely as a result of external factors, the possibility of a culture war over epistemology – what we know and how – was already given in the contradictory roles of knowledge and information, as previously outlined: (1) to further the human subject in the further objectification of our world; (2) to consolidate existing social relations by converting their inherent contradictions into a manageable sequence.

In our discussion, as it appears on these pages, we have arrived back at the distinction between investigative activity that addresses social reality in its lively contradictions, and mediating activity, which also forms part of social reality but which addresses such contradictions in order to deactivate them. Newspaper journalism, as previously observed, undertook both of these tasks, but the second has tended to override the first. Thus, the newspaper encompasses a wide range of human experience, but the way in which this experience is written up places it all on the single plane where we meet each other as equal individuals with something to sell; meanwhile, the exploitation of labour by capital – the unequal societal relation that also informs every minute of our everyday existence – has been 'cut from the back' (like paragraphs that do not fit the page), so that its conflict with essentially egalitarian, interpersonal relations disappears from the story altogether.

Moreover, in reducing societal relations to interpersonal ones, coverage of this kind also defaults to the historically specific personae of alienated labourer and inactive capitalist, and their mutual estrangement from the self-affirmation of the human subject in making the world our object. In that they are estranged from productive activity, this pair can only meet each other as merchants of the two, key commodities in their possession, i.e. capital and labour power (as noted, the combination of these commodities serves to unlock productive activity, but their bearers are barely integrated into this process). Thus, the world in all its lively contradiction has been brought to a standstill, and journalism fulfils its mediating role by limiting the volatile contradiction between societal and interpersonal relations, which is necessarily contained as and when they are ordered to appear on the same level.

During the 1970s and 1980s, academic analysis of journalism frequently failed to distinguish between non-alienating objectification that affirms the human subject and mediation that ultimately affirms objects over subjects, thereby alienating subjects from themselves as from the objects they themselves have produced. Instead, objectivity as a whole, including that aspect of it which even now corresponds to the self-affirmation of the human subject, was wrongly identified with the alienated version incorporated in mediating activity. Similarly, when contemplating the grievous actions of the unseen hand of the market (and its accomplices), the most radical thinking of the period tended to dismiss outright journalism's ambition to detect causes and solve cases by cracking them open. Instead, this progressive aspiration was wrongly identified with journalism's other, related task of resolving social contradiction (provisionally) by closing it down. This was the case of mistaken identity that prompted so many Foucauldians to subsume journalism and every other kind of knowledge into the powers that be.

Radical intellectuals made a category error for which they are culpable. But given the conditions pertaining at the time, their mistake is also understandable. At this time, there was little sign of the working class putting itself forward as the realisation of the human subject or harbouring the ambition to objectify the world on its own terms. In such a context, the fact that only one form of (alienated) objectification was readily available prompted even the best minds of their generation to see this as the only possible form of objectification. Accordingly, in their (imperfectly) laudable eagerness to oppose alienated objectivity, radical intellectuals rushed to identify with the dynamism discernible in subjectivity. In doing so, they lost sight of both the relation between objectification and the human subject and the distinction between being-the-subject, which combines subjectivity and objectification in original activity, and the kind of subjectivity that depends on prior objectification but does not actively re-engage with it, thereby consigning both parties to a life of mutual hostility. In their criticism of alienated objectivity, therefore, they prepared the intellectual ground for the further development of alienated subjectivity.

There is no space here in which to ask when the progressive aspirations of this generation began to take on regressive effects (answers to this question appear in Calcutt 1998). It is pertinent, however, that from the early 1990s onwards Western elites began to behave in accordance with the radical critique of alienated objectivity. They reneged on their previous insistence that mediating activity should occur in well-defined episodes, culminating in clear, if temporary, resolution. Whereas in the 1970s and 1980s, being open-ended entailed some measure of opposition to the institutionalised finitude of capitalist society, during the 1990s openness and inclusivity lost their exclusively oppositional character; instead, these qualities were welcomed as new moral values by members of a new power elite, who entered them into the rubric of their 'governance'.

From fortress to network

The recent change in social protocol is exemplified in mainstream journalism, where there is no longer a uniform requirement that stories should have a beginning, middle and end – still less the previously predominant expectation that the story's end must determine the beginning and the middle. Similarly, even the most established news organisations, such as the British Broadcasting Corporation (BBC), have moved beyond their erstwhile, analogue disposition and assumed many of the dynamics associated with being digital. In this respect, widespread enthusiasm for all things digital is partly a technical metaphor for non-technical developments. Not only on our pages but also in the outside world, 'digital' is as much a metaphor for dynamism as a direct reference to the technical properties of new media.

New protocols in mainstream journalism were first signalled in the 1980s with the development of rolling news broadcast on dedicated, cable television channels such as Cable News Network (CNN). Again, the technicalities involved were hardly as significant as the changing attitudes and practices which they came to represent. The idea that news could roll, and would continue rolling indefinitely, differed sharply from the previous idea that news came as a sequence of distinct packages – successive editions and separate issues or time-specified bulletins – each of which attempted to be more definitive than the last. Rolling news, on the other hand, was largely defined by the absence of the definitive. There was more to this than recognising the provisional character of news, since that recognition was already as old as the adage that journalism is the first draft of history, and therefore not the last. Yet until recently, professional journalism also aspired to make its first draft everlasting. Only in the past two decades has it become acceptable for mainstream journalism to see itself going with the flow.

In the 1990s, a latter-day version of 1960s-style New Journalism also entered the mainstream. Confirmation that New was no longer the alternative version of journalism came in the form of Martin Bell's declaration (1998) that reporters were no longer bystanders and should make a point of not pretending otherwise. Writing about 'the journalism of attachment' in a personal capacity, Bell (a BBC man to his bones) nonetheless represented the changing priorities of perhaps the most venerable news platform in Britain, when he declared for the comparatively free play of subjectivity (on the part of journalists and their subjects) and against the outdated straitjacket of alienated objectivity, from which even senior journalists in the most established organisations now felt increasingly estranged. It was almost as if these journalists were reproducing the criticisms of their own erstwhile journalism which the radical academy had first formulated twenty to thirty years before.

In the first decade of the twenty-first century, the hitherto dominant expectation that reporters should aim for exclusives that were also conclusive was further diminished. As we write on the cusp of the next decade, new priorities for mainstream journalists now include being inclusive and open-ended – the very values that once marked out the counterculture from that which it set out to counter. Based in established institutions such as the BBC and the London School of Economics, influential journalists and prominent commentators on journalism talk of the fall of 'fortress journalism' and the rise of 'networked journalism' in its place (Beckett 2010). They observe that journalism is no longer operable from walled enclosures of privilege and relative security, with occasional forays into the wilderness of plebeian experience. Instead, professional journalists should see themselves partly as originators but also as curators and facilitators of content generated by users (the people formerly known as readers). In the wider discussion, journalists are reconstituted as nodal points in networks of content producers and arrangers, encompassing professionals and non-professionals alike; and Web 2.0 (delivering digital dreams, for real this time) is taken to be the engine for reworking journalism into a networked world and reconceptualising journalism itself as a network.

This package of expectations is the most recent in a long-running series of manifestos aiming to take journalism out of the alienated objectivity associated with monetised, centralised and bureaucratised news organisation. Unfortunately, the current escape programme tends to retain journalism in an alienated state, confined this time to alienated subjectivity (rather than the alienated objectivity which is its mirror image). But in this latest example, which combines ideas of networks and subjectivity into an ideal of networked subjectivity, the realisation of these ambitions is intimately associated with journalism becoming truly digital, i.e. aligning itself organisationally with the technical character of digital media.

In our presentation, we have made metaphorical reference to journalism being digital, i.e. we refer to moments in journalism which have been as dynamic as the technical composition of digital media content. Though some of the moments to which we refer predate the actual development of digital technology, we make no apology for mixing up the timing in cavalier fashion, since our reference to being digital is indeed metaphorical. Conversely, we have been careful not to use the term too literally, i.e. to suggest that the technical process of digitisation could or should determine the recomposition of journalism. To us, this has no more salience than ascribing the development of journalism to the existence of the printing press. (If so, why two centuries between alleged effect and supposed cause?) We regard digital technology as the platform upon which journalism is being restaged, and, while we have noted that the technical properties of this platform are conducive to the lively humanity of the characters acting upon it, we also note that the play's directions originate elsewhere. However, in order to identify these directions and their real determinations, it is necessary to address the dominant view of digital technology and the fetishised interpretation of what it does. By working our way backwards from its distorted expression, we aim to arrive at the underlying reality.

Setting analytical levels

Every professional journalist working in the West today will have experienced at least one moment when the arrival of a new piece of kit in the newsroom has been as momentous as the appointment of a new editor. Equally momentous, if not more so, has been the spread of new communications kit outside the newsroom, among the people formerly known as readers. In this context, it appears that technology itself is acting on the lives of journalists and non-journalists alike. Among those inclined to counter the tendency towards technological determinism, an old argument just as readily appears: namely, that every piece of new technology and any number of new editors are all answerable to economic pressures beyond both the internal politics of the 'silo' and the white boxes containing computers, software, etc.

Step forward, market forces! Unfortunately, the standard argument that the neo-liberal market is responsible for most things that happen in journalism has not kept pace with non-standard developments, particularly the way in which digital media content has begun to flout the law of value by standing partly outside the market (Anderson 2009); its aptitude for doing this, i.e. the discernible but by no means unilateral tendency towards de-commodification, being one and the same as the threat it poses to business models based on the standardisation of commodities.

In the light of this experience, it really does seem more accurate (and less hackneyed) to suggest that we are all actors involved in creating interpersonal networks, whose lives, in turn, are shaped by the process of network creation. Furthermore, when our experience is reviewed in this light, it is sensible enough to theorise these relations as 'actor-network' (Latour 2007) or 'network society' (Castells 2009); even to suggest that digital technology is almost like another person operating in the newly expanded networks of interpersonal relations.

According to the terms in which we have made our presentation, the problem with both these depictions is that the societal relation is left out of the picture. While the labour–capital relation is mentioned both in the attack on 'neo-liberalism' and in the tendency towards technological determinism, each of these accounts refers to this relation as if it were only one among any number of relations. Thus they both gloss over its uniquely associative role. To reiterate, this relation acquires general significance because labour in general is constituted as a consequence of it. Resulting from the engagement of labour power by capital in production for exchange, all labourers come to be related to each other (indirectly), just as the commodities they produce are directly related and rated according to the amount of labour they contain. Thus, the labour–capital relation first makes for a uniquely universal form of human association before separating the products so produced from their producers and translating the quality of their active association into a quantity of value contained in each commodity.

The vantage point from which to establish this in thought is only as abstract as the abstract labour that occurs in practice, the universality of the latter being the basis for universalism in the former. Similarly, those aspects of our consciousness that depend on abstract labour in its uniquely transferable character are also imbued with the characteristics of their patron so that in some ways this kind of consciousness is disposed towards the universality of human activity and is sometimes able to make this activity its starting point. Under these terms, neither technology nor even market forces are given in advance of productive activity and the historically specific form of its organisation. Whereas technology is seen to drive social reality when the latter is reconstructed (erroneously) as if all of it occurs on a single, interpersonal plane, if we operate in thought at only the same level of abstraction as already operates in the social construction of abstract labour, technology is put back in its box and the definitive role is rightly accorded to concerted, human activity.

Why, then, is it so difficult to acquire this insight and to maintain the viewing position from which it can be acquired? The answer lies in our previous observation that in circumstances conditioned by capital, observation itself is typically disposed towards the containment of contradiction rather than full appreciation of it. Moreover, this disposition is formed by the standard position from which to make observations, which corresponds to the position of sellers and buyers at the point of exchange, up to and including sellers and buyers of commodity labour power. At this point there are only interpersonal relations between human subjects, for this is the point at which the productive association of labour has been entered into the commodity, having been transplanted from the labourer and now all but evacuated from him. After activating the social character of labour, capital now reclaims it for itself, along with the products of labour. This point, at which labourers are as alienated from each other as they are from the objects they have produced, tends to promote alienated objectivity; moreover, it is also the point at which the distinction between subjectivity and objectification is hardened into contradiction so that they confront each other as opposites rather than complementary moments in the integrated process of being the subject.

In capitalist society, therefore, the relation between subjectivity and objectification tends to acquire a confrontational character. But this is not an eternal verity. Rather, their estrangement occurs only when human subjects are alienated from the process of objectification that they themselves have undertaken. Capitalist relations are inscribed with such alienation; but the form which it takes is not prescribed. Instead, alienation is repeatedly reformulated along with successive reformations of capital. For example, the onset of capitalist production relations on a national scale was accompanied by the formulation of alienated objectivity in the format of national newspapers. By contrast, now that the capitalist economy has been globalised, there is scope for a borderless kind of journalism – networked journalism, in other words. But we suggest that this journalism is no further estranged from alienation than its predecessor. Instead, it accords with a revised and more comprehensive form of alienation between tendencies towards subjectivity in the West and the transfer of systematic objectification to the East.

We also suggest that the unstable character of alienation points to the possibility of professional and political intervention to reintegrate subjectivity and objectification in the interests of the human subject, but, of course, there is no guarantee that this will be accomplished. On the other hand, we can be sure that the estrangement of subjectivity and objectification will not become absolute (except perhaps in conditions so extreme that they are barely conceivable). Instead, there are already new forms and revised versions of the mediating activity which we have previously identified as an integral part – more accurately, the integrating part – in the continuous composition of contradictory social relations under capital. However, whereas earlier generations of mediating activity typically tended to promote the resolution of social contradiction in one country, not least through the production of alienated objectivity on a national scale, now that the capitalist economy has moved to a global scale of operations, mediating activity has divided largely along geographical lines, in accordance with a world economy subdivided between productive and non-productive activity.

We are not in a position to establish the exact status of this subdivision. There is wide recognition of 'financialisation' (Dore 2008) in contrast to the accelerated growth of production in Brazil and Russia but especially in South Korea and

'Chindia' (Engardio 2007; Dicken 2007) and widespread concern about the ensuing economic imbalance between East and West (Legrain 2010; Wolf 2009). However, some analysts go much further, pointing to deep structural decline in the productive economies of the West, which has been only superficially offset by 'palliative' developments such as the growth of financial services and increased state support (Mullan 2008, 2009; Poynter 2009, 2010). Phil Mullan has noted that 'if you add up the profits of financial institutions and the financial activities of non-financial companies, it is about 50 per cent of the economy' of the USA. This draws him to the conclusion that in the UK and USA, 'virtually the entire economy has become dominated by financial-style activity' (Mullan 2009).

There is no space here to examine Mullan's proposition in detail, but there is surely sufficient evidence to suggest that the centre of capitalist production has been moving from West to East (especially if the definition of 'East' is promiscuous enough to include Russia and Brazil). Moreover, we suggest that long-standing forms of mediating activity have travelled in broadly the same direction. Thus, the newest and most productive economies, mainly in the East, are also producing alienated objectivity that lends itself to episodic resolution in roughly the same, old ways first seen in British mediating activity nearly 200 years ago. At the same time, older, Western economies are newly disposed to revised forms of mediating activity that tend towards unresolved, open-ended sequences of alienated subjectivity – alienated, especially, from the objectification now occurring in Eastern production.

While alienated subjectivity seems to be among the chief characteristics of that part of Western mediating activity which is defined as journalism, just as alienated objectivity is a feature of its contemporary Eastern counterpart, nonetheless the conditions in which media and mediation are proliferating also offer the chance to turn mediating activity against the regressive estrangement of subjectivity from objectification and towards their progressive reintegration. But this inviting prospect will not accomplish itself. Even though digital media technology is conducive to this task – even more so now it is becoming more widely available throughout the world – the international realignment of objectification and the human subject requires an especially conscious kind of subjective intervention, not least on the part of journalists.

Recent origins of alienated subjectivity

The current composition of subjectivity in many of the most prominent regions of the West follows an important episode in which the alienation of subjectivity from objectification was first marked out in the demise of substantive politics and in popular estrangement from the political. This episode preceded the most recent reconfiguration of production and non-productive activity along geographical lines; indeed, the completion of the previous episode, and with it the final closure of a long-diminished political cycle which had opened so bravely with mid-nineteenth-century journalism, has been a precondition for the substantial (not unilateral) displacement of production from West to East and the further alienation of subjectivity from objectification.

As previously noted, modern politics has served to mediate the contradictions latent in the social relations of capitalist production. But in containing these contradictions, i.e. establishing them in what came to be their boundaries, the political has also contained, i.e. presented, a contradiction of its own between, on the one hand, the likelihood of social reproduction (with current contradictions reproduced and contained accordingly) and, on the other hand, the possibility of social transformation, at which point current contradictions would become neither tolerable nor reproducible. While acting as a bridge between subjectivity and objectification in the era of capitalist social reproduction, the conduct of politics has confirmed their separation but will also have alluded to their unification, to be accomplished, potentially, by human subjects coming together in political activity to form the historical subject – humanity making history for itself.

The possibility of such transformation was both presented and contained in social democracy, exemplified in the written constitution of the British Labour Party which was ratified in 1921. For more than half a century afterwards, politics in Britain were conducted by reference to this possibility and the containment thereof, typically through the mediating activity (political activism) of the organised labour movement (the Labour Party and the unions) and its Right-wing counterparts, such as the Conservative Party. During the course of these decades, however, successive generations identified less and less with the political, which came to be thought of (if anyone was thinking about it at all) as 'the god that failed' (Crossman 1950). Instead of regarding politics as the means to unify their subjectivity with the objective world, thereby enacting social change and affirming themselves in the history-making role of the human subject, growing numbers of increasingly disaffected individuals came to regard the political as yet another form of objectification from which their subjectivity was already alienated. Conversely, their disaffection became increasingly individuated. Trends towards both disaffection and individuation came together in a series of cultural forms including 'the birth of the cool', beat, mod and punk. Although each of these was initiated by the young, as they matured so did their disaffection. Over time, the youth cult of alienation expanded to include larger numbers of young people with each of its successive manifestations. Taken together, these subcultures amounted to an accumulation of disaffection, representative of growing acceptance among the now-adult population of the West that there is 'no future' for anything but further expressions of disaffection. Instead of the declaration that 'we're all socialists now', which rang partly true in Britain during the 1950s, by the beginning of the 1990s it would have been more accurate to say 'we're all alienated now'.

Alienation from politics, and increased cynicism towards the possibilities once afforded by the political, were ratified in 1989 by the fall of the Berlin Wall and 'the end of the end of ideology' (Jacoby 1999). Lacking even the idea of an alternative to capitalism, there was still less motivation to maintain traditional political allegiances either for or against the status quo. Meanwhile, without the degree of definition derived from standing out against both sides of the (now non-existent) political divide, displays of disaffection soon lost even the remnants of their distinctively youthful character. When Tony Blair became UK prime minister in 1997, the generation of forty-somethings who entered government along with him were well versed in the discourse of alienation. In government, in the attempt to continue society by post-political means, they were obliged to speak a counter-language of (first) shared national experience, and (latterly) community. Nonetheless, New Labour's managerialists relied on the alienation of most of the electorate from the possibility of social transformation as previously acknowledged in labour movement politics. Alienation from this possibility was their own formative experience (Mulgan 1994); it was the predicate for their preferred mode of address; and they used it repeatedly in the attempt to formulate the next generation of shared experience. Under New Labour between 1997 and 2005, estrangement from both agency and collectivity was instrumentalised into a domestic 'culture of fear' (Furedi 2002). Alienated subjectivity emerged as one of the few communication channels left open to the British elite in its efforts to reach the wider population.

Today, the continuous composition of alienated subjectivity serves as a (poor) substitute for mediating activity in the form of social democratic politics, but without the political pressures associated with social democracy, perhaps it is as robust as mediation now needs to be. Regardless of its long-term viability, however, the adoption of alienated subjectivity as a form of mediation among Westerners presaged a further round of alienation in which much of the West has become estranged not only from the political possibility of transforming production relations but also from the economic transformations occurring spontaneously in capitalist production. Without the precedent provided by the recent alienation of subjectivity from its objectification in politics, it is doubtful whether so much of the West could have moved as quickly, or as far away from the objectifying activity entailed in the social relations of capitalist production.

Currency of alienated subjectivity

Capitalism makes objectification into an alienating process because it excludes human subjects from their own subjectivity for as long as they are active in the production process, and in the range of mediating activities between rounds of production, we are ultimately bound to a fixed existence, largely separated from our own capacity to make the world anew. Accordingly, when human subjects are made again in consciousness, whether the latter is formulated as, for example, journalism or sociology, we are normally made into fixed objects which seem to lack the capacity to make ourselves more than we already are. This is the fixative effect of objectivity derived from alienation: alienated objectivity. In fleeing from objectification, on the other hand, alienated subjectivity is a constant movement. But its flights of fancy are grounded in the fixed assumption that making the world our object is necessarily an alienating process, best left behind (politics), or, in the case of production, better left to someone else (preferably on the other side of the world). Thus, in this instance, subjectivity also defaults to alienation, even though it promises escape from objectification and the alienation associated with it.

The movement of alienated subjectivity resembles the movements of fictitious capital, i.e. capital that accumulates not by entering into the production process but by remaining some considerable distance from it. Thus, fictitious capital is also the movement of capital values among themselves, without entering into production. When capital enters into production, people are prompted to enter into commodities, or, at least, living labour is entered into them, such that finished commodities are also containers of dead labour. Compared to this mortifying process, fictitious capital has considerable advantages. In its estrangement from the production of objects, it avoids not only the regulatory pressures of all kinds of production but also the mortification of humanity that occurs specifically and spontaneously in the capitalist production of dead labour laid out in its own casket – the commodity. Similarly, its counterpart in consciousness, alienated subjectivity, is much livelier for not being weighed down by constant reference to the ponderous process of production. In short, fictitious capital is an easier way for social groups, regions or now perhaps even whole nations to make a living. Recently, it has become the economic component in a whole way of life so that fast-moving fictitious capital combined with flights of subjective fancy are now reciprocally reinforcing parts in a Western culture that blithely assumes that production is a job for other parts of the world.

Yet it is still an alienated culture. Escape (for some people, mainly in the West) from capital's death wish for labour is also exclusion from transformations currently occurring in the social relations of production and further occlusion of the potential for transforming production and its social relations. Thus, alienated subjectivity is the mirror image of alienated objectification. From their different positions, now formulated along geographical lines, they both amount to the vanishing point of the human subject.

It could be said that a Western culture that thrives on the exchange of commodities while not deigning to enter into their production is reminiscent of, for example, London's way of life in the age of mercantilism, in which case it might also be thought that our criticism of today's alienated subjectivity is wholly inconsistent, since we previously praised the merchant city of London for setting the progressive, social scene which the first incarnation of journalism went on to describe. But this is to isolate the exchange of commodities and the accompanying trade in subjectivity from the wider context of human, historical development. Again, the question of objectivity in its historical specificity will serve to remind us of these relations. It will also suggest why mercantilist London led to journalism's first success, whereas London as the fictitious capital of alienated subjectivity has been less conducive to the successful development of journalism.

In the age of Enlightened mercantilism, objectivity could only have come from the empirical tradition of picking up found objects – a way of accumulating knowledge corresponding to merchants picking up objects as they found them, appropriating ready-made artefacts which became commodities as and when they were brought to metropolitan markets. Thus, mercantilist culture was subdivided between the collation of found objects and the formation of subjectivity based on dealing in these objects commercially. Moreover, the journey between the two – moving from the wilderness where objects were found to the society where subjectivity would be formed – was an especially delicate operation (hence the significance of the highwayman in eighteenth-century English literature). Furthermore, this subdivision was also reflected in the parallel lines of philosophical development: empiricism and idealism.

But if it was one (progressive) thing to create a new level of socialisation through trade while remaining largely estranged from separate clusters of production which were not yet associated with one another, it is quite another to be estranged from the unified system that now integrates a wide range of human activities into a process of productive objectification. Similarly, for Western journalism to estrange itself from the possibility of objectivity, in much the same way that Western economies are moving further away from the social system of productive objectification, is setting up journalism to fail in its social role. Unfortunately, judging by recent coverage of finance, the journalism of alienated subjectivity has been only too ready to accept this invitation.

Finance and alienated subjectivity

It is now a common complaint that in the first decade of the twenty-first century journalism failed to interrogate finance, and, moreover, that journalism's failure meant there was little or no check on tendencies that culminated (for the time being) in the financial crisis of 2008–9. This is a complaint to the effect that financial journalists did not do enough to intervene and, at the same time, a demand for journalism to objectify its subject matter – to stand outside financial activity and look back at it as an object. Perhaps unbeknown to itself, therefore, it is also a petition for objective journalism. Ironically, the petition is voiced by some of the same people who have been railing against the supposed myth of objective journalism, and, in a further irony, it transpires that the failure arose largely because Western journalism has in the main replaced the pursuit of objectivity with a preference for alienated subjectivity – a preference that concurs both with the established criticism of alienated objectivity and now with the workings of the financial world itself. Precisely because it has been chasing after a version of subjectivity that is opposed to objectivity (alienated or not), Western journalism has become more like the financial activity which it is now less able to externalise and objectify.

From the beginning of the nineteenth century onwards, the primary role of finance has been to mediate between successive rounds of capitalist production and the concomitant accumulation of capital. Until recently, finance has served as yet another form of mediating activity that partially resolves contradiction by building bridges between its polarities. Thus, capitalist finance began by addressing commercial aspects of the contradiction between private appropriation and social production. This contradiction is problematic not only for labourers but even for capital, which is normally obliged to fund the next round of social production even before surplus value from the current round has been realised as private profit; hence the development of finance capital in a mediating role. Performance of this role was especially notable towards the end of the nineteenth century and around the turn of the twentieth, when the expansion of production could not have continued without the formation of joint stock companies and the imperial export of capital, both of which were underwritten by financial institutions. Ever since the mercantilist period and the days of the South Sea Bubble, there have been bouts of speculative activity in which financiers gained temporary freedom from the objective demands of production and gave free rein to their collective subjectivity. But for as long as the demands of production were contained largely in the same national economy as the free play of financial speculation, the latter was always liable to be reined in by the former, and speculative activity remained a subsidiary element within even the most advanced capitalist economies.

In the recent period, however, many of the limitations on financial activity have been lifted. Since 1989, when the fall of the Berlin Wall finally removed even the idea of the working class restricting the movement of capital, productive activity has shipped out East, leaving the West free not only to indulge in bouts of speculation but also to construct an entire way of life which is locally based on the continuous movement of capital through various financial 'products'. The variety of these 'products' is truly fantastic, yet they are uniformly distant from the production of new value in the manufacture of goods; thus, they are all equally estranged from the process of objectification.

This is the continuation of finance as mediation, but, instead of mediating activity designed to restart production by bringing finance to bear upon it at the earliest opportunity, nowadays a great deal of ingenuity goes into devising profitable schemes that delay, almost indefinitely, the re-entry of capital into production (Tett 2009). The proliferation of such schemes does not entirely preclude the traditional role of finance in mediating between rounds of productive accumulation. Indeed, if the performance of this role were brought to an abrupt end, the most recent round of capitalist production would also have been the last. But it does mean that in particular countries and regions financial services have now expanded to the point where the financial form of mediating activity is almost an end in itself. Furthermore, in so far as it is estranged from the objectification that occurs in production and distanced from the objective laws to which capitalist production remains answerable (as it must also remain profitable), this activity is unusually subjective – even for finance; hence the monetary value of such 'products' is given mainly by the mood of the financial markets.

While finance, taken as a whole, continues to perform a mediating role, the performance of this role is much changed. Whereas finance formerly looked towards production as the point where the mediating episode would eventually come to an end, now its attention is primarily concentrated on activities which, though not entirely speculative, amount to a kind of communal conjecture indefinitely expressed in the markets. As a credit note issued against profits to be realised from future production, finance had always anticipated the social process of objectification, beyond the limited range that strictly private capital could reach by itself. Today, by contrast, financial services and even large numbers of apparently productive Western companies anticipate nothing more objective than further rounds of anticipation, operating in a continuum of mediating activity that spirals away from objectification towards the most rarefied forms of subjectivity.

Occasionally, however, the separation of subjectivity from objectification is seen to have become implausibly prolonged, even in the further, subjective judgement of those who profit most from prolonging it. The 'credit crunch' of 2008–9 was just such a self-reflexive occasion, and its damaging consequences were in this sense self-inflicted; yet it was also a reflection of the disjuncture between finance and production, subjectivity and objectification, as seen in a dramatic and far-reaching episode which now seems only to have pushed Western finance even further away from production and the investment it requires.

The same sort of ratio is discernible in Western journalism. Taken as whole, it continues to operate on an axis of mediating activity with objectification at one end and subjectivity at the other. As mediating activity, it still contains the possibility of integrating these two in ways that point to the further realisation of the human subject. But this possibility will remain remote for as long as the majority of Western publishers and broadcasters continue to position themselves stiflingly close to subjectivity and unusually far away from objectification.

Not that this is an entirely comfortable position for professional media organisations to arrive at. Though their executives are little concerned about how they got here, they are horrified to find their costly organisations occupying much the same, subjective position as millions of non-professional producers with independent access to publishing technology and less inclination to refer, still less defer, to professional journalists.

When, as in the West it has recently been inclined to do, professional journalism prioritises networked subjectivity, it privileges a form of mediating activity which it cannot make its own, since so many other media users are already practising it on their own and generating their own content for each other – for free. Thus, financial crisis across the world economy and the financial crisis of journalism have more in common than their timing: they are both driven by the alienation of subjectivity from objectification – a form of estrangement first given by capitalist society, now given greater significance in trends towards the re-division of the world between regions of productive activity and areas dedicated to finance-led mediation.

Similarly, when professional writers abrogate the responsibility to objectify, they also release readers from the obligation to pay them (or pay their employers to pay them), for what they are no longer doing. In the digital age, now that so many erstwhile readers have the capacity to function as self-publishing writers, we can only expect to see a premium on writing that makes a point of coming from that other position, first held in London by the likes of the *Spectator*, to which the actions of directly self-interested parties are re-directed for measurement and assessment. This is the objectifying position in which all manner of human actions is literally accountable – the objective account is written here. In today's context, the only kind of journalism worth paying for is that which occupies this position, which is also to say that objectivity is the collective standard that its individual journalists are striving to reach. Conversely, there can be no premium on journalism that pays little attention to the demands of objectification, since reader-writers already have free access to countless expressions of networked subjectivity in a wide variety of no-fee formats. Professional writers who would have dispensed with the alleged pretence of objectivity have been writing a suicide note for professional writing. On business grounds alone, objectivity must be at the core of journalism, if journalism is to have a commercial future.

Reciprocal alienation

In Western media as in the financialised economies of the West, mediating activity now tends towards networks of subjectivity formed not in proximity to objectification but at a particularly protracted distance from it. Accordingly, in the West, the workings of finance and media have come to resemble each other closely, whereas media in the East are more likely to take their cue from the productive activity taking place nearby.

Throughout the West, millions of Internet users are putting derivative icons of themselves into circulation for others to interpret and speculate upon. In social media and also on the websites of corporate media brands, they are launching representations of themselves into circuits of mutual interpretation, just as financiers issue representations of value into economies of reciprocal speculation. Imitating shares, perhaps seeking some kind of shared experience, whether financial, or cultural or somewhere in between, the common purpose of all this activity seems to be that mediation should continue in an unending spiral away from objectification and towards subjectivity.

Though often overlooked, the use of social media in the East both preceded and is now surpassing their usage in the West. Norman Lewis (2008) noted that South Korea spawned the first social media site, CyWorld, in 1999. He also observed that China is host to QQ, 'the largest instant messaging social network in the world'. In 2008, there were 300 million registered user accounts with QQ, and in 2007 the enterprise reported revenues of $523 million and operating profits of $240 million, while 'Facebook recorded a $50 million *loss* in the same year' (Lewis 2008). These figures point not only to the (then) diverse fortunes of their respective companies but also to significantly different usage of social media, East and West. Though in both instances young people make up the majority of users, in the West the young are more likely to put a moral and aesthetic premium on anti-consumerism; hence, their self-presentation in social media aspires to be 'the real me', without deference to (too many) consumer goods (even their interest in corporate brands is partly to do with making commodities less material and more ethereal). Meanwhile, their Eastern counterparts show less compunction towards consumerism; hence, QQ's profits are largely generated by users paying to display digital goods such as background music and fashion items for their avatars (Lewis 2008). Thus, the personalised pages of Chinese social media users have come to resemble the cluttered interiors characteristic of British, middle-class households of the Victorian period. Though they are more than a century apart, in each example a fetish for objects is similarly displayed. Whereas in the East, the personal identity of social-media account holders is only guaranteed by their display of previously paid-for objects, in the West the free play of subjectivity is acted out by the demographic cohort dubbed 'Generation Y-Pay?' (Sweeney 2009), and their antipathy to things, especially things that have to be paid for, is indicated by the years it took Facebook to move into profit. Thus, the various expectations of social media, East and West, confirm the suggestion that mediating activities, West and East, are variously oriented towards subjectivity and objectification.

In the West, where they are located between networked finance and social-media networks, mainstream media companies are attempting to monetise the free play of subjectivity, first by inviting domestic users onto their corporately owned websites to form so-called communities, then recording their presence there and selling it on to advertisers. However, it is questionable whether this amounts to a viable business model, and it is also doubtful whether much of this activity amounts to journalism, even if it is facilitated by paid 'journalists'.

There is no doubt, however, that these networks of subjectivity are not as untrammelled as they may seem to those caught up in them. The irony of subjectivity in its estrangement from objectification is that it too becomes objectified; moreover, it is objectified in ways which are doubly alienated from the affirmation of the human subject.

Seen from the point of view of production in the East, Western culture is an external object that performs mediating services. Though the object furnished by the West is subjectivity, this particular form of subjectivity has been devised by Westerners who are also its primary participants, and, as such, it is hardly derived from the activity of Easterners – except indirectly, in that it is ultimately paid for out of the surplus accumulated from their productive activity. Thus, for the people of the East, Western subjectivity is a thing largely outside themselves, although it must also contain something of themselves for it to mediate some of the contradictions which they themselves experience.

In these aspects, the relationship between Western culture and Eastern audiences is not dissimilar to that of 'the culture industry' and those consuming its commodities, as identified by Adorno (2001) in mid-twentieth-century Europe and the USA. Though the menu of that which is consumed by today's Easterners is not as fixed as it was when the mid-Western working class dined almost exclusively on Hollywood movies and hamburgers, the 'culture industry' comparison holds good if we think of a whole city like London as something close to a reality TV format, an unending real-time play of subjectivity, available not only to the local population, who are in the show as well as watching it, but also to millions of 'read-only' viewers throughout the East. The productive activity of the West may be relatively smaller, but in the continuous performance of subjectivity Western media are like a mediating *Big Brother* to the objectifying East.

In the new home of labour-intensive objectification, Western-made subjectivity is received as a package from which Easterners are objectively alienated, even as many are also subjectively inclined to identify with it. Meanwhile, in the West, inasmuch as we have been retreating further into our alienated subjectivity, we have only confirmed our unprecedented estrangement from objectification.

Yet the inclination towards one-sided subjectivity is not entirely unbalanced in Western culture. There are counter-tendencies, with both subjective and objective origins. For some journalists and commentators, the undisciplined cultivation of subjectivity is simply too much of an insult to their innate sense of professionalism; hence, Andrew Keen's influential riposte, *The Cult of the Amateur: How Today's Internet Is Killing Our Culture and Assaulting Our Economy* (2007). When Keen identified today's cultural trends as a threat to the previous achievements of Western culture, he was effectively holding up the past as a defensive weapon against the present. But the demand for robust media and substantial mediating activity is not only nostalgic. Across the world as a whole, capitalist production is increasing at a faster rate now than ever before, and, accordingly, its ensuing contradictions can only become more intense. Moreover, in China and India, the largest of the expanding economies, the political realm is hardly more habitable than in the West. From the productive regions of the East, and also from other developing nations that seek to replicate their productive capacity, comes the growing demand for mediating activity, including journalism, that is authoritative and definitive in the style traditionally associated with the West.

The possibility of this demand being met by non-Western media organisations may have accelerated the transformation, but, in any case, the BBC World Service has enjoyed something of a makeover since the launch of Al-Jazeera, and especially since Al-Jazeera English came on air in 2006. From being mainly a mouthpiece for the British way of life, complete with a Loyalist marching song as its theme tune, the BBC World Service has developed into a news-based mediation service offered to worldwide audiences. Its recent development shows both the demand for robust journalism on the part of non-Western populations and the enthusiasm among Western professionals for supplying it.

Thus, the domestic tendencies for Western mediating activity to move even further towards the subjective are offset by the demand, often initiated from outside the West, for Western media to undertake well-defined forms of mediating activity, more in accord with the objectification that now takes place largely in the East. Many journalists believe that journalism should be plural enough to encompass both of these, and, again, the idea of the network serves to suggest the possibility of stringing them together in an inclusive, open-ended process. Under this sort of loose arrangement, journalism that aspires to objectivity can coexist with highly subjective media content that is tending towards non-journalism. But unless the distinction between these two is made clear (and it rarely is), the effect of their relativisation is to undermine the specific character of objectivity and the aspiration to attain it.

Accordingly, though there is some pressure for a robust, objectifying journalism, in Western media circles the stronger inclination is to think of journalism as the facilitator of many subjectivities, preferably without presuming to measure other people's subjectivity – what they make of their own experience – against standards which only purport to be universal. Hence the cliché of the new professionalism: there is always someone who knows more about the story than we do. Although this is said as if it emancipates the people formerly known as 'our' sources, freeing them from the fixed position in which journalism previously placed them, in current conditions this sentiment also undermines the journalist's capacity to abstract from other people's experience. If allowed to go unchallenged, it would confine our consciousness to the plane of the present and particular, where further particulars are ever present, and there is no vantage point from which to come to anything except arbitrary conclusions. Appropriately enough for the journalism of networked subjectivity, this is the same plane on which interpersonal networks operate in a similarly indefinite process.

At this level, and in so far as writers, readers, viewers and listeners are confined to this level, 'inclusivity' segues into being permanently inconclusive, which to journalists of old would have been as unprofessional as silence on the radio. In the circles that influence today's journalism, however, their reciprocity is seen as cause for celebration, hence the widespread hope that the widening of networked subjectivity – millions more people having access to digital networks which support reciprocal self-expression – will also support journalism (part-professional, part-user-generated) in the further realisation of a network society. In its most explicit, self-consciously grandiose formulation, the suggestion is that saving journalism by making it more inclusive can also save the world (Beckett 2008).[1] While there is no question that access to digital communications should be universal, this hope is sadly misplaced: it weakens journalism by resting it on a peculiarly weak social formation: the network. Moreover, it projects the local experience of networked subjectivity onto the wider world of objectification. Thus, production as a whole is identified with media production, and the whole world is assimilated into an idea that pertains mainly to that part of it where the local way of life really does consist of networked subjectivity (hence some of the locals are inclined to mistake their peculiar experience for that of the whole world).

Networked subjectivity is problematic not only because of its almost exclusive orientation to subjectivity but also because it is, indeed, networked. When conditioned by estrangement from objectification, as they now are, the social relations of networking are necessarily narrow and thin, and they lack the societal substance of capitalist production relations. No matter how much any number of networks are widened to include more people, networked subjectivity has only an indirect relationship to the production of the world, our object, in the form of objects (commodities) for market exchange. Accordingly, its connection to the connectedness of all the labourers involved in the social production of value is equally tenuous. Similarly, relations internal to networks, i.e. between networked individuals, do not acquire the general character which is both given by abstract labour and taken away when abstract labour is absent or marginalised from the local, social formation.

In localities characterised by networking, production relations amounting to the general relation between everyone and everyone else are only a dim and distant reference point. The local reality consists almost exclusively of present and particular relations which must be personally activated for them to exist at all. In twenty-first-century Western culture, this is most clearly expressed in the recently acquired habit of using mobile phones almost constantly. Bordering on the compulsive, this behaviour is consistent with a way of life where there is no society except the networked variety which we must constantly call into existence. It is not much of an exaggeration to say that in regions that depend on networked subjectivity, you are who you're phoning. We phone therefore we are. PhonesRUs.

Journalists, of course, are used to the idea that you are only as good as your last story (and perhaps the phone call that got you the key quote or anecdote). But in this well-worn phrase, the idea of a 'good story' implies a position from which to judge how good it is; moreover, it implies a position not entirely bound up within the pressure to produce particular stories but abstracted from that process, at least to the point where observers (our *Spectator*, once more) can look back at stories, even the ones they are still writing, and assess the writing of them according to general standards drawn from all the other stories they have ever written or read. Furthermore, the generalisation of this position – the fact that it has been formally available to all, all the time – could only have come about in a general system of social production based as much on abstract labour as on the materialisation of labour in commodities.

Abstract labour is the hub of this social system. The point at which labour has been stripped of all its particular properties is the point to which all particular forms of labour refer, since at this point they lose their particularities long enough to be measured as portions of labour in general. Here, labour is entered into the general system of social production; conversely, the entire system of social production originates here. Without abstract labour as its focal point, production would be neither as systematic nor as socialised as it now is – even under capitalism. Of course, the corollary of abstract labour is its materialisation in particular commodities, which are akin to the spokes of a wheel radiating in and out of the hub. Thus, the objects resulting from productive activity on the part of human subjects are both incorporated into a general system of abstract labour and sent out from there to meet particular needs and desires, also on the part of human subjects.

We have previously noted the correspondence between productive objectification and objectivity in thought. Moreover, as the productive system of objectification encompasses abstract and concrete labour, so objectivity combines abstract thinking and concrete analysis. Likewise, the development of objectivity has depended on historically specific production relations, though it has never been a simple cipher for them. Conversely, in those regions increasingly given over to networks and networked subjectivity, where social relations have been revised in the absence or marginalisation, locally, of production relations and objectification, the basis for objectivity will have been similarly scaled back so that it is plausible to suggest that in these locations objectivity might become as scarce as productive objectification already is.

Thankfully, the realisation of this tendency is not inevitable. The very same technology which has been used for networking purposes can also be used for the purpose of transcending networks and reconnecting us to the universe that hinges on abstract labour. Similarly, there is the potential for those whose lives are consumed by productive activity to make a less alienated connection with Western subjectivity, and this, in turn, points to the possibility of curtailing the geographical estrangement of subjectivity from objectification.

None of this can be accomplished by the technology itself. But some of it could be accomplished by journalists using digital technology to reclaim objectivity. To achieve this, however, journalists will have been obliged to reject ideas of journalism as a network, unless and until networks are themselves reconfigured along with the realignment of subjectivity and objectification.

News from everywhere

Though already implicit in our commentary, we think it wise to make an explicit distinction between the self-congratulatory idea of networked subjectivity, which only exacerbates the tendency towards Western estrangement from objectification, and, on the other hand, the technical capacity of networked technologies. Technically speaking, the commensurate character of digital media content, its replicability, and its continuous construction from reciprocal moments of abstraction and materialisation are all consonant with the truly social aspect of capitalist relations, i.e. the extent to which capital has already enlarged the scope of subjectivity and objectification by mediating, both regressively and progressively, between the two.

This also suggests that digital communication can offer technical support for reconfiguring relations between subjectivity and objectification. The capacities of digital media technology readily articulate with the further possibility of realising more of the human subject. It seems plausible that the very best media content could prefigure this possibility in consciousness, just as Enlightenment philosophy prefigured, though without fully realising it, the social content of capitalism.

The suggestion is that digitally supported media content can mediate between subjectivity and objectification so as to reduce the extent of their current estrangement. If so, the preceding question then becomes: what can be done with digital journalism that could enable it to develop further as a predominantly progressive form of mediating activity?

The portability of digital equipment and the replicability of digital media content are enough to indicate the further reach that is now within our grasp. In terms of what can be described, how near or far we can be in describing it, and how many and varied will be the people submitting initial descriptions, we can expect digitally supported journalism to cover a much wider arc of human experience with considerably greater accuracy. Thus, there is technical capability to support what we have known for a while: that neither of the previously available viewing positions is wholly satisfactory – not the fixed position of traditional reporters, as alienated as it is abstracted, nor the fixations of their 'attached' counterparts. Instead of those impossibly fixed positions, digital technology is a note to the effect that it is not only possible but also necessary to move the camera eye, not just for the gimmick of seeing it move but to obtain moving pictures of the dynamic human beings we have in our sights.

Even moving pictures would be flat without perspective. But there is now the possibility of involving more people in establishing what that perspective should be. With input from a wider range of sources, some of whom might already have published their source material in relatively raw form, we should expect professional journalism to achieve a standard of objectivity which is more comprehensive in its scoping movements, more robust in its definitive moments and open and self-conscious about the transition between these two.

Digital media technology allows many more people to enter their version of events into the pre-production phase of journalism. Similarly, in the blogosphere and on Twitter, larger numbers of people can contribute to the post-production phase of journalism, putting journalism under more pressure to correct itself and making better use of journalism, now as robust as it is also reflexive, in order to intervene in society. But integrating the wider public into journalism's pre- and post-production phases should not mean discarding the specific role of journalists in producing journalism, i.e. taking in what they have seen for themselves and what has been reported to them, but also taking it to a new level of understanding by a combination of abstract thinking and specific technique – just as Tom Wicker did with his portable typewriter in Dallas on the day Kennedy was killed. In contrast to the currently fashionable idea of journalists as curators or facilitators, the production phase of journalism must be recognised as original work; again, not in the sense of making it up but in the sense of making something more out of human experience than is available to those directly experiencing it.

Professional journalists, it seems to us, should be people whose (paid-for) time is taken up by crafting observation (other people's as well as their own) into a more developed form of objectification, who previously spent time learning their craft and rehearsing the techniques required for them to accomplish this. Those without so much dedicated time or this particular training are unlikely to contribute as much in the composition of objective journalism, yet we would still expect them to play the key, public role of assessing what does and does not qualify as such.

This is to reiterate our previous observation that subjectivity and objectification are complementary as well as opposite. Though their relation has been distorted for centuries, nonetheless, objectification necessarily entails not only the consumption but also the production of subjectivity, while the application of subjectivity in objectification also entails the affirmation of both. Accordingly, raising the standard of objectivity means incorporating more subjectivity into its composition, both to enrich the available material and also to discipline the process of abstracting from it.

Instead of the view from nowhere on the part of a faceless, isolated individual, as we envisage it, the collective process of creating objectivity will need to incorporate, test and sometimes discard more subjectivity than ever before, so much so that 'news from everywhere' would be a far more fitting description.

Part III

The public

Chapter 5

The fragmenting public

The twenty-first-century news audience is seen, paradoxically, as both exceptionally passive and unprecedentedly active. On the one hand, the news audience is thought to be made up of apathetic and easily distracted consumers rather than active and engaged citizens; on the other, they are 'the people formerly known as the audience' (Rosen 2006), not consumers but 'prosumers', creative 'generators' of media content. The first view, often connected to discussions of 'trivialisation' and 'dumbing down' since the 1990s, would seem to confirm Habermas's (1989) contention that the commercialisation of media has led to the public sphere becoming 'refeudalised'. Even among analysts who emphasise the creative and interactive dimensions of the audience's engagement with new media, there is disagreement between those who make the largely optimistic argument that we are witnessing the development of a 'transnational public sphere' (Higgins 2008: 145) and more sceptical diagnoses of a public sphere fragmented into countless versions of the 'Daily Me' (Calcutt 1999: 73–7), with the blogosphere and web-based personalised news services feeding a process of individuation in which news no longer constructs 'the commons'.

Contemporary attitudes to the public – frowned upon as passive consumers or flattered as content-generating users – are often explained in terms of recent technological and commercial developments but are better understood, we argue, as the product of long-term political changes and, accordingly, changes in the way that 'the public sphere' and 'the public' have been conceived by both journalists and academics. As part of this longer-term shift, both journalism and Journalism Studies have tended to favour 'difference', as variously identified with niche markets, segmented readerships and the politics of cultural identity. This development has often been seen as an improvement on the monolithic national political culture of old, but it threatens to undercut the purpose of journalism as a wider, public forum. Today, against the backdrop of declining viewing figures and falling newspaper sales in the West, there is much discussion of how to engage the public. But the general trend is to think in terms of 'public spheres' in the plural and to repudiate past unity as being necessarily false. While the terms in which society has previously imagined a unified public and a unitary public sphere have indeed been problematic, it is nevertheless important, we argue, to hold on to the *universalist* conception of the public sphere.

The idea of the public

Who is 'the public'? It may seem too obvious a question, yet it is now commonplace in the academic study of journalism and politics to argue that the public has no existence prior to its construction through discourse. 'There is no *a priori* public,' contend Stephen Coleman and Karen Ross, 'the public is always a product of representation' (2010: 3). This is an 'anti-essentialist' view: it holds that there is no 'essence' within people that makes them who they are. Instead, people's identities are understood as constructed and as therefore malleable and open to change. From this point of view, the public has no prior existence which political discourse is obliged to acknowledge. Rather, the public is only called into being by political discourses which address it as such. There is an element of truth in this presentation: after all, 'the public' is only one of a number of possible ways to imagine the people who comprise it. In addition to being thought of as the public, we are also routinely addressed as a nation, for example, or as taxpayers, families or communities. Such different modes of address carry political implications and indicate particular perspectives: from one point of view, we might be thought of as the citizenry or the electorate; from another, we appear as the crowd or the mob.

The anti-essentialist approach also draws attention to the fact that different ways of representing people are not fixed or unchanging. In the past, for instance, it was common for news organisations to represent large numbers of people as 'workers' or 'trade unionists' and to employ specialist 'industrial relations correspondents' who would report on matters concerning this significant social group. Over the past twenty years or so, the same people have instead come to be represented more often as 'consumers', who apparently need their own 'consumer affairs correspondents' to report on their concerns. As this example suggests, however, we should be wary of overemphasising the role of representation or imagining that it is an entirely arbitrary process. The shift from 'trade unionists' to 'consumers' may encourage us to see ourselves in one way rather than another but it is not as if this change in the mode of address is a haphazard occurrence, nor does it bring a new reality into being by itself; rather, it is bound up with much larger political and social processes. Indeed, part of what we want to suggest in this chapter is that the anti-essentialist perspective, with its emphasis on discourse, representation and social construction, has itself developed in the context of a broader political shift which is not, after all, explicable solely or even largely in terms of representation.

In principle, if not always in practice, conceptualising people as 'the public' implies something positive and progressive. 'The public' is an inclusive, open, universal category: nobody is formally barred from it (though large numbers of people have been variously excluded at different times). In political terms, it signals a democratic and egalitarian orientation, suggesting that society should be organised for the public good, for the public or general interest rather than for the benefit of private interests. In practice, of course, people have had to fight for equal treatment and to force their way into the 'inclusive' public sphere, and the 'public good' has often tended to be defined in ways that benefit powerful private interests rather than transcending them. Nevertheless, the existence of a public sphere oriented towards politics and couched in terms of formal equality is entirely positive in that it provides a space where people can potentially formulate ideas about how to challenge and transform society's unequal relationships.

There is a real basis for representations or discourses of 'the public', though this does not mean that the discourse is fully in line with social reality. Not only a principled expression of formal equality, it transpires that the idea of the public is also an attempt to straighten out some of the recurring contradictions of capitalism. As James Heartfield (1996: 14) suggests, we live in an 'anti-social society', in which the social aspect of our being – our connections with society at large, beyond our immediate, interpersonal relationships – is indirect, mediated through the market. We make millions of connections with other people every day, in the course of our most mundane, taken-for-granted activities. Turning on a tap, making a cup of coffee, driving a car: all these ordinary actions depend upon – and thereby connect us to – the labour of countless other people around the world whom we never meet. Our social, human connections are strangely impersonal, mediated through non-human objects, commodities exchanged in the market. Moreover, we join in with this process and become part of the life of society when we take our own commodity – our ability to work – to the marketplace and exchange it for wages. In our peculiarly antisocial society, the abstract, exchangeable quality of labour power as a commodity is the basis of the equally abstract category of 'the public'. The basis of our public existence as members of society, in other words, is not wholly public but partly private: it originates partly in the world of self-interest and even 'private enterprise'. This is perhaps one of the reasons why 'the public' can sometimes seem an insubstantial or elusive idea – appearing to analysts as a product of discourse rather than a solid fact. It really is abstract – in the sense that our membership of the 'general public' takes no account of our concrete particularity – and its promise of formal equality is based on a socio-economic system that is at the same time the very thing that perpetuates inequality.

The modern idea of politics gained currency in the eighteenth century, around the same time as the emergence of a public sphere. As we demonstrated in Chapters 2 and 3, in Britain these developments were driven by the nascent bourgeoisie, whose burgeoning power in the spheres of commercial trade and, subsequently, commodity production led them to confront the question of political power, and the *ancien régime* that was obstructing their development of it. English capitalists created a new space in which to challenge the aristocracy and new methods of exerting a different kind of pressure which is both more encompassing and more focused than the interplay of particular commercial interests but generally less comprehensive and coercive than warfare or military occupation. 'Politics' is the generic term for the modus operandi comprised of such mediating activity. Conversely, having found the means to pursue their class interests most effectively, the British bourgeoisie also felt the need to establish a private sphere of liberty from the state – even though the state itself was coming to resemble their collective concerns. Again, the public sphere emerged as the space in which not only to debate and challenge but also to ratify the exercise of limited authority by the state.

The public sphere as it first developed was in principle universal and open but in practice partial and restricted. For those admitted into polite society there was a new social space for reasoned debate and criticism, but not everyone was invited. Still, Habermas (1989: 125) suggests that although, over the course of the nineteenth century, the concept of the public sphere became 'mere ideology' – a pretence of free and open debate – in its original, albeit limited, incarnation it did represent something truly valuable and progressive. Following Habermas, many commentators have sought to uphold the positive 'in principle' aspect of the public sphere, treating it as a 'normative ideal' to which we might aspire (for example, Curran 1991: 83; Dahlgren 1995: 11; Sparks 2004: 140). If it is to be taken as an ideal, however, it is important to clarify just what is positive about it and how in practice the public sphere has failed to live up to its promise.

Among British and American writers who have taken up Habermas's ideas since 1990, the ideal tends to be marshalled in defence of public-service broadcasting and in support of programmes for media reform (for example, Curran 1991; McCauley et al. 2003). Though this more policy-oriented discussion is somewhat removed from Habermas's specific historical concerns, it is broadly in keeping with his ideas, since for Habermas the thing to be celebrated about the eighteenth-century public sphere is the ideal of 'rational–critical debate'. Hence, he highlights its 'firm rules' and code of conduct as key positive features. He celebrates the broad agreement concerning 'reasonable forms' that public discussion should take, and endorses eighteenth-century expectations of acceptable 'standards' and 'goals' of critical argument (1989: 131). In this respect, Habermas's historical inquiry in *The Structural Transformation of the Public Sphere* anticipates ideas later developed in his philosophical works, where he elaborates a 'theory of communicative action'. Habermas's philosophical notion of the 'ideal speech situation' suggests that the route to progress and emancipation lies in 'normatively grounded communication', governed by 'binding consensual norms' (Dahlgren 1991: 5; Heartfield 2002: 76). This ideal of rational, rule-governed intersubjective communication could be seen as having been embodied in the eighteenth-century public sphere, but only to the extent that 'within the public – presupposing its shared class interest – friend-or-foe relations were in fact impossible' (Habermas 1989: 131). The fact that fundamental differences were not at stake, in other words, is what allowed the public sphere to work in the consensual, rule-bound way that Habermas idealises. The intrusion of different, clashing interests would spoil the picture because reasonable discussion would become secondary to the pursuit of those interests: 'instrumental reason' would supplant 'rational–critical debate'; the assertion of subjectivity would displace intersubjective communication. And this, indeed, is exactly what Habermas sees as having happened.

According to Habermas's account, a number of factors led to the decline of the public sphere as a forum for 'rational–critical' debate. The expanded role of the state, the commercialisation of the media and the reorientation of private life around leisure and consumption have all helped to change and blur the distinction between public and private. Both are diminished in the process so that on the one hand, 'The world fashioned by the mass media is a public sphere in appearance only', while on the other, 'the integrity of the private sphere which they promise to their consumers is also an illusion' (1989: 171). But the primary reason for the decline of the public sphere is that its initial character as a space of rational discussion was disturbed by the intrusion of clashing interests. Habermas (1989: 131–2) notes that as the public sphere expanded and lost its 'social exclusiveness', so it became increasingly difficult to maintain the idea that it was a forum for reasonable dialogue among equals; the conversation of polite society was rudely interrupted by 'coarser forms of violent conflict' as the different interests of different social classes came into conflict. As he observes, 'Laws passed under the "pressure of the street" could hardly be understood any longer as embodying the reasonable consensus of publicly debating private persons. They corresponded more or less overtly to the compromise between competing private interests' (Habermas 1989: 132).

However, what is understood here as a clash of 'private interests' was actually something much bigger. The significance of the public sphere is not so much its idealised status as a rule bound space of rationality but more its practical function as a forum for debating and working out a general, or public, interest – that is to say, what should be done in the interests or to the benefit of the whole of society. This is what gives it its democratic character. The problem is that this universalistic orientation suggests a social unity which has never existed (this is not to say that under different conditions it never could). Whereas the rising bourgeoisie of the eighteenth century could be said to have been acting in the general interest (as a historically progressive social force), as the ruling class of the new capitalist order the bourgeoisie's claim to represent the public interest was soon open to challenge by a class which had different, contrary interests. That challenge – at least in its most developed political forms – took the form of an alternative claim to universalism rather than a sectional 'private' interest. The working class, Marx argued, could potentially act as the 'universal class' because its revolution would represent the interests of the whole of society in a way that the bourgeois revolution could not. The ideals of the capitalist class, as boldly stated in France's Declaration of the Rights of Man and of the Citizen, or in the American Declaration of Independence, would never be fully achieved under a system in which the wealth created by the many was owned by the few. As Habermas (1989: 177) observes, 'In Marx's opinion the masses would employ the platform of the public sphere [...] not to destroy it but to make it into what, according to liberal pretence, it had always claimed to be.' Although Habermas's criticism is directed against top-down developments that have turned a 'culture-debating public' into a 'culture-consuming public', his critique also implies a rather disapproving view of the masses, understood as being under the 'tutelage' of the media (1989: 171). Perhaps this is why, where Marx had proposed the working class as the 'universal subject', the social actor whose interests coincided with historical progress, Habermas distrusts self-interest *tout court* (up to and including the possibility of the collectively self-interested human subject) and instead prefers rule-governed intersubjectivity (Heartfield 2002: 75–8).

While many commentators (for example, Dahlgren 1995: 101; Garnham 1992) have noted that the issue of universalism lies at the heart of Habermas's argument about the public sphere, the most common criticism is that his conception of the public is *too* universalistic. Critics complain that he is wrong to think in terms of a single public sphere; instead, they suggest multiple public spheres for multiple publics or 'counter-publics', usually defined in terms of identity politics, such as a 'gay public', or 'radical feminist public' (Calhoun 2005: 286). One of the best-known critics of Habermas in this respect is Nancy Fraser, who challenges the notion that 'a single, overarching public sphere is a positive and desirable state of affairs', arguing instead that this imposes a spurious unity on what is in reality 'a multiplicity of publics'. Members of 'subordinated social groups – women, workers, peoples of colour, and gays and lesbians – have repeatedly found it advantageous to constitute alternative publics', she suggests, claiming that a properly democratic and inclusive approach should emphasise 'subaltern counterpublics' in opposition to 'dominant publics' (Fraser 1992: 122–3). While some have questioned this 'rainbow coalition' (Garnham 1992: 370–1), Fraser's emphasis on difference and diversity is now the most widely accepted approach. Curran, for example, in trying to model a media system that would promote 'social cohesion' and 'affirm common identities, values and memories', assumes that such goals are best achieved by a system that 'connects to different segments of society, in order to enhance its diversity' (2002: 240–1; see also Curran 1991: 103–5). The danger of this approach, as Curran acknowledges, is that it may encourage 'fissiparous tendencies' (2002: 240), driving people apart rather than drawing them together into a common dialogue.

Today, such fragmentation of the public is indeed the key problem, rather than any imposition of false unity. As we argue in what follows, the problem of how to maintain the integrity of the public sphere while opening it up to truly universal participation is not one that can be resolved, either in theory or in practice, by emphasising difference. The next section looks at the history of public-service broadcasting in Britain, as an illustration of the way that 'the public' has come to be understood in terms of multiplicity and diversity rather than a single unified entity.

Serving the public

In the early years of radio broadcasting the medium was widely utilised as a means of creating and sustaining national unity, whether it was Adolf Hitler's speeches transmitted on the mass-produced *Volksempfänger* ('people's receiver'), or President Franklin D. Roosevelt's Depression-era 'fireside chats'. In Britain, broadcasting was less directly political – its regulation by a board of governors keeping it at arm's length from government – but John Reith's vision of broadcasting as a public service was equally grounded in an understanding of radio's potential for bringing society together, for 'making the nation as one man' in Reith's phrase (Scannell and Cardiff 1991: 10).[1] While some programming was explicitly concerned with promoting national cohesion – for example, through broadcast coverage of royal occasions or talks and features on the national character – the distinctive feature of British broadcasting was its sense of *cultural*, rather than overtly political, mission. This was encapsulated in the Reithian idea of 'uplift': the British Broadcasting Corporation (BBC) would not merely entertain its listeners but would improve and educate them. Yet the circumstances that made this vision of public-service broadcasting seem desirable also made it difficult to realise in practice.

Accounts of the early days of the BBC often draw attention to the resemblance between the Corporation's paternalistic conception of public service and the ideas of the Victorian poet and critic Matthew Arnold. In his 1869 work *Culture and Anarchy*, Arnold had argued that the promotion of culture – defined as 'the best which has been thought and said in the world' (Arnold 1993: 190) – was the means, in effect, to manage the enlargement of the public sphere. The 'anarchy' of his title was really working-class organisation and agitation for political enfranchisement: Arnold was horrified by 'multitudinous processions in the streets', such as the Reform League's 1866 demonstration for franchise reform, which ended in violence after the police refused the marchers access to Hyde Park (Arnold 1993: 100). Arnold's response was 'to recommend culture as the great help out of our difficulties': education and the inculcation of traditional values through the appreciation of art and literature would, he hoped, have a calming and civilising influence (1993: 190). In the period before the outbreak of the Second World War in 1939, when the new mass medium of radio took on a somewhat similar mission of cultural education in Britain, it did so not from a position of confidence in shared national values but rather, in the wake of war, revolution and ongoing economic crisis, against a backdrop of elite anxiety and cultural pessimism. The contemporary heirs to Arnold's tradition, such as the poet T. S. Eliot and, particularly, the literary critic F. R. Leavis, felt that they were fighting a rearguard action against inevitable cultural decline and recognised that theirs was a minority approach (Leavis 1930: 1, 25; Mulhern 1979: 174–5). Whereas in the 1860s Arnold had talked unselfconsciously about spreading 'sweetness and light', by the 1930s it seemed to be more a question of whether the torch of culture could be kept alight against the encroaching darkness.

Nevertheless, culture, rather than politics, seemed the more promising terrain on which to promote broadcasting's national mission. Under pressure from the Left, elites found to their dismay that ideas which had in the past been a source of ideological strength – such as 'race' or Empire – were now more likely to cause discomfort and discord. As Paddy Scannell and David Cardiff observe in their *Social History of British Broadcasting*: 'Empire Day was a constant source of embarrassment to producers who were aware that its traditional celebration involved aggressive and ultra-patriotic sentiments which might offend supporters of internationalism and the League of Nations' (1991: 288–9). While Reith's fledgling BBC was able, at the time of the 1926 General Strike, to establish itself as a national institution in the eyes of government, it was unable to achieve the same recognition from its audience, some of whom branded it the 'British Falsehood Corporation' (Pegg 1983: 180). The bitter social divisions manifest in the General Strike and starkly visible throughout the 1930s were hard to negotiate for an organisation such as the BBC which presented itself as serving the nation as a whole. Thus, when broadcasters handled sensitive subjects such as unemployment or slum housing, they frequently ran into problems, censoring working-class representatives and then being denounced in the Left-wing press for their bias. As Mark Pegg observes, the problems encountered by the early BBC 'represented the tremendous social void which existed between political authority and most of the British working class' (1983: 223).

The BBC's difficulties in relating to its audience – either politically or culturally – was a cause for some concern in the 1930s but became a more urgent problem with the outbreak of the Second World War. Audience perceptions of the BBC as aloof and patronising threatened to undermine its aspiration to be 'one of the essential weapons of the war' (Briggs 1970: 16). As late as 1944, George Orwell was still criticising the use of a 'BBC dialect' that, he argued, working-class people 'instinctively dislike and cannot easily master' (cited in Briggs 1970: 57). Broadcasts were failing to make an impression on listeners, he observed, because they were 'uttered in stilted bookish language, and, incidentally, in an upper-class accent' (cited in Briggs 1970: 57). Orwell's comments notwithstanding, in fact the war had eased the problems of addressing a unitary national public, not least because of the degree of real political consensus, encouraged by the Labour Party, trade unions and Communist Party shop stewards, around the war effort itself. Yet, while the Reithian ideal of addressing the whole nation 'as one man' was now a more realistic prospect – with huge audiences tuning in to its wartime programming – the BBC's strategy for increasing its mass appeal entailed moving away from the model of a single, national service. At the start of the war, the BBC divided its broadcasting into the Home Service and the Forces Programme, the latter catering to a mass audience with a more informal style, light entertainment, comedy and popular music. The listening public did not necessarily divide in quite the same way – *The Brains Trust* discussion programme attracted substantial numbers of listeners to the Home Service, for example (Curran and Seaton 2010: 129–30) – but the broadcasters seem to have imagined it as two distinct sections: a majority and a minority. At a moment of national crisis, in an organisation formally dedicated to national unity, they still found it necessary to reproduce the division between the working class and its betters.

After the war, there could be no return to the *status quo ante*, particularly since it was the Forces Programme that attracted the majority of listeners, including those who had previously been lost to Continental European commercial radio (Briggs 1970: 587–8). The Forces Programme became the Light Programme, the Home Service continued, and the Third Programme was added in 1946. While the latter's focus on the arts and high culture seemed to preserve the early BBC ideal of 'uplift', it also signalled a further move away from the Reithian vision of broadcasting as a unified service for a single audience. The audience was now firmly segmented into 'highbrow', 'middlebrow' and 'lowbrow', with the public-service ideal revised and increasingly restricted to the middle-to-upper-class minority not served by popular programming.

In the decades that followed, the development of television broadcasting followed a similar pattern. No sooner had the BBC established the importance of its Television Service, with the 1953 coronation of Queen Elizabeth II – just the sort of unifying national event to gladden the Reithian heart – than it was challenged by the introduction of commercial television in 1955. Independent Television was to be regulated in line with the established public-service ethos of British broadcasting, but the introduction of a second, different channel inevitably eroded the position of the BBC as the national broadcaster. As Tom Burns (1977: 43) suggests, 'Competition meant the intrusion of other renderings of Britishness and of right-mindedness, and the consequent shrinking of BBC values to something sectional and questionable.' Moreover, this development led to a further rethinking of public service: if the BBC was competing for the same audience as commercial broadcasting, how was its distinctive mission to be defined? The answer came with the introduction of BBC 2 in 1964 as the channel with an educational emphasis and a remit to provide programming of minority interest. As in radio, the implicit definition of public-service broadcasting moved from a single inclusive channel addressing everyone to an idea of specialist provision for the minority not catered for by programming for the mass audience.

This model of public service was consolidated and extended in the plans for a second commercial channel, Channel 4, launched in 1979. As with BBC 2, Channel 4 had a particular public-service remit to provide programming that would address 'tastes and interests not otherwise catered for'. Though politicians from the Right might have had regional audiences in mind, by the time of its launch Channel 4's executive was taking this to mean catering for politicised minority identities – women, gays and lesbians, ethnic groups and youth – rather than simply minority tastes. Critics, supporters and many of those working at the new channel all understood that its task was to provide for 'those previously silenced or excluded by mainstream broadcasting' (Harvey 1982: 162); to draw in 'previously excluded or alienated constituencies' (Landry 1982: 167); to 'give voice to [the] voiceless' (Docherty et al. 1988: 15). For radical critics of broadcasting, the 'central issue' that the new channel had to address was: 'Who are the "British" in British Broadcasting? Does "British" effectively mean *English* [...] does it

mean *white* [...] does it mean *male* [...]?' (Blanchard and Morley 1982: 2).
A product of the late 1970s, Channel 4 reflected the times in which it was conceived: a moment when, as the post-Second World War political consensus broke
down, the Left abandoned a universalist orientation in favour of 'minoritarian
zeal' (Docherty et al. 1988: 120). Yet, although developments in broadcasting
converged with the Left-wing cultural politics of the era, they also dovetailed
with the emphasis of Margaret Thatcher's Conservative government, which presided over the channel's birth, on free enterprise and entrepreneurialism. Another
innovative aspect of Channel 4 was its distinctive business model: it would operate like a publishing house, commissioning content from independent production
companies rather than making its own programmes. While the post-1968 Left
invested its hopes in the new broadcaster's 'alternative' content, for the Right the
content was secondary to the way that the channel's structure embodied the 'new
entrepreneurship' (Docherty et al. 1988: 49). As John Corner perceptively noted
at the time, the context for Channel 4's new model of public-service broadcasting
was a 'shift towards privatisation [...] [and] "free market" ideologies in communications, with their attendant "philosophies" of consumer choice' (1982: 163–4).
Gitlin (1998: 170–1) points to similar trends in US cable broadcasting and
niche magazine publishing, driven by 'advertisers' interest in direct targeting of
audience segments'.

The trend towards fragmentation of the audience – in television, a move
towards 'narrowcasting' rather than broadcasting – accelerated with the development of new technologies. The growth of cable and satellite TV from the mid-
1980s, terrestrial digital channels from the late 1990s and the development of
Internet-based viewing platforms all seemed to splinter the viewing public by
making myriad choices available. As the foregoing sketch of British broadcasting
history suggests, however, the trend towards fragmentation was much older than
these technical innovations and their comparatively recent implementation. Of
course, there are good grounds for the critique of the false unity attempted by
the early BBC, whose claim to speak to the whole nation was really an ideological
response to circumstances of intense social division. Yet, in attacking the specious
character of bourgeois universalism – the Reithian nation – the Left's celebration
of difference segued surprisingly well into market segmentation.

More recent work in Journalism Studies has begun to address the problem of a
disengaged public and a fragmented public sphere, assessing how news organisations might be able to reconnect with the audience (see, for example, Dahlgren
2009; Gans 2003; Coleman and Blumler 2009; Lewis et al. 2005). Some of these
suggestions are constructive but rarely get to the real nub of the problem, which
at root is the crisis of political agency identified by Nick Couldry et al. (2010:
194–5). Thus, on the whole, Journalism Studies is not yet well placed to address
this issue, largely because its inheritance is a political and intellectual tradition
which, as we discuss in the following section, has deconstructed the category of
'the public', distrusted claims to universalism and either questioned the capacity
for agency or understood it in a narrow and limited way.

Ideology and representation

As we noted earlier, 'the public' is today commonly understood as being a discursive construction, a 'product of representation'. In this section we examine how the theoretical development of Media and Cultural Studies around textual representation was closely bound up with the more practical question of *political* representation and specifically with the issue of why people's class position does not translate neatly into a shared political outlook. Developing out of the post-1968 Left, in an era of student radicalism, feminism, the civil-rights movement and Third World solidarity causes, Media and Cultural Studies brought in new theories of identity, gender, ethnicity and youth subcultures to supplement – and ultimately to replace – the traditional Marxist focus on the working class. In the process, critics maintain, the discipline gradually shifted its focus, 'from class struggle to the politics of pleasure' (Harris 1992); and early preoccupations with the theory of ideology gave way to a less critical, even celebratory attitude to popular culture. One of the main points of contention has been the question of how far the news is understood to influence people's beliefs and opinions about the world in line with dominant ideologies and how far news audiences are viewed as active creators of meaning, able to subvert 'hegemonic' ideas. This continuing debate – represented today in contradictory views of the audience, noted at the beginning of this chapter, as both 'active citizen' and 'couch potato' (Lewis and Wahl-Jorgensen 2005) – can be traced back to Stuart Hall's influential notion of 'decoding'.

Hall's (1980) 'encoding/decoding' thesis models audience responses to the ideological meanings given to events by the news media. The news, Hall suggests, is ideologically 'encoded': structured – through its choice of images and words – in such a way as to reproduce dominant or hegemonic meanings (the example he gives is of strikes being presented as detrimental to the national interest). But while media texts offer a 'preferred reading' – inviting us to agree with 'dominant definitions' of the significance of events – people do not automatically accept what is offered. Audience 'decodings do not follow inevitably from encodings' (Hall 1980: 136). Instead, he suggests, audience responses might be 'dominant-hegemonic', accepting the preferred interpretation as encoded by the news; but they could also be 'oppositional', rejecting such interpretations in favour of an alternative world view, or – by implication, the more likely outcome – they could be 'negotiated', not fully accepting the dominant discourse but falling short of outright opposition (1980: 136–8). The work of Hall and his colleagues was an attempt to steer a middle course between two established positions: on the one hand they wished to highlight the importance of ideology, in contrast to the American tradition of communications research which tended to minimise media effects and influences, but, at the same time, they also sought to avoid earlier (Frankfurt School) views of ideology as brainwashing by an all-powerful culture industry (Hall 1982).

Clearly such a model could be developed in contradictory ways, depending on whether one were to emphasise the ideological, encoding side of the proposition or the active-audience, decoding aspect. The conventional story of how it did develop is that, over the course of the 1980s, researchers increasingly stressed the autonomous power of audiences as arbiters of textual meaning, to the point that ideology, if it was considered at all, was not really treated as a problem. James Curran (2002: 111) describes this in terms of a 'new revisionism in media and cultural studies', whereby the emphasis on the active role of audiences produced fantasies of 'semiotic democracy', largely abandoning the discipline's 'radical tradition' and converging with liberal-pluralist approaches. Similarly, Greg Philo and David Miller (2001: 50) argue that active-audience theories are one of a number of theoretical 'dead ends' in the discipline, leading away from critical engagement with the world and ultimately losing touch with reality. There is much truth in this critique, particularly Philo and Miller's point that theories about audience identities 'tend to lack any sense of agency' (2001: 61). In general, however, the critique of 'active audience' theories tends to emphasise not a lack of agency but the opposite: a lack of determination. Hence, for example, Philo and Miller complain that, according to many media theorists, 'identities are not determined by socioeconomic forces, but are "creatively" put together', and that such theorists suffer from an 'inability to analyse or discuss the real natural, material and historical circumstances in which identities are forged' (2001: 59–60). We wish to argue that, on the contrary, the essential fault is not a lack of determinism but a surfeit of it, leading to descriptions of audiences which contain only a weak sense of their agency. In this respect, the seemingly radical tradition was flawed to begin with.

The theoretical basis for the 'new and exciting phase' of audience research that Hall sought to inaugurate was 'the semiotic paradigm' (1980: 131). This paradigm, derived from Ferdinand de Saussure's structuralist linguistics, was important not so much because it produced semiotic analyses of news language and images (though sometimes it did) but more because it allowed other phenomena – in particular, ideology – to be conceived of as working 'like a language'. According to Hall, the adoption of this linguistic metaphor, sometimes referred to as the 'cultural turn', constitutes 'the theoretical revolution of our time' (Grossberg 1996: 145). For Saussure, language is a self-contained sign system (he insists that language must be studied as it exists at one moment in time, not as it develops historically) which produces meaning through differences. The meaning of a sign (a word) derives not from any relationship between the sign and what it represents, nor from any hidden essence in the word itself, nor even from the intended meaning of the speaker who utters it, but from the place of that word within the overall sign system (the language), in relation to all the other signs. The particular characteristics of linguistic signs, therefore, are arbitrary: they convey meaning only through their place in an agreed system of linguistic conventions. This is a straightforward proposition in terms of the formal properties of signs (the 'signifier' in Saussure's terminology), since we know that different languages use different words for the same thing – 'dog' could just as easily be *chien* or *Hund*. But the same must logically also apply to the conceptual aspect of the sign – the meaning associated with it (Saussure's 'signified'). Different languages do not simply sound different, they conceptualise the world in different ways (though the differences are not as dramatic as is sometimes suggested). This is the key point which is taken up in extending the semiotic paradigm beyond linguistics: it suggests that language is a kind of conceptual map which makes sense of the world in particular ways, depending on which language we speak, and other 'signifying systems', including ideology, may be seen as doing the same thing (Hall 1980: 134).[2]

We might note in passing that although structuralism was seized upon as an exciting new way to develop the critique of ideology, in practice the semiotic approach tended to be concerned less with challenging particular ideas than with unpicking the mechanisms through which, supposedly, ideology works in general. Whereas a more effective critique of ideology would have been premised on contrasting the true state of affairs with its misleading ideological representation, the semiotic approach implied that *any* discourse is merely a conventional view of the world – Hall (1982: 67) notes the family resemblance between semiotics and social-constructionism in this respect. Hence, as we saw in Chapter 3, there was a tendency towards relativism in the semiotic approach, which became more pronounced as its focus shifted away from ideology; and still more so, as events outside the academy moved even further away from class conflict and the competition between classes to establish a universal mandate.

At least to begin with, however, ideology was the key question, and in reworking the concept in line with the semiotic paradigm, Hall and his colleagues at Birmingham University's Centre for Contemporary Cultural Studies were initially influenced by the French 'structuralist Marxist' Louis Althusser. Largely forgotten today, Althusser's work was once a powerful, and unfortunately doleful, influence on media studies, providing theoretical ballast for a view of ideology which was simultaneously anti-determinist and rigidly deterministic. It was anti-determinist in the sense that it insisted on the 'relative autonomy' of ideology – that it is not straightforwardly determined by socio-economic circumstances. In practice, this tended to mean simply 'autonomy', since determination was deferred to a 'last instance' which 'never comes' (Althusser 2005: 113).[3] The anti-determinist approach, treating ideology as an independent sphere, was meant to avoid economic reductionism or essentialism, thereby opening up a more sophisticated and nuanced understanding of the role of the media. At the same time, however, Althusser's anti-essentialism produced an avowedly anti-humanist version of Marxism which was extremely deterministic. Rejecting Marx's humanistic approach as an 'essentialist' aberration, Althusser (1984: 48–9) equated subjectivity with subjection, arguing that we become subjects when we are 'interpellated', that is to say when we recognise ourselves as being addressed by, and subjected to, ideology. From this perspective, history was conceived as 'a process without a subject', leaving little, if any, room for agency (Althusser 1971: 90). This was a nominally Marxist version of the post-structuralist proposition that human subjectivity is a product of language rather than the other way round.

Translating encoding/decoding into Althusserian terms, we would see the media as 'relatively autonomous' institutions performing distinct 'ideological work' to encode events with a preferred reading, and we would expect to find audience responses to texts determined by the 'subject position' into which they are 'inserted' by social and cultural forces.

When researchers began to test Hall's encoding/decoding hypothesis by investigating actual audience responses, they quickly found that people were not as passive as they ought to have been according to Althusser's theory. Hall's former student, David Morley, undertook a study, *The 'Nationwide' Audience*, based on the encoding/decoding model, in which he found that people were more aware of the constructedness of the TV message than he had anticipated:

> I expected to find a clear division so that decoding practices would either be unconscious [...] and as such, in line with the dominant code or else, if conscious, they could recognise the construction of preferred readings and reject them. In fact [...] the awareness of the construction by no means entails the rejection of what is constructed.
>
> (Morley 1980: 140)

People did recognise that there was a process of 'encoding' going on, in other words, but might nevertheless choose to accept the 'preferred reading' if it coincided with their own outlook. Perhaps the most revealing thing here is that the audience was expected to be largely 'unconscious' and unable to read the text with the same sophistication as media researchers. Morley's work, however, is seen by critics as marking the point when scholars started to overemphasise the active, interpretive process of decoding (Curran 2002: 115; Philo and Miller 2001: 53). In a second study, *Family Television*, Morley did explicitly question how 'the Althusserian drift of much early cultural studies work [...] would reduce [an individual viewer] to the status of a mere personification of a given structure, "spoken" by the discourses which cross the space of his subjectivity' (Morley 1986: 43). Yet his explanation of how audiences 'decode' texts remained within the same paradigm. He describes a hypothetical viewer – a 'white male working-class shop steward' – who watches a news item about factory redundancies from an 'oppositional' viewpoint. But the next item is about the Brixton riots, and he produces a 'negotiated' reading, suspicious of both black youth and the police. He then changes channels and watches a sitcom portraying traditional gender roles, and, as a man, he produces a dominant reading. Morley's argument about this hypothetical viewer is that:

> He is indeed a 'subject crossed by a number of discourses', but it is a *he*, the particular person (who represents a specific combination of/intersection of such discourses), who makes the readings, not the discourses which 'speak' him in any simple sense.
>
> (Morley 1986: 43)

As criticisms of rigid Althusserian determinism go, this must surely be among the mildest: Morley tentatively suggests that, even though people are hardly more than nodal points for various discourses, they might have some small measure of agency in interpreting a television programme. Indeed, Morley's (1986: 43) call to 'examine in detail the different ways in which a given "deep structure" works itself out in different contexts, and to try to reinstate the notion of persons actively engaging in cultural practice' does not sound substantively different from Philo and Miller's (2001: 59) demand for an 'empirical account of how people actually construct their sense of self in real social relationships in the context of competing forces and interests'.

As we indicated earlier, these debates about how audiences respond to ideologically encoded news were not only theoretical but also turned on more practical questions. The contradictory view of 'ideology-in-general' that was worked out in the Althusserian jargon of 'relative autonomy' and 'interpellation' expressed a particular political problem, which persisted even after Althusser was abandoned in favour of a different theorist, Antonio Gramsci, whose ideas about hegemony suggested that ideological dominance was a more contingent and fluid phenomenon. The problem was that, having emerged from the Second World War in what were thought to be promising historical circumstances, the political outlook of the working class appeared to be conformist rather than revolutionary. Yet, rather than taking the perhaps more obvious course of challenging the conservative influence of state-socialist ideas in the British labour movement, the intellectuals of the New Left focused their concern on the cultural erosion of traditional working-class identity. Hall wrote in *Universities and Left Review* in 1958 of the new 'sense of classlessness' that characterised Britain in the 'affluent' 1950s. In part, this was explained away as a product of socio-economic changes resulting in a shift towards 'consumerism'. As Hall put it: 'Capitalism as a social system is now based upon consumption' (Hall 1958: 29). At the same time, however, this was also an argument about the 'changing pattern of life, attitudes and values' which were part of this consumerism and an argument against 'vulgar-Marxist' determinism (Hall 1958: 27).

Here we can already see the main lines of the debate about ideology, whereby Hall simultaneously cautions against determinism while making a determinist argument. Doubts about the working class as the potential agent of historical change led him to reject 'economic reductionism, a too simple correspondence between the economic and the political': ideology is thereby made into an autonomous sphere, working according to its 'own laws of development and evolution' (Hall 1983: 70, 83). The anti-determinist approach is at the same time heavily deterministic, in two senses. First, ideology is understood as exerting tremendous power over people, whether 'interpellating' them in Althusserian terms or recruiting them to some 'hegemonic project' in Gramscian terminology. Second, supposed objective changes are seen to have an inexorable influence in determining political responses: early on, the supposed shift towards consumerism; in later work, an alleged shift to 'post-Fordist' production (Hall 1989).

The rather dim view of the working class persisted, culminating in Hall's 1988 obituary for 'that single, singular subject we used to call Socialist Man', in which he comes close to gloating over the corpse:

> Socialist Man, with one mind, one set of interests, one project, is dead. And good riddance. Who needs 'him' now, with his investment in a particular historical period, with 'his' particular sense of masculinity, shoring 'his' identity up in a particular set of familial relations, a particular kind of sexual identity? Who needs 'him' as the singular identity through which the great diversity of human beings and ethnic cultures in our world must enter the twenty-first century? This 'he' is dead: finished.
>
> (Hall 1988a: 169–70)

Hall's supporters, and they are legion, might defend him by saying that their champion was not dismissing the working class per se but rejecting the discourse of the working class, personified as 'Socialist Man'. But by their own analysis, in which representation is primary, these are one and the same thing. Even if in some ways they would prefer to maintain the distinction, within the terms of their analysis it is not possible to hold onto it. In any case, well before this point, 'socialist man' had been demoted from the position of the 'universal class' to merely one particular identity among many others. In the adverse political circumstances of the late 1970s and 1980s, with traditional labour-movement politics on the defensive, the previous orientation towards the working class started to seem like nothing more than a prejudice, dismissed by some as 'classism' (Laclau and Mouffe 1985). Theorists increasingly turned from ideology to questions of identity and difference, hoping to find more political life in the so-called 'new social movements' of feminism, gay liberation and anti-racism.

The growing emphasis on cultural differences and identities did not arrive out of the blue, however. It echoed a long-standing theme in New Left thought, namely, the deconstruction of what Raymond Williams (1980: 39) calls 'the *selective* tradition: that which, within the terms of an effective dominant culture, is always passed off as "*the* tradition", "*the* significant past."' Media and Cultural Studies writers commonly questioned the pretension to universality of a particular (elite, British, Western) culture as it pertains, for example, to broadcasting. Increasingly, however, the aim of the critique was not to realise the universal by challenging false universals but to question all claims to universalism. As the American critic Cornel West elaborates:

> Distinctive features of the new cultural politics of difference are to trash the monolithic and homogenous in the name of diversity, multiplicity and heterogeneity; to reject the abstract, general and universal in light of the concrete, specific, and particular; and to historicise, contextualise, and pluralise by highlighting the contingent, provisional, variable, tentative, shifting, and changing.
>
> (West 1993: 203–4)

Moreover, work on identity and difference in the 1980s and 1990s imported the same theoretical framework that had been developed in relation to the issue of ideology. Cultural identity was understood, in other words, not in terms of any hidden essence to be uncovered but as an active process of representation or discursive construction. Hall explains:

> I use 'identity' to refer to the meeting point, the point of *suture*, between on the one hand the discourses and practices which attempt to 'interpellate', speak to us or hail us into place as the social subjects of particular discourses, and on the other hand, the processes which produce subjectivities, which construct us as subjects which can be 'spoken'.
>
> (Hall 1996: 5–6)

The persistence of the Althusserian vocabulary may seem surprising, but from the 'anti-essentialist' point of view it makes perfect sense to see identity as constructed by discourse.

The radical-sounding agenda of 'trashing' universals, however, undermines the critique it seeks to make by adopting the relativist approach of celebrating difference. As Kenan Malik has pointed out, the particularist elevation of identity and difference represents a drastic lowering of horizons: from the demand for equality to 'the right to be different'. As he observes, to retain a concept of essential humanity it is necessary to maintain a universalist outlook: 'Without such a common essence, equality would be a meaningless concept. If humanity did not form a single category [...] then equality between different human individuals and groups would be [...] meaningless' (Malik 1996: 258). This need not imply a biological concept of essence, as in supposedly 'natural' categories such as 'race' or gender, but can be understood in terms of social essence: Malik's argument here invokes Marx's (1978: 67) view that 'the human essence is no abstraction inherent in each single individual. In its reality it is the ensemble of social relations.' As we suggested earlier, there is a real basis for social categories such as 'the public'. The constructionist approach, in contrast, tends to see identities as provisional – no more and no less. According to Homi K. Bhabha, for example, '"The people" always exist as a multiple form of identification, waiting to be created and constructed' (Rutherford 1990: 220). Similarly, Hall (1988a: 173) argues that the task of intellectuals is to seize the means of 'making new human subjects and shove them in the direction of a new culture'. This is not to exclude the possibility of agency outright; rather, it is confined to the contingent. Accordingly, the diversity of lifestyle choices offered by contemporary 'post-Fordist' capitalism is said to 'allow the individual some space in which to reassert a measure of choice and control over everyday life and to "play" with its more expressive dimensions' (Hall 1988b: 28). He means that when we buy commodities we also make a statement about ourselves and our identities:

> [I]n the modern world, objects are also signs, and we relate to the world of things in both an instrumental and a symbolic mode. In a world tyrannised

by scarcity, men and women nevertheless express in their practical lives not only what they need for material existence but some sense of their symbolic place in the world, of who they are, their identities.

(Hall 1989: 130)

Ironically, in view of Hall's earlier critique of consumerism, agency here becomes centred around the act of consumption, as we 'actively' construct our identities from the symbolic resources on offer in the shops or in the media. As we have pointed out, the confluence of the politics of difference with developments in broadcasting in the 1980s represented an accommodation to the niche marketing of 'post-Fordist' capitalism.

Conclusion: prosumers and public sphericles

As we have discussed in this chapter, contemporary views of the news audience are highly contradictory. According to Brian McNair (2000: 172), for example, there are now 'unprecedented levels of *mass participation* in politics and, through the expansion of access, of *mass participation* in the public sphere'. He even claims that we are witnessing a 'defeudalisation' of the public sphere, 'meaning the *restoration* [...] of the critical publicity and scrutiny of elites which (for Habermas) characterised its early, ideal form; and the extension of access to the level of, if not the universal, then at least the masses, constituted as citizens irrespective of property or other qualifications' (2000: 176). In contrast, Stephen Coleman and Jay Blumler (2009: 1) maintain that 'A pervasive anxiety characterises liberal democracy in the early twenty-first century [...] citizens seem to be increasingly disenchanted by and disengaged from the processes and institutions of the democratic state.' Both views are, in a sense, correct, but McNair's is only superficially so. It is true that we are encouraged by the media to see ourselves as 'active audiences', continually invited to press the red button, phone in with a vote, email a photo or a comment, even to suggest news stories that ought to be covered. Yet such 'activity' tends to be largely reactive and shallow. Even as content-generators, bloggers or amateur journalists, the audience is still restricted to an essentially passive role – perhaps not consigned to the armchair in couch-potato mode but still sitting down to produce commentary on events rather than acting in or leading the events themselves. This might change, of course, and new communications technologies could potentially support new sorts of relationships between the media and the public. Yet, so far at least, the idea of the 'prosumer' seems more like a logical development from the twin tendencies in conceptions of the audience that we have discussed above – as both passive consumer of commercialised media and 'active' producer of textual meaning. Unfortunately, it is Coleman and Blumler's diagnosis of disenchantment that offers the more accurate account, but in this chapter we hope to have indicated some points of departure for thinking about a way to resolve the problem they describe. As we have argued, while there may once have been good reason to criticise the false unities previously imposed by national institutions such as the BBC, that is not the problem we face today. Indeed, it is doubtful how far it was ever the case that, as Hall argues, the BBC *'produced* the nation which it then *addressed* [...] [and] *constructed* its audience by the ways in which it represented them' (1993: 32, original emphasis). Certainly the BBC tried to do this but, as we have seen, it had some difficulties in doing so. Hall's characterisation of the Corporation as 'an instrument, an apparatus, a "machine" through which the nation was constituted' (1993: 32) surely attributes too much power to broadcasting, in line with exaggerated claims about ideological 'interpellation' as constitutive of the subject. The extent to which 'the nation' is produced as a meaningful shared identity is dependent on extra-discursive factors, not least the social and political context in which broadcasting operates. The continuing preference for critiques of 'monolithic' cultures and imposed unities seems like a hangover from the past, a relic of the post-war consensus that critics such as Hall attacked as it broke down in the 1970s.

Just as the technology of broadcasting could not, on its own, engender unity, so too it would be mistaken to view newer media technologies either as producing fragmentation in the recent past or as offering a magic solution to disengagement in the near future. Rather, in reviewing theoretical developments from the 1980s and 1990s and highlighting their relation to the convergence between a cultural politics of diversity and the growth of specialisation and market segmentation in contemporary news media, we have sought to suggest that the fragmenting public is more a product of political trends – in particular, the decline and eventual collapse of the Left, formerly the most reliable defender of universalist values. Today, more optimistic diagnoses of 'critical publicity and scrutiny of elites' would seem to confuse public cynicism about political leaders and institutions with critical scepticism. While there is no shortage of people questioning political elites today, the vantage points from which questions are asked rarely imply political critique let alone a serious discussion of alternatives and future possibilities. Rather, as we have noted a number of times throughout this book, with the end of Left and Right and the hollowing out of the public sphere, we are all undergoing the absence of a meaningful political framework. This is the key to the 'crisis of disengagement' described by Coleman and Blumler (2009: 1).

The first flush of excitement about the democratising force of the Internet has given way to more realistic appraisals which, while appreciating its potential, are also sensitive to the fact that new technologies cannot, in themselves, automatically engender meaningful public participation (Fenton 2010: 14). Instead, one might see current uses of social media or Web 2.0 as examples of active 'identity-construction', though not in the resistant, politicised mould envisaged by cultural theorists. As users of Facebook, Twitter or YouTube construct a persona for their networks of friends and followers, they are partly engaged in sociable activity, but of a solipsistic sort, preoccupied with personal display as much as with engagement with others. It might be characterised in terms of the 'triumph of the concrete over the abstract' (Calcutt 2005), which can also be seen in other aspects of contemporary culture, from the exposure of the intimate affairs of celebrities to the emotive 'personal narratives' of politicians (even George W. Bush wept on *Oprah* when campaigning for office). In the absence of competing visions and ideologies (political practices which require abstraction to a contested idea of the general interest), it is perhaps inevitable that more attention is paid to the personalities and personal lives of individual politicians (the concrete). Likewise, when there has been considerable weakening of the politicising processes which formerly abstracted us from the realm of the particular, we should not be surprised if the concrete world of interpersonal relationships takes on a disproportionate importance. In this context, rather than encouraging further fragmentation or even narrower emphasis on the particular, we propose that Journalism Studies should shrug off the hangovers of the recent past and reclaim the idea of the universal public.

Conclusion
Journalism and Journalism Studies

This concluding essay is written in the hope that Journalism Studies will not waste the current crisis of journalism. Rather, that the threats now posed to journalism's commercial basis and its definitive stance will also serve as the opportunity for Journalism Studies to be reconfigured for the sake of journalism's renewal. Journalism is too important to be left entirely to journalists. On the other hand, if Journalism Studies continues to talk past journalism, as it has done in the past, it will render itself supremely unimportant.

Mindful of the need for journalism and Journalism Studies to get better acquainted, and on the basis of our prior analysis, we (the authors of this book) would like to offer some, minimal definitions of what we (journalism and Journalism Studies) are here to talk about, and how best we might talk about it:

Journalism: the concerted activity of reporting and commenting on recent human activity, disseminated in well-crafted forms for the benefit of others more often engaged in other activities.

Journalism Studies: detailed consideration of activities specific to journalism (see above) and logical reconstruction of their relations with the wider field of historically specific human activity.

Thus, Journalism Studies is characterised as consciousness of journalism (not its conscience), as journalism itself is consciousness of the actions performed by human subjects in making the world our object – a process which, in so far as it is human, already entails consciousness and its application.

This last point should also be the starting point in our understanding of subsequent levels of consciousness and their application in journalism and Journalism Studies. We must bear in mind that, in the way people go about making their world, for all that their making of it is distorted by the obstructive intervention of capital, there is already a reciprocal relationship between subjectivity and objectification. In making the world our object, as also in making our world of objects, all of us think about what we are making and about ourselves making it. This is a very important part of what makes us human; and in so far as journalism and

Journalism Studies are successive extensions of this quality of human life, they are also the continuation of our humanity.

But more often than not, the potential for subjectivity and objectification to complement each other fully is diminished by capital interposing itself between them and turning them against each other. Accordingly, journalism and Journalism Studies alike (and also their history of mutual hostility) have been largely (though by no means entirely) composed of the estrangement between subjectivity and objectification.

Thus, the traditional journalist, alienated from the people who are his or her subject matter, often sneers at them as he or she contemplates them. There is normally no need for smears, since his or her contempt is enough to write them off. But his or her habit of fixing them, putting them in their place just as his or her stories of their lives are placed on the page, is not only directed at the people it purports to describe but is also derived from the alienation of his or her own subjectivity from the collective enterprise of making the world we live in, i.e. objectification. Thus, even his or her eventual contribution to objectification – the news report that reproduces in thought what has already been produced in action – is writ large with alienation: it is written on the basis that subjectivity and objectification are necessarily estranged; as indeed they generally, spontaneously are in the historical conditions particular to capitalism.

In its original, anti-capitalist incarnation, this is what Journalism Studies found objectionable about 'objective' journalism – and rightly so. But in its increasingly unconvincing efforts to right this wrong, the academy produced its own iteration of alienated objectivity even while polemicising against it in journalism. As journalism was traditionally alienated from the people it described, the academy has also been alienated from them, and, again, in this particular field, from the journalism it describes. It's hardly surprising, then, that the stock characterisation of campus radicals shaking their fists at 'the meedja' is uncannily reminiscent of stereotypical *Daily Mail* feature writers railing against immigrants or the European Union. Subjectively, they are polar opposites, but objectively they have much in common. Outrage, as bitter as it is impotent, is their lingua franca, alienation their common experience.

The reconfiguration of human activity in the world today, with its gross imbalance between the concentration of mediating activity in the West and the centralisation of productive activity towards the East, reposes the problem of alienation in a newly expanded form. It also offers us the chance of bringing fresh significance to the old declaration against alienation: *Homo sum: humani nil a me alienum puto* (I am a man: I believe that nothing human is alien to me). To be able to live by this humanist principle, however, we will have to struggle against pressures which would negate it; and it will not be possible to wage this struggle now by reliving battles first fought in the 1970s and 1980s.

On the other hand, Journalism Studies is currently facing the biggest opportunity in its history: in today's conditions and because of these conditions, there is a serious possibility that the realisation of our (academic) subject will make a significant contribution to the realisation of the human subject. But for Journalism Studies to attain its full significance, it is the responsibility of those involved in it to demonstrate that journalism at its best can suggest (in mediating activity) how to overcome (in mediation but also in production) the historically specific, now also geographically particular, estrangement between subjectivity and objectification.

Not that this estrangement is now or has ever been absolute (the day that it became so would be the end of our world). Instead, there is a host of activities which mediate between subjectivity and objectification, but, peculiar to capitalism, the normal effect of such mediating activity is not to align these two but to line them up in opposition. Thus their separation is ratified, while falling far short of divorce.

Similarly, successive rounds of mediating activity often compound the alienation effects that the previous rounds were intended to address. For example, episodes of intergovernmental mediation have done little to address the imbalance between productive activity in the East and financial mediation in the West. These diplomatic episodes were prompted by financial crisis, itself brought on not only by this same imbalance but also by the attempts to guard against its effects, i.e. to mediate the contradiction between previous rounds of mediation (finance) and originating, productive activity. Ironically, the earlier efforts to mediate between (financial) mediation and production, which turned out to be especially destabilising, had been developed in the interests of 'securitisation', i.e. they consisted of yet another layer of financial 'products' designed to secure the mediation between already existing layers of finance (mediation). We would apologise for this amount of repetition, except that this really is how it is: spiralling rounds of mediation that ratify the estrangement of subjectivity from objectification.

Yet mediation is as contradictory as the contradictions it addresses. Just as there is mainstream mediating activity which makes the societal contradiction manageable by ratifying the separation of subjectivity and objectification, so there is scope for mediating activity that highlights contradiction and the reasons underlying it. Moreover, in so far as this latter activity refers to our social reality in its lively, contradictory character (not seeking to deaden it by explaining away the contradiction), of necessity it is active in aligning subjectivity with objectification and overcoming the contradiction between them. Furthermore, when this kind of activity is cognitive, when it occurs in thought, objectivity is what it is moving towards. Thus, objectivity is that quality of thought which we arrive at (or near) when subjectivity is connected to objectification and at the same time disconnected from any mediating activity which would reiterate their alienation. Subjectivity and objectification both flourish whenever they are independent from mediation that turns them against each other. In these moments of freedom, the movement towards objectivity complements the active realisation of the human subject instead of negating it.

The possibility of moving towards objectivity is widely discernible in all manner of activity on the part of human subjects: in the historical and the contemporary, at global level and in the *minutiae* of our daily lives.

In the mercantilist era, the abstracted position which human subjects must occupy in thought in order for objectivity to begin to materialise, was confined to the markets of mercantile cities and their immediate surroundings. With the onset of commodity production as a general mode, this position was first generalised across the nation, and barely contained within its borders; indeed, the pressure to mark out this viewing platform as if it were a national enclosure was an important factor in the formulation of alienated objectivity. More recently, the same developments which have internationalised the growing separation of subjectivity and objectification have reinforced the international dimension of objectivity, i.e. they confirm that the movement of thought towards objectivity is also movement into a position equidistant from the demands of alienated subjectivity in the West and the requirements of alienated objectification in the East. In this context, objectivity has to be international; and, at a time when the whole world's media are technically connected, digitally supported journalism is well placed to stake out a suitably internationalist position.

Thus, the global scale of subjectivity's alienation from objectification has its obverse: the international stature of the objective means with which to address it. Similarly, though East and West are opposites as regards the form of alienation which their respective mediating activities are tending towards, on both sides there are also subjective trends that counteract these tendencies and again suggest the possibility of realigning subjectivity with objectification.

On the part of Easterners, especially the young, there is widespread desire to subvert their designated role in objectification by acquiring something like Western subjectivity. Meanwhile, many young Westerners yearn for a form of association more substantial than interpersonal networks; hence the turn to religion on the part of many young people, ostensibly as a return to tradition but really a new-found quest for social relations with more depth than the flat, horizontal lines that shape their networked subjectivity. Thus, millions of people on each side of the divide are expressing a desire to overcome it, however fetishised their expressions are. If their aspirations were to go past each other like the proverbial ships in the night, it would be a missed opportunity of historic proportions. This is no exaggeration: we really would have missed the opportunity to reconfigure relations between subjectivity and objectification, West and East; and thus make history.

The first step in this epic journey is there on the page or screen in front of us all: writing. In these historically specific conditions, the very act of writing signals the objectification of subjectivity and the possibility of bringing them into alignment. This much is suggested by placing our thoughts outside ourselves so that you can hear them, propelling them onto a surface which makes them a thing that you can see and launching them into a space which belongs to neither you nor us exclusively but is shared by all.

Writing has not always been like this. There were times when it was primarily a technique for explaining away the powerlessness of people in the face of nature, and in such circumstances even apparently straightforward records were couched in those terms. But they are not the terms we are obliged to live by, thankfully; instead, in these times, the well-rehearsed combination of expressing and checking, release and control, which finds its form in the written object, is already the kernel of objectivity, no matter how many times it goes unrecognised as such.

Others will judge whether or not we have succeeded, but in this book we have tried to be objective and propagandistic at the same time. Instead of propaganda for the manufacture of consent, which we have described as alienated objectivity, and in place of propaganda for inconclusive dissent, which we have described as alienated subjectivity, we are propagandising for the realisation of the human subject, beginning with the remaking of objectivity in journalism and Journalism Studies.

We believe there is an objective basis for our propaganda. Unless you have cheated and skipped to the end of the book, by now you will have read the case we make to this end.

Notes

Introduction: Journalism in question

1 See 'Putting the Crisis in Local Journalism on the Political Agenda', Goldsmiths, University of London, available online at http://www.gold.ac.uk/global-media-democracy/events/localjournalismcrisis (accessed 6 July 2010).

2 Its two major academic journals – *Journalism Studies* and *Journalism: Theory, Practice and Criticism* – both began publishing in 2000. For an interesting account of the tensions generated between Cultural Studies and journalism training in the emergence of Journalism Studies (in an Australian context), see Turner (2000).

3 See: 'The BBC UGC Hub', *BBC College of Journalism*, available online at http://www.bbc.co.uk/journalism/skills/citizen-journalism/citizen-journalism-guide/the-hub.shtml (accessed 6 July 2010).

1 Ownership and the news industry

1 We only have access to the edition of 23 November. However, our colleague, Richard Sharpe, found a copy of the 22 November special edition in his mother-in-law's loft in Detroit and got in touch with Tom Wicker to ask him about writing the story. Although our reading of Wicker's writing is different from Sharpe's, it was his initial detective work that found us the thing to read.

2 From Richard Sharpe's conversation with Tom Wicker, we understand that the segment of the story which is not to shape, concerning the arrest of Lee Harvey Oswald, was inserted by a subeditor in New York.

3 See http://www.youtube.com/watch?v=WNmhTlLKcB8 and http://www.youtube.com/watch?v=GF1gUKQcVpE.

4 Although we must be careful not to impute our interpretation of Johnson in his historically-specific ambitions to the poet, novelist and essayist John Wain, nonetheless we should acknowledge the inspirational influence of Wain's biography of Samuel Johnson, first published in 1974.

2 Media and mediating activity

1 It is important to recognise that the analytical sociology of Galtung and Ruge was gradually superseded by the more biographical approach associated with Cultural Studies; nonetheless, the Cultural Studies literature continues to refer back to the original formulation of 'news values' by Galtung and Ruge.

2 Mandy Rice-Davies was the close friend of Christine Keeler, whose affair with Minister of War John Profumo led him to resign from the UK government in

1963. As a witness in the trial of Stephen Ward, charged with living off immoral earnings from Keeler and Rice-Davies, she was informed by prosecuting counsel that Lord Astor denied having an affair with her, or even having met her. Famously, Rice-Davies replied, 'Well, he would, wouldn't he?'

3 The rise and fall of objectivity

1 For information on declining voter turnouts in UK general elections (1945–2010) see http://www.ukpolitical.info/Turnout45.htm (accessed 15 June 2010). A UK parliamentary survey of declining membership of political parties is available at http://www.parliament.uk/commons/lib/research/briefings/snsg-05125.pdf (accessed 15 June 2010). Gitlin (1998: 169) describes a similar situation in the USA.

2 For an excellent discussion of the difference between Marxism and social construction see Heartfield (1996).

3 They note here that 'Our use of the term "ideology" in this context and throughout refers to sets of ideas which represent or serve the interests of social groups or classes. It is not intended to convey the meaning of merely illusory or false thinking' (GUMG 1980: 402). As we have indicated, this formula avoids the issue of whether ideas serving the interests of particular 'social groups or classes' are true or not.

4 *Today*, BBC Radio 4, 3 March 2010. The presenter, James Naughtie, responded to Robinson's remarks by saying: 'I'm glad we got some agreement there.'

4 The future of objectivity

1 Beckett refutes the idea that his work lends itself to what we have called 'networked subjectivity', and we acknowledge that he has not abandoned objectivity outright. We agree with him that objectivity is socially constructed and he agrees with us that digital media can increase the likelihood of realising it; but we part company when he concedes that objectivity itself is relative (Beckett 2008: 62), not only the attempt to achieve it. In our analysis, this is just the kind of concession that puts networked subjectivity in the driving seat.

5 The fragmenting public

1 As the Ullswater Committee put it in 1936: 'The position of the Corporation is [...] one of independence in the day-to-day management of its business, and of ultimate control by His Majesty's Government'. Report of the Broadcasting Committee (The Ullswater Report), Cmnd 5091, 1936, p. 18.

2 As Hall observes here (1980: 133–4), the French literary critic Roland Barthes (1973) makes a similar point, attempting to discover a direct equivalent of the signifier/signified relationship for 'myth'.

3 Having proposed that ideology is determined by material factors 'in the last instance', Althusser (2005: 113) then says that 'From the first moment to the last, the lonely hour of "the last instance" never comes.' Hall (1977: 327) endorses the point, even though a last instance which never comes is not in fact a last instance.

References

Adorno, Theodor W. (2001) 'The Culture Industry Reconsidered', in *The Culture Industry: Selected Essays on Mass Culture*, London and New York, NY: Routledge. First published 1948.

Allan, Stuart (1997) 'News and the Public Sphere: Towards a History of Objectivity and Impartiality', in M. Bromley and T. O'Malley (eds.), *A Journalism Reader*, London and New York, NY: Routledge.

Allen, Charles (2007) *Kipling Sahib: India and the Making of Rudyard Kipling*, London: Abacus.

Althusser, Louis (1971) *Lenin and Philosophy, and Other Essays*, London: New Left Books.

——(1984) *Essays on Ideology*, London: Verso.

——(2005) *For Marx*, London: Verso. First published 1965.

Anderson, Chris (2009) *Free: The Future of a Radical Price*, London: Random House Business Books.

Arnold, Matthew (1993) *Culture and Anarchy and Other Writings*, Cambridge: Cambridge University Press. First published 1869.

Atton, Chris and Hamilton, James (2008) *Alternative Journalism*, London: Sage.

Avery, John (1997) *Progress, Poverty and Population: Re-Reading Condorcet, Godwin and Malthus*, London: Frank Cass.

Barthes, Roland (1973) *Mythologies*, London: Paladin.

Baugh, Albert C. and Cable, Thomas (1978) *A History of the English Language*, 3rd edn, London: Routledge & Kegan Paul.

Beckett, Charlie (2008) *Supermedia: Saving Journalism So It Can Save the World*, London: Wiley-Blackwell.

——(2010) *The Value of Networked Journalism*, London: Polis. Available online at http://www.polismedia.org (accessed 14 June 2010).

Behr, Edward (1982) *Anyone Here Been Raped and Speaks English?*, London: New English Library.

Bell, Martin (1998) 'The Journalism of Attachment', in Matthew Kieran (ed.), *Media Ethics*, London and New York, NY: Routledge.

Bennett, W. Lance (1990) 'Toward a Theory of Press–State Relations in the United States', *Journal of Communication*, 40 (2): 103–25.

Bernays, Edward L. (1947) 'The Engineering of Consent', *The ANNALS of the American Academy of Political and Social Science*, 250: 113–20.

Blair, Tony (2003) 'Statement Opening Iraq Debate in Parliament', 18 March, available online at http://www.number-10.gov.uk/output/page3294 (accessed 15 June 2010).

Blanchard, Simon and Morley, David (1982) 'Introduction', in Simon Blanchard and David Morley (eds.), *What's This Channel Fo(u)r?*, London: Comedia.

Boyce, George (1978) 'The Fourth Estate: The Re-Appraisal of a Concept', in George Boyce, James Curran and Pauline Wingate (eds.), *Newspaper History from the Seventeenth Century to the Present Day*, London: Constable.

Boykoff, Maxwell T. (2007) 'Flogging a Dead Norm? Newspaper Coverage of Anthropogenic Climate Change in the United States and United Kingdom from 2003 to 2006', *Area*, 39 (4): 470–81.

Boykoff, Maxwell T. and Boykoff, Jules M. (2004) 'Balance as Bias: Global Warming and the US Prestige Press', *Global Environmental Change*, 14 (2): 125–36.

Briggs, Asa (1970) *The History of Broadcasting in the United Kingdom, Vol. Three: The War of Words*, Oxford: Oxford University Press.

Brock, George (2010) 'Is News Over?', Inaugural Lecture, City University, London, 17 March, available online at http://www.scribd.com/doc/28560140/george-brock-is-news-over (accessed 11 June 2010).

Broersma, Marcel (2010) 'The Unbearable Limitations of Journalism: On Press Critique and Journalism's Claim to Truth', *International Communication Gazette*, 72 (1): 21–33.

Brown, Richard (1991) *Society and Economy in Modern Britain, 1700–1850*, London and New York, NY: Routledge.

Burns, Tom (1977) *The BBC: Public Institution and Private World*, London: Macmillan.

Calcutt, Andrew (1998) *Arrested Development: Pop Culture and the Erosion of Adulthood*, London: Cassell.

——(1999) *White Noise: An A–Z of the Contradictions in Cyberculture*, Basingstoke: Macmillan.

——(2005) 'Celebrity Turns and the Return of Politics', paper presented to the Celebrity Culture Conference, University of Paisley, 12–14 September.

Calhoun, Craig (2005) 'Public', in Tony Bennett, Lawrence Grossberg and Meaghan Morris (eds.), *New Keywords: A Revised Vocabulary of Culture and Society*, Oxford: Blackwell.

Castells, Manuel (2009) *Communication Power*, Oxford: Oxford University Press.

Chalaby, Jean K. (1998) *The Invention of Journalism*, Basingstoke: Palgrave Macmillan.

Chibnall, Steve (1977) *Law and Order News: An Analysis of Crime Reporting in the British Press*, London: Tavistock.

Choonara, Esme (2009) 'Stop the BBC "Rolling Out the Red Carpet" for Nazi BNP Leader on Question Time', *Socialist Worker*, No. 2169, 12 September, available at http://www.socialistworker.co.uk/art.php?id=18949 (accessed 15 June 2010).

Cobbett, William (1812), cited in George Spater (1982) *William Cobbett: The Poor Man's Friend*, vol. II, Cambridge: Cambridge University Press.

Cobbett, William (1967) *Rural Rides*, ed. George Woodcock, Harmondsworth: Penguin. First published 1830.

Cohen, Stanley and Young, Jock (eds.) (1973) *The Manufacture of News*, London: Constable.

Coleman, Stephen and Blumler, Jay (2009) *The Internet and Democratic Citizenship*, Cambridge: Cambridge University Press.

Coleman, Stephen and Ross, Karen (2010) *The Media and the Public*, Chichester: Wiley-Blackwell.

Corner, John (1982) 'Rethinking Public Service TV: A Note on "New Images for Old"', in Simon Blanchard and David Morley (eds.), *What's This Channel Fo(u)r?*, London: Comedia.

Couldry, Nick, Livingstone, Sonia and Markham, Tim (2010) *Media Consumption and Public Engagement*, Basingstoke: Palgrave Macmillan.

Crossman, Richard (ed.) (1950) *The God That Failed*, New York, NY: Harper.

Cunningham, Brent (2003) 'Re-Thinking Objectivity', *Columbia Journalism Review*, July–August, pp. 24–32.

Curran, James (1991) 'Mass Media and Democracy: A Reappraisal', in James Curran and Michael Gurevitch (eds.), *Mass Media and Society*, London: Arnold.

——(2002) *Media and Power*, London and New York, NY: Routledge.

Curran, James and Seaton, Jean (1981) *Power Without Responsibility: Press and Broadcasting in Britain*, Glasgow: Fontana.

——(2010) *Power Without Responsibility: Press, Broadcasting and the Internet in Britain*, 7th edn, London and New York, NY: Routledge.

Dahlgren, Peter (1991) 'Introduction', in Peter Dahlgren and Colin Sparks (eds.), *Communication and Citizenship*, London and New York, NY: Routledge.

——(1995) *Television and the Public Sphere*, London: Sage.

——(2009) *Media and Political Engagement*, Cambridge: Cambridge University Press.

Davies, Nick (2008) *Flat-Earth News: An Award-Winning Reporter Exposes Falsehood, Distortion and Propaganda in the Global Media*, London: Chatto & Windus.

Dear, Jeremy (2009) 'The NUJ's Economic Stimulus Plan for Local Media', London: National Union of Journalists, available online at http://www.nuj.org (accessed 10 July 2010).

Deuze, Mark (2009) 'The Future of Citizen Journalism', in Stuart Allan and Einar Thorsen (eds.), *Citizen Journalism: Global Perspectives*, New York, NY: Peter Lang.

Dicken, Peter (2007) *Global Shift: Mapping the Changing Contours of the World Economy*, 5th edn, London: Sage.

Dickens, Charles (1852) 'A Sleep to Startle Us', *Household Words*, 13 March, Reprinted in Jon E. Lewis (ed.) (2003) *The Mammoth Book of Journalism*, London: Robinson.

DiMaggio, Anthony (2008) *Mass Media, Mass Propaganda*, Lanham, Md.: Lexington Books.

Docherty, David, Morrison, David and Tracey, Michael (1988) *Keeping Faith? Channel Four and Its Audience*, London: John Libbey.

Dore, Ronald (2008) 'Financialisation of the Global Economy', *Industrial and Corporate Change*, Special Issue, 18 (2): 1097–112.

Eldridge, John (ed.) (1972) *Max Weber: The Interpretation of Social Reality*, London: Nelson University Paperbacks.

Eldridge, John, Kitzinger, Jenny and Williams, Kevin (1997) *The Mass Media and Power in Modern Britain*, Oxford: Oxford University Press.

Engardio, Peter (ed.) (2007) *Chindia: How China and India Are Revolutionising Global Business*, New York, NY: McGraw-Hill.

Evans, Harold (2009) *My Paper Chase: True Stories of Vanished Times*, London: Little, Brown.

Fenton, Natalie (2010) 'Drowning or Waving? New Media, Journalism and Democracy', in Natalie Fenton (ed.), *New Media, Old News*, London: Sage.

Fishman, Mark (1980) *Manufacturing the News*, Austin, Tex.: University of Texas Press.

Franklin, Bob (1997) *Newszak and News Media*, London: Arnold.

Fraser, Nancy (1992) 'Rethinking the Public Sphere: A Contribution to the Critique of Actually Existing Democracy', in Craig Calhoun (ed.), *Habermas and the Public Sphere*, Cambridge, Mass.: MIT Press.

Frayn, Michael (2005) *Towards the End of the Morning*, London: Faber & Faber. First published 1967.

Furedi, Frank (2002) *Culture of Fear*, London: Continuum.

Gaber, Ivor (2008) 'Three Cheers for Subjectivity: Or, The Crumbling of the Seven Pillars of Journalistic Wisdom', conference paper presented at *The End of Journalism: Technology, Education and Ethics*, University of Bedfordshire, 17–18 October, available online at http://theendofjournalism.wikidot.com/ivorgaber (accessed 15 June 2010).

Galtung, Johann and Ruge, Marie (1973) 'Structuring and Selecting News', in Stanley Cohen and Jock Young (eds.), *The Manufacture of News*, London: Constable. First published 1965.

Gans, Herbert J. (1980) *Deciding What's News*, New York, NY: Random House.

——(2003) *Democracy and the News*, Oxford: Oxford University Press.

Garnham, Nicholas (1992) 'The Media and the Public Sphere', in Craig Calhoun (ed.), *Habermas and the Public Sphere*, Cambridge, Mass.: MIT Press.

Gay, Peter (1979) *The Enlightenment: An Interpretation, Volume 2: The Science of Freedom*, London: Wildwood House.

Gillmor, Dan (2004) *We the Media*, available online at http://www.authorama.com/book/we-the-media.html (accessed 2 July 2010).

——(2006) *We the Media: Grassroots Journalism by the People, for the People*, Sebastopol, Calif.: O'Reilly Media, Inc.

Gitlin, Todd (1998) 'Public Sphere or Public Sphericules?' in Tamar Liebes and James Curran (eds.), *Media, Ritual and Identity*, London and New York, NY: Routledge.

Glasgow University Media Group (1980) *More Bad News*, London: Routledge & Kegan Paul.

Gouldner, Alvin (1970) *The Coming Crisis of Western Sociology*, New York, NY: Basic Books.

Gowing, Nik (1997) *Media Coverage: Help or Hindrance in Conflict Prevention?* (Report to the Carnegie Commission on Preventing Deadly Conflict), Washington, DC: Carnegie Corporation.

Grossberg, Lawrence (1996) 'On Postmodernism and Articulation: An Interview with Stuart Hall', in David Morley and Kuan-Hsing Chen (eds.), *Stuart Hall: Critical Dialogues in Cultural Studies*, London and New York, NY: Routledge.

Guardian (n.d.) *Newsroom: The Guardian Past and Present*, London: The Guardian.

Habermas, Jürgen (1989) *The Structural Transformation of the Public Sphere*, Cambridge: Polity.

Hackett, Robert and Zhao, Yuezhi (1998) *Sustaining Democracy? Journalism and the Politics of Objectivity*, Toronto: Garamond Press.

Hall, Stuart (1958) 'A Sense of Classlessness', *Universities and New Left Review*, 5 (autumn 1958); quoted in Michael Kenny (1995) *The First New Left: British Intellectuals after Stalin*, London: Lawrence & Wishart, pp. 58–9.

——(1973) 'A World at One with Itself', in Stanley Cohen and Jock Young (eds.), *The Manufacture of News*, London: Constable. First published 1970.

——(1977) 'Culture, the Media and the "Ideological Effect"', in James Curran, Michael Gurevitch and Janet Woollacott (eds.), *Mass Communication and Society*, London: Edward Arnold/Open University Press.

——(1980) 'Encoding/Decoding', in Stuart Hall, Dorothy Hobson, Andrew Lowe and Paul Willis (eds.), *Culture, Media, Language*, London: Hutchinson.

——(1982) 'The Rediscovery of "Ideology": Return of the Repressed in Media Studies', in Michael Gurevitch, Tony Bennett, James Curran and Janet Woollacott (eds.), *Culture, Society and the Media*, London and New York, NY: Routledge.

——(1983) 'The Problem of Ideology: Marxism Without Guarantees', in Betty Matthews (ed.), *Marx 100 Years on*, London: Lawrence & Wishart.

——(1988a) *The Hard Road to Renewal*, London: Verso/*Marxism Today*.

——(1988b) 'Brave New World', *Marxism Today*, October, pp. 24–9.

——(1989) 'The Meaning of New Times', in Stuart Hall and Martin Jacques (eds.), *New Times*, London: Lawrence & Wishart.

——(1993) 'Which Public, Whose Service?', in Wilf Stevenson (ed.), *All Our Futures: The Changing Role and Purpose of the BBC*, London: BFI.

——(1996) 'Introduction: Who Needs "Identity"?', in Stuart Hall and Paul Du Gay (eds.), *Questions of Cultural Identity*, London: Sage.

Hall, Stuart, Crichter, Chas, Jefferson, Tony, Clarke, John and Roberts, Brian (1978) *Policing the Crisis: Mugging, the State and Law and Order*, London: Macmillan.

Hallin, Daniel C. (1989) *The 'Uncensored War': The Media and Vietnam*, Oxford: Oxford University Press. First published 1986.

Hammond, Philip (2002) 'Moral Combat: Advocacy Journalists and the New Humanitarianism', in David Chandler (ed.), *Rethinking Human Rights*, Basingstoke: Palgrave.

Harris, David (1992) *From Class Struggle to the Politics of Pleasure*, London and New York, NY: Routledge.

Harvey, Sylvia (1982) 'New Images for Old? Channel Four and Independent Film', in Simon Blanchard and David Morley (eds.), *What's This Channel Fo(u)r?*, London: Comedia.

Heartfield, James (1996) 'Marxism and Social Construction', in Suke Wolton (ed.), *Marxism, Mysticism and Modern Theory*, London: Macmillan.

——(2002) *The 'Death of the Subject' Explained*, Sheffield: Sheffield Hallam University Press.

Hegel, Georg Wilhelm Friedrich (1820) 'Preface', in *The Philosophy of Right*, available online at http://www.marxists.org/reference/archive/hegel/index.htm (accessed 12 July 2010).

Higgins, Michael (2008) *Media and Their Publics*, Maidenhead: Open University Press.

Hindman, Matthew (2009) *The Myth of Digital Democracy*, Princeton, NJ: Princeton University Press.

Houghton, Walter (1957) *The Victorian Frame of Mind, 1830–1870*, New Haven, Conn.: Yale University Press.

Hume, Mick (1997) *Whose War Is It Anyway? The Dangers of the Journalism of Attachment*, London: Informinc.

——(1998) *Televictims*, London: Informinc.

Jacoby, Russell (1999) *The End of Utopia: Politics and Culture in an Age of Apathy*, New York, NY: Basic Books.

Jenkins, Simon (1986) *The Market for Glory: Fleet Street Ownership in the Twentieth Century*, London: Faber & Faber.

Jennings, Humphrey (1995) *Pandaemonium 1660–1886: The Coming of the Machine as Seen by Contemporary Observers*, London: Macmillan.

Keane, Fergal (1996) 'Letter to Daniel', *From Our Own Correspondent*, BBC Radio 4, 15 February, available online at http://news.bbc.co.uk/1/hi/programmes/from_our_own_correspondent/41784.stm (accessed 15 June 2010).

Keeble, Richard (2004) 'Information Warfare in an Age of Hyper-Militarism', in Stuart Allan and Barbie Zelizer (eds.), *Reporting War: Journalism in Wartime*, London and New York, NY: Routledge.

Keen, Andrew (2007) *The Cult of the Amateur: How Today's Internet Is Killing Our Culture and Assaulting Our Economy*, London: Nicholas Brealey Publishing.

Kenny, Michael (1995) *The First New Left: British Intellectuals after Stalin*, London: Lawrence & Wishart.

Laclau, Ernesto and Mouffe, Chantal (1985) *Hegemony and Socialist Strategy*, London: Verso.

Landry, Charles (1982) 'Users' Guide to Channel Four', in Simon Blanchard and David Morley (eds.), *What's This Channel Fo(u)r?*, London: Comedia.

Latour, Bruno (2007) *Re-Assembling the Social: An Introduction to Actor-Network Theory*, Oxford: Oxford University Press.

Leavis, F. R. (1930) *Mass Civilization and Minority Culture*, Cambridge: Minority Press.

Legrain, Philippe (2010) *Aftershock: Reshaping the World Economy after the Crisis*, London: Little, Brown.

Lewis, Justin and Wahl-Jorgensen, Karin (2005) 'Active Citizen or Couch Potato? Journalism and Public Opinion', in Stuart Allan (ed.), *Journalism: Critical Issues*, Maidenhead: Open University Press.

Lewis, Justin, Inthorn, Sanna and Wahl-Jorgensen, Karin (2005) *Citizens or Consumers?*, Maidenhead: Open University Press.

Lewis, Norman (2008) 'To See the Future of the Internet, Look East', *Spiked*, 19 May, available online at http://www.spiked-online.com/index.php?/site/article/5166 (accessed 16 July 2010).

Lichtenberg, Judith (1991) 'In Defense of Objectivity', in James Curran and Michael Gurevitch (eds.), *Mass Media and Society*, London: Arnold.

Lindner, Rolf (2006) *The Reportage of Urban Culture: Robert Park and the Chicago School*, Cambridge: Cambridge University Press.

Lippmann, Walter (1997) *Public Opinion*, New York, NY: Free Press. First published 1922.

Mackie, Erin (ed.) (1998) *The Commerce of Everyday Life: Selections from* The Tatler *and* The Spectator, New York, NY: Bedford/St Martin's.

Malik, Kenan (1996) *The Meaning of Race*, Basingstoke: Macmillan.

Malthus, Thomas R. (1826) 'Preface to the Second Edition', in *An Essay on the Principle of Population; or, A View of Its Past and Present Effects on Human*

Happiness, with an Inquiry into Our Prospects Respecting the Future Removal or Mitigation of the Evils Which It Occasions, vol. I, 6th edn, London: John Murray. First published 1803.

Mare, Eric De (1972) *London 1851: The Year of the Great Exhibition*, London: Folio Society.

Markham, Tim (2010) 'The Case Against the Democratic Influence of the Internet on Journalism', in Sean Tunney and Garrett Monaghan (eds.), *Web Journalism: A New Form of Citizenship?*, Brighton: Sussex Academic Press.

Marx, Karl (1842a) Supplement to *Rheinische Zeitung*, No. 135, 15 May, available online at http://www.marxists.org/archive/marx/works/1842/free-press/ch06. htm (accessed 6 April 2010).

——(1842b) Supplement to *Rheinische Zeitung*, No. 139, 19 May, available online at http://www.marxists.org/archive/marx/works/1842/free-press/ch06.htm (accessed 6 April 2010).

——(1978) 'Theses on Feuerbach', in Friedrich Engels, *Ludwig Feuerbach and the End of Classical German Philosophy*, Moscow: Progress. Written in 1845; first published 1888.

——(1983) *Capital: A Critique of Political Economy*, vol. 1, London: Lawrence & Wishart. First published 1887.

——(1989) 'Letter to Ludwig Kugelmann, 27 July 1871', in Karl Marx and Friedrich Engels, *Marx and Engels Collected Works*, vol. XLIV, London: Lawrence & Wishart.

Marx, Karl and Engels, Friedrich (1998) *The German Ideology*, New York, NY: Prometheus Books. First published 1845–6.

——(2010) *The Communist Manifesto*, London: Arcturus. First published 1848.

Matheson, Donald and Allan, Stuart (2009) *Digital War Reporting*, Cambridge: Polity.

Mayes, Tessa (2000) 'Submerging in "Therapy News"', *British Journalism Review*, 11 (4): 30–5.

McCauley, Michael, Peterson, Eric, Artz, B. Lee and Halleck, Deedee (2003) 'Introduction', in Michael Mccauley, Eric Peterson, B. Lee Artz and Deedee Halleck (eds.), *Public Broadcasting and the Public Interest*, Armonk, NY: M. E. Sharpe.

McCombs, Maxwell E. and Shaw, Donald L. (1972) 'The Agenda-Setting Function of Mass Media', *Public Opinion Quarterly*, 36 (2): 176–87.

McKeen, William (2008) *Outlaw Journalist: The Life and Times of Hunter S. Thompson*, London: Aurum Press.

McNair, Brian (1998) *The Sociology of Journalism*, London: Arnold.

——(2000) *Journalism and Democracy: An Evaluation of the Political Public Sphere*, London and New York, NY: Routledge.

——(2006) *Cultural Chaos: Journalism, News and Power in a Globalised World*, London and New York, NY: Routledge.

Meikle, Graham (2009) *Interpreting News*, Basingstoke: Palgrave.

Mermin, Jonathan (1999) *Debating War and Peace*, Princeton, NJ: Princeton University Press.

Mindich, David T. Z. (1998) *Just the Facts: How 'Objectivity' Came to Define American Journalism*, New York, NY: New York University Press.

Morley, David (1980) *The 'Nationwide' Audience*, London: BFI.

——(1986) *Family Television*, London: Comedia.

Mulgan, Geoffrey (1994) *Politics in an Antipolitical Age*, Cambridge: Polity Press.

Mulhern, Francis (1979) *The Moment of 'Scrutiny'*, London: New Left Books.

Mullan, Phil (2008) 'The "Credit Crunch" and the SAD Economy', *Spiked*, 3 November, available online at http://www.spiked-online.com/index.php/site/article/5884 (accessed 17 July 2010).

——(2009) 'It's a Recession, Jim, But Not as We Know It', *Spiked*, 28 May, available online at http://www.spiked-online.com/index.php/site/article/6890 (accessed 17 July 2010).

Nagel, Thomas (1986) *The View from Nowhere*, Oxford: Oxford University Press.

O'Malley, Thomas (1986) 'Religion and the Newspaper Press, 1660–85: A Study of the *London Gazette*', in Michael Harris and Alan Lee (eds.), *The Press in English Society from the Seventeenth to the Nineteenth Centuries*, London and Toronto: Associated University Press.

O'Neill, Brendan (2006) 'Global Warming: The Chilling Effect on Free Speech', *Spiked*, 6 October, available online at http://www.spiked-online.com/index.php?/site/article/1782 (accessed 15 June 2010).

Observer (n.d.) *The Observer: A Short History of the World's Oldest Sunday Newspaper*, London: *The Observer*.

Pedelty, Mark (1995) *War Stories: The Culture of Foreign Correspondents*, London and New York, NY: Routledge.

Pegg, Mark (1983) *Broadcasting and Society, 1918–1939*, London: Croom Helm.

Philo, Greg (1990) *Seeing and Believing*, London: Routledge.

Philo, Greg and Miller, David (2001) 'Cultural Compliance', in Greg Philo and David Miller (eds.), *Market Killing*, Harlow: Longman.

Pilger, John (1999) *Hidden Agendas*, London: Vintage.

Poynter, Gavin (2009) 'The Crunch and the Crisis: The Unravelling of Lifestyle Capitalism?', *Rising East Essays*, 1 (1), 8 April, available online at http://www.uel.ac.uk/risingeast/essays/2009-04-01.htm (accessed 17 July 2010).

——(2010) 'London's Economy in the Long Recession', *Rising East Essays*, 2 (1), 4 March, available online at http://www.uel.ac.uk/risingeast/essays/2010-03-10.htm (accessed 17 July 2010).

Price, John V. (1982) 'The Reading of Philosophical Literature', in Isabel Rivers (ed.), *Books and Their Readers in Eighteenth Century England*, Leicester: Leicester University Press.

Quinn, Adrian (2007) 'Contrary to Claims, Conventions and Culture: An Apologia for the Glasgow University Media Group', *International Journal of Media and Cultural Politics*, 3 (1): 5–24, available online at http://www.gla.ac.uk/centres/mediagroup/quinn%20apologia.pdf (accessed 15 June 2010).

Raymond, Joad (ed.) (1993) *Making the News: An Anthology of the Newsbooks in Revolutionary England, 1641–1660*, Moreton-in-Marsh: Windrush Press.

Ricchiardi, Sherry (1996) 'Over the Line?', *American Journalism Review*, 18 (September): 24–31.

Rock, Paul (1973) 'News as Eternal Recurrence', in Stanley Cohen and Jock Young (eds.), *The Manufacture of News: A Reader*, Beverly Hills, Calif.: Sage Publications.

Rosen, Jay (2006) 'The People Formerly Known as the Audience', *Pressthink*, 27 June, available online at http://journalism.nyu.edu/pubzone/weblogs/pressthink/2006/06/27/ppl_frmr.html (accessed 2 July 2010).

Rubin, Isaac Ilyich (1979) *A History of Economic Thought*, trans. and ed. by Donald Filtzer, London: Pluto Press. First published 1929.

Russell, William Howard (2003) 'The Battle of Balaclava', in Jon E. Lewis (ed.), *The Mammoth Book of Journalism*, London: Robinson. First published 1854.

Rutherford, Jonathan (1990) 'The Third Space: Interview with Homi Bhabha', in Jonathan Rutherford (ed.), *Identity: Community, Culture, Difference*, London: Lawrence & Wishart.

Scannell, Paddy and Cardiff, David (1991) *A Social History of British Broadcasting*, vol. I: *1922–1939: Serving the Nation*, Oxford: Blackwell.

Schlesinger, Philip (1997) *Putting 'Reality' Together*, 2nd edn, London and New York, NY: Routledge.

Schudson, Michael (1978) *Discovering the News: A Social History of American Newspapers*, New York, NY: Basic Books.

——(1991) 'The Sociology of News Production Revisited', in James Curran and Michael Gurevitch (eds.), *Mass Media and Society*, London: Arnold.

Scott, Charles Prestwich (1921), 'A Sufficiency of Grace', editorial for the centenary edition of the *Manchester Guardian*, reproduced in *Newsroom: The Guardian Past and Present*, London: *The Guardian* (undated).

Smith, Anthony (1978) 'The Long Road to Objectivity and Back Again: The Kinds of Truth We Get in Journalism', in George Boyce, James Curran and Pauline Wingate (eds.), *Newspaper History from the Seventeenth Century to the Present Day*, London: Constable.

Sparks, Colin (2004) 'The Global, the Local and the Public Sphere', in Robert C. Allen and Annette Hill (eds.), *The Television Studies Reader*, London and New York, NY: Routledge.

Spater, George (1982) *William Cobbett: The Poor Man's Friend*, vols. I and II, Cambridge: Cambridge University Press.

Speck, William (1986) 'Politics and the Press', in Michael Harris and Alan Lee (eds.), *The Press in English Society from the Seventeenth to the Nineteenth Centuries*, London and Toronto: Associated University Press.

Steele, Richard and Addison, Joseph (1988) *Selections from the Tatler and the Spectator*, ed. Angus Ross, Harmondsworth: Penguin.

Strupp, Joe (2008) 'The End of "Objectivity" in New Journalism Era: A Good Thing?', *Editor and Publisher*, 12 November, available online at http://www.reclaimthemedia.org/journalistic_practice/end_objectivity_new_journalism1346 (accessed 15 June 2010).

Stuart, Charles (ed.) (1975) *The Reith Diaries*, London: Collins.

Sweeney, Mark (2009) 'Anti-Piracy Campaign Aims to Win over Generation Y-Pay of Internet Users', *The Guardian*, 7 September, available online at http://www.guardian.co.uk/technology/2009/sep/07/anti-piracy-campaign-bill-filesharing (accessed 17 July 2010).

Tett, Gillian (2009) *Fool's Gold: How Unrestrained Greed Corrupted a Dream, Shattered Global Markets and Unleashed a Catastrophe*, London: Little, Brown.

Thussu, Daya Kishan (2007) *News as Entertainment*, London: Sage.

Tuchman, Gaye (1972) 'Objectivity as Strategic Ritual: An Examination of News-men's Notions of Objectivity', *American Journal of Sociology*, 77 (4): 660–79.
——(1978) *Making News: A Study in the Construction of Reality*, New York, NY: The Free Press.
Tunstall, Jeremy (1971) *Journalists at Work: Specialist Correspondents, Their News Organizations, News Sources, and Competitor-Colleagues*, London: Constable.
Turner, Graeme (2000) '"Media Wars": Journalism, Cultural and Media Studies in Australia', *Journalism: Theory, Practice and Criticism*, 1 (3): 353–65.
Wahl-Jorgensen, Karin and Hanitzsch, Thomas (2009) 'Introduction: On Why and How We Should Do Journalism Studies', in Karin Wahl-Jorgensen and Thomas Hanitzsch (eds.), *The Handbook of Journalism Studies*, London and New York, NY: Routledge.
Wain, John (1974) *Samuel Johnson*, London: Macmillan.
Ward, Stephen J. A. (2004) *The Invention of Journalism Ethics: The Path to Objectivity and Beyond*, Montreal: McGill-Queen's University Press.
Wardle, Claire (2010a) 'User Generated Content and Public Service Broadcasting', Clairewardle.com, 19 May, available online at http://clairewardle.com/2010/05/19/user-generated-content-and-public-service-broadcasting (accessed 2 July 2010).
——(2010b) 'What Makes People Send in Their Stuff?', BBC College of Journalism, 17 June, available online at http://www.bbc.co.uk/journalism/blog/2010/06/what-makes-people-send-us-thei.shtml (accessed 2 July 2010).
Wardle, Claire and Williams, Andrew (2008) 'Ugc@thebbc' (research report), Cardiff: Cardiff School of Journalism, Media and Cultural Studies, available online at http://www.bbc.co.uk/blogs/knowledgeexchange/cardiffone.pdf (accessed 2 July 2010).
Waugh, Evelyn (1951) *Scoop: A Novel about Journalists*, Harmondsworth: Penguin. First published 1933.
Weber, Max (1949) 'Objectivity in Social Science and Social Policy', in *The Methodology of the Social Sciences*, trans. and ed. by Edward A. Shils and Henry N. Finch, New York, NY: Free Press.
——(1972) 'The Psycho-Physics of Industrial Work', in John Eldridge (ed.), *Max Weber: The Interpretation of Social Reality*, London: Nelson University Paperbacks. First published 1924.
West, Cornel (1993) 'The New Cultural Politics of Difference', in Simon During (ed.), *The Cultural Studies Reader*, London and New York, NY: Routledge.
Williams, Kevin (1997) *Get Me a Murder a Day! A History of Mass Communication in Britain*, London: Hodder Education.
——(2010) *Read All About It! A History of the British Newspaper*, London and New York, NY: Routledge.
Williams, Raymond (1963) *Culture and Society, 1780–1950*, Harmondsworth: Penguin.
——(1965) *The Long Revolution*, Harmondsworth: Penguin.
——(1980) *Problems in Materialism and Culture*, London: Verso.
Wilson, Richard (1978) 'Newspapers and Industry: The Export of Wool Controversy in the 1780s', in George Boyce, James Curran and Pauline Wingate (eds.), *Newspaper History from the Seventeenth Century to the Present Day*, London: Constable.
Wolf, Martin (2009) *Fixing Global Finance: How to Curb Financial Crisis in the Twenty-First Century*, New Haven, Conn.: Yale University Press.

Wolfe, Tom (1968) *The Kandy-Kolored Tangerine-Flake Streamline Baby*, London: Mayflower Books.

Wolfe, Tom and Johnson, E. W. (eds.) (1975) *The New Journalism, with an Anthology*, London: Picador.

Wright Mills, C. (1970) *The Sociological Imagination*, Harmondsworth: Penguin. First published 1959.

Index